CO-OP VILLAGES

The Next Evolution

Co-op Villages: The Next Evolution

Published by:
Co-op Village Foundation, Inc.
6692 E. Magnolia Street
Milton, FL 32570
Phone: 850-623-8753
Email: costa4669@bellsouth.net
www.co-opvillagefoundation.org

Cover design by David Sand

ISBN: 978-0-9794865-0-0

Publisher's Cataloging in Publication

Data available upon request

CO-OP VILLAGES

The Next Evolution

Jack Reed

Jen Chendea

Jim Costa

DEDICATION

This book is dedicated to
Mike, a planetary hero extraordinaire.

Jim

ABOUT THIS BOOK

Very seldom does one hear about a viable plan to transform the planet and to address all its problems. *Co-op Villages: The Next Evolution* offers such a plan, a plan that could change everything. The authors trace the challenges we face to the legacy of the everyone-for-themselves paradigm that has ruled this planet unquestioned for thousands of years.

But what if we instead choose to have this planet work for everyone and for all life on the planet? The heart of this book lays out that vision. The basic building block that is needed is how we live together and relate together in Community, and the author meticulously describes how that would look in a Highest Good for all model. Envision a world that enjoys the latest technology, yet respects the natural resources of the planet and keeps them intact. Imagine living in a diverse, sustainable Community where everyone is well cared for, with all their needs being met.

This is not a utopian fantasy. This *IS* the next evolution—literally a blueprint for transforming our world through realistic and practical solutions to the present-day political, environmental, economic, and social problems of the entire planet.

Table of Contents

Chapter 1

WHY ARE YOU DOING THIS?

by Jim Costa

How do you ...?

How do you ...? Change the world? Help many instead of a few? Stop the madness? Find peace within yourself while surrounded by insanity? How do you ...?

I had spent years asking myself this same question over and over again—pushing for answers, squeezing out "you must be out of your mind" solutions one at a time. But now I was really stuck. No answer was forthcoming no matter how many times I asked myself, "How do you ..." Nothing.

I was so consumed with the "how do you" that I had dropped out of the workforce ten years earlier and walked around with my head in a proctologist's workspace visualizing the details of the "how do you's." But now I was seeing it. It was real—a true doable solution to the madness. Now, to tell the world was all that remained to be done. But how do you? Whom do you tell? How do you tell somebody that even though society can't seem to be able to solve just one of its problems, it can easily solve most of them at one time? That's like saying you can't pick up just one jack by itself, but you can pick them all up on just one bounce of the ball. How do you tell somebody that?

Then I knew. Who, that is. He was a nationally renowned attorney who had taken up the plight of the world himself. Well connected nationally, an environmentalist, a philanthropist. Above all, one of the most intelligent persons in the area. If I was on the wrong track, he could convince me to give it up. I respected his thinking. However, if I was right, he could tell me whom to deliver the message to. Mike could resolve the "Whom do you tell" dilemma and send me to that person.

God almighty! Always just one more "how do you ...?" How do you reach the busiest man in town? Reach someone way out of your league who doesn't even know you? Reach someone who has been out of state for two months on an international case? How do you ask someone to help you get $2 million in sixty days for your crazy idea? How do you get your letter to his attention knowing he is finally coming home one week before Christmas with two months of mail stacked on his desk? God almighty! Always just one more "how do you ...?"

Mike was my only hope, but I knew it was a lost cause. I resigned myself that our Co-op Village land offer would just have to expire—no down payment; no saving mankind. It would just expire, like we all do eventually.

Then an angel appeared! He looked just like me. He was my brother. I have seen him in action many times. He's the finest outside salesman I have ever seen. He can talk his way into any office. They actually welcome him when he breaks through. He's amazing. He knows everybody.

I am eating my guts out and tell him that I'm packing it in because I can't figure out "how do you ...?"

"No biggie," John told me. "Mike goes to such and such church. Just give the package with a short cover letter to his pastor and tell his pastor your problem. Don't compete with the magazine renewals on his desk."

Dear Mr. —:

Please forgive me for the way that you have received this package. I am just the messenger here and feel that you are the only person who will know to whom to deliver the message. I knew of no other way to bring this to your attention.

This package is part of our website showing how to house

500 persons on 500 acres sustainably forever. This Co-op Village will provide all housing, food, utilities, health benefits, transportation, job training or advanced education, and living-wage jobs for life for its residents. The cost to each resident is $40,000 and we hope to finance that for those who need it. This is the culmination of years of work.

I believe that after one village is built, hundreds — then thousands — of others will pop up around the country since this will be the only viable option that millions of people will have to live in dignity. This will transform the country. These villages will provide what our culture and governments promise but cannot deliver.

These villages will produce their own organic food, produce their own utilities, reduce oil demand, and truly be concerned about the land they live on. Governments can't change the world, but a grass-roots movement such as this can. It's the only way the ill affects of global warming, globalization, and governmental manipulation by multinational corporations can be reversed — on a local level.

This is probably the only current viable option for mankind to mitigate the disasters that lie ahead globally both financially and environmentally. Cowboys know that you can turn a bull's body simply by turning its head; so too can the world be turned if the U.S. culture can be turned. This project is a means to accomplish that quickly before governments can stop it. Currently we are just silently marching towards a cliff. But if enough villages are built, society will then have an option to choose how it will create its future.

We have designed a village for which there is a strong demand and which is a sound business investment, is blueprinted so that it can be replicated anywhere, and economically dovetails nicely with our current capitalistic system.

Our local think tank has advanced this idea as far as we can go by ourselves. We are now ready to give it to the world, but do not know to whom to give it. We are prepared to build the first village in Marianna, Florida, but will need some investor financing to continue on. We need to be picked up on a national level by someone who will understand the value of this project. We need a hero for the planet!

I hope that you will see this for what it can be and hope you will pass it on to whoever you feel needs to see it. We have no intention of ever making money on this idea. However, whoever you pass this to could make quite a deal in brokering the land or by providing a minimal amount of financing for the villages that follow.

In order to build the first village, we are seeking a $2 million construction loan pledged against a $40 million asset at a high interest rate to be repaid in five years. Hopefully, you will know who will recognize the potential and need of this project.

Thank you for your time.

I waited.

Finally a response—those magical words. I have been told that during wrecks, horrible accidents, or emergencies, time seems to slow down. The actions seem to take forever to unfold and somehow lock themselves in your memory forever, one frame at a time. Then later it just replays itself as a perfect recording, no flaw in the memory, transporting with it the physical and emotional feelings from the original experience. So, too, those magical words keep playing back in my mind. "Lo, Jim, this is Mike—We need to talk today."

We agreed to meet at the sushi restaurant at 11:45. The last thing Mike said before hanging up was, "Just what is it you want from me? Do you want me to set up a meeting with some investors for you?" This was like dangling a dead fish over the water at Sea World! Yes! "Oh, my God," I thought. "I hit the jackpot." This is exactly what I wanted. Just a chance was all that I needed; just a few minutes in a room with a few deep pockets to plead my cause. The $2 million would give us the land down payment, make all the land payments the first year so that we could focus on building, and give us a million for infrastructure. Fish can be so beautiful.

"No, Mike." I heard my voice say it, but it couldn't be me saying it. It couldn't be. Maybe I was just hearing things. "This thing has gotten much bigger than I ever could have imagined," I said. "I just need fifteen minutes to tell you what's not in the package." I needed direction.

Our meeting started with the normal pleasantries. I had to ask him to order for me; I'm just a common slob. Then he asked those six little probing questions. The same ones I had heard him ask twenty times before in my mind. "How are you going to admit residents?" "Is anybody else doing this now?" And so on. But then he asked a question that told me he had read only half of the package. Why just half?

Around the age of forty-five, about four years before I stopped working, I began to open up as an intuitive, a psychic. I denied it until a few months before I quit working. When it started I would see business meetings a few days before they occurred. In those visions I would see everyone's positions, arguments, and personal feelings. It was like seeing another card player's hand. But the strange thing was that usually these meetings were with total strangers! I could understand if they were with persons I had prior dealings with. But these were total strangers and there was no way I could have guessed the things I saw beforehand. There was no way. So I just ignored it and figured I was just a good guesser until I realized I had to deal with it because it was real. I quit work, slowed down, and developed that gift. I learned to listen.

Many a night during the two months before Mike and I met, I woke from dreams visualizing our discussion. He asked those exact questions over and over again. Each time I answered them better than before. Then one night out of the clear blue he hit me with it, that one question. Until then I had had the whole world figured out. With that one question he destroyed ten years of work. That one question rocked my very foundation. My footing was gone and I collapsed. Why did he have to ask that? He asked the question. I couldn't think of a thing to say in response. I just sat there. Mike got up and walked away. That was how the dream ended. He just walked away and I had no response. Why did he have to ask that question? "How can just a few of these villages change the nation?"

I was depressed for about a week after that dream because I still had nothing to say to him in response. Nothing.

Then he went higher with the questions. I saw those coming too. The answers were exactly as I had rehearsed them. Then he started moving to THE question. I could feel him going there. He asked why I thought there might be a financial meltdown in this country. In about a minute, I summarized the six-page paper I had written on it the prior week in trying to figure out how I was going to respond to that big question he was pushing me to.

I told him about the baby boomers overloading the SSI system in 2008 and how the big people were predicting that SSI, Medicare and Medicaid, and federal, state, and municipal pensions probably would have to be cut in half.

I told him about petro-dollars and how oil is sold in U.S. dollars only and is causing foreign countries to invest in business and real estate here in order to get those dollars. I talked about how the rest of the world was beginning to feel our dollar may not be stable enough and may start quoting in Euro dollars and how that would cause those investors to pull out of the United States and wreck our economy.

I told him about our overwhelming trade deficits and how the big people are saying our dollar may go the path of third-world currencies.

I told him about global warming and how it could destroy our economy if we tried to stop our damaging acts.

I told him about globalization and how it was destroying our jobs more each year.

And then... I told him about how our economy for the past 100 years had been based on cheap energy and now that was a thing of the past. Our suburbia was and continues to be built based on cheap fuel, and now cheap fuel too is becoming a thing of the past.

When I had finished, he corrected me and said the dollar would not be replaced by Euros but instead by the Chinese yen. We were seeing the same thing.

Then he discussed how the village could help people. He could see the benefit of villages. He agreed that they could provide jobs and dignity for the working poor and the middle class. "A village would be a great socioeconomic experiment," he said.

Then Mike asked THE question. He had been playing with me. He had been stalling. He had set me up. And now he was going there. "How can building a few of these villages save this country? It won't make that big of an impact quickly enough," he said.

He was right. It would take ten years, in my mind, to make an impact. If we had a meltdown in six months it would destroy our economy. Ten years would not help anything. For a month I had brooded over that question of his. But now I was prepared. He had pushed me in my dreams and he had inspired me once again to ask "how do you ... ?" In my dreams, Mike had pushed me to give him the answer he was looking for.

"When we build the first village we will write operating manuals on raising food, building a local commerce, utility production, alternative healthcare systems, truly sustainable living, sharing, etc.," I said. "In the event of a meltdown our manuals could be used to retrofit suburbia across the United States in just a few months and bring up a new economy. This country could survive," I said.

We briefly discussed the how's and wherefores of the retrofit and concluded that desperate people would be willing to do desperate things, but all in all it might work.

Then Mike said, "Of course this will never happen because as oil gets harder to get, there are alternative fuels, so suburbia is safe."

I immediately responded. "All of the big people tell us that it will be at least thirty years before alternative fuels can be brought on line, Mike. In the meantime, we have no at-worst fallback position."

The conversation was over. Not another word was said. That was the longest ten seconds of silence I ever heard. Our meeting was through. It was decided. We had talked as equals but that too was over.

Finally, after that long ten seconds: "This is how it works," Mike said. "You need two million. Ten people will put up $300,000 each. But Jim, you have to put up first. You have to publish your idea in a book. As soon as you publish you will have your money."

"But Mike," I protested, "I'm not a writer."

"Look," he said, "you have already done all of the detail describing the building and running of the village. All you have to do is download your website and add three chapters in the front. You have already done all of the hard work, so just finish it. Until you publish, you do not exist nor does your idea exist. Finish it."

Then he stopped being nice. I soon learned how an old rag-doll feels when it is no longer a child's favored toy. He came after me like a banshee. He was merciless and wouldn't let up. I never saw it coming in my dreams. I never got a heads up. I need to talk to somebody about that.

"Jim, why are you doing this?" he asked. Then he faced those steely eyes at me. I don't know where they came from. I hadn't noticed them before. Maybe he put in contacts?

"I was born to do this," I said. "I opened up as an intuitive when I slowed down after not working anymore. I started seeing the village in dreams. I went there in my mind. I can't stop seeing it. I have to make it real. I have no choice in the matter—I have to do it." There. I said it. It's hard to tell people you are weird. But I couldn't lie to Mike. I had to tell him my predicament.

"No. That's not what I mean. Why are you doing this?" he repeated. There he goes—those eyes again.

I don't even remember what I told him. I went higher, I know that. My instincts took over—autopilot. Something about people living with dignity, having security, grandchildren having an option. I think I probably said something like that. I see myself as saying things like that, thinking how I would answer that question if he asked me that now. So I suppose I told him something like that. I guess. Whatever I told him, I felt good about it. There, I gave him a great answer and now he will stop with the eyes.

"No. Why are you doing this?" he demanded. Then I saw it. His forehead had wrinkles when there were none before. His voice had anger in it. His eyes were now squinted a little and his face was clearly red. What had I done? Why is he upset with me? What the heck is going on?

What does he want out of me? Maybe he wants the highest answer I can give him. If I can just calm down, I can give it to him and he will go away. I took a deep breath of air and let it come out of me. Let's get this over with. "A snake has to shed its skin in order to grow. Maybe what's been holding us back is our economic system. It's causing us to step all over each other. It's making us physically ill from the stress. It's killing families. Its making us consume more because we are afraid of losing it. It's making us kill the planet we are standing on."

Oh, God. Now he's madder than ever. He's leaning over the table coming after me. Those eyes again. He sticks his finger just a foot in front of my face and demands again, "WHY ARE YOU DOING THIS?"

So much is randomly going through my mind. I have no control of the thoughts. I haven't felt like this since high school, standing on my feet wondering myself why I never studied, all while a nun was going after me. I saw an image of a punch-drunk fighter trying to keep balance on his legs. I saw several episodes of Perry Mason and how the badgered witness suddenly confesses to murder. Yeah, like anyone would really be so stupid as to say that in court. I wished that cute waitress would walk back by so maybe he would sneak a quick peek, but I knew he wouldn't. I felt defenseless and exposed. The only way I could have felt more exposed was to stand butt-naked on the courthouse steps at high noon.

Then I felt it. I knew what I had to do. Now I was mad. The adrenaline kicked in. I was on top and I knew what I had to do and I was going to do it, by God. I was in total control. In my mind's eye I saw myself jumping up and saying, "I did it to Mr. Mustard in the library with the wrench!" I had to stop those eyes. "For God's sake, Mike, to stop war!" I hollered out.

I would like to say I stopped him. I would like to. But I can't.

He calmly leaned back in his chair and softly began talking about Thoreau and his book Walden Pond. He said something about man being at peace, serenity; finding self, contentment, joy, away from materialism. I remember hearing some of those words but not all that he was saying. I was still trying to figure out what had just happened.

Mike said, "Jim, you did an amazing job describing the village and how it would work. Now you have to add three chapters in the front discussing the higher philosophical approach as to why the village. Philosophically tell the reader all that you just told me. Oh yeah, add a chapter comparing and contrasting the village to the Amish, Jim Jones, The Farm (the large commune leftover from the hippies), kibbutzim in Israel. Then you've got it. How hard can that be? Then you get your money. I'll monitor your progress. Got to go, I have a one-fifteen."

Mike stood up and pushed his chair back. I looked up at him and said,. "The rush is on, but the first one cannot be a premature ejaculation." He calmly looked at me but didn't say anything. He put on his sunglasses and headed towards the front door. I stood up and turned and took two steps towards the back door.

"Jim," I heard. I turned around and saw Mike two paces from the front door. He took off his sunglasses and held them in his right hand. With the same hand he pointed his index finger angled down towards the floor. With each word said, his hand went towards the floor and bobbed back up again. Looking right through me, he slowly announced—no, declared—no, ordered:

"This ... experiment... MUST ... be ... done."

Write a book. Yeah, easy for you. I can think philosophy, I think, but I can't write it.

What he's asking for is what Jack Reed did. Now that was a great job! His book, *The Next Evolution*, now that was something. In it he described the philosophical needs for such a village. He challenged the world to build just one. The challenge: Put 500 persons on 1,000 acres to live sustainably forever. But he never described the makeup of the village.

That's what I had been seeing: the makeup of the village. When I read Jack's book, I knew I had to write down all that I saw. I didn't know why. I just knew it felt good writing it. But that's technical writing and anybody can do that.

"How can I do this?" I asked Jack."It was easy for you. You did such a great job of it. But how can I do that?"

Jack had infected me with his dream—to build a village. We were both addicted. Couldn't swear off it. But it would take so much backing, and no banker in the world would touch the first one.

"No problem," he said. "Let's cooperate. Rip the first three chapters out of my book and stick it in yours. Mike will never know the difference!"

I told Jen about Mike and then about Jack. "Great." She was so enthusiastic. She lives in Virginia, where Andrei is stationed in the Navy. She spent four months home last year while he was in another Navy school. She was a godsend at our meetings. About twenty-six, I guess. Finished in art history and philosophy, I think she said. What the heck can you do with that?

I only called Jen whenever I got cut or scraped in our meetings and the group wouldn't do "right." She was always so supportive. Always said she wished she was here so she could contribute. It was the same every time. "What can I do to help?" Of course, what could she do? She was there; we were here.

I don't think she ever got it. Simply by asking, she always did. Just to hear her say, "can I help" was more than enough.

But today it wasn't to be. She sounded terrible. A cold made her voice sound husky; I could actually hear her nose dripping over the phone. "Babies are just incubators for germs" she said.

"Mike said I had to write a book first. I'm not a writer. I flunked English Comp," I freely admitted.

"What can I do to help?" she asked.

"He even said I have to compare and contrast the village to other eco-villages, communes, etc.,"

She said, "Great! that I can do from here. Any particular style? How long do I have? A few days? A week? A month? How many pages?"

"Yep," was all I said. "Call me when it's finished. All I have to do now is explain all of this."

Where should I say that we would build the first village near Pensacola, Florida, starting in the fall of 2007? I will just have to work that in somewhere in the book. It will come to me. We were actually going to do it! God! We are actually going to do it!

Because of the time constraints, I knew we would have to let our land option die. But now we had money and could purchase land near home. That would be so much easier and safer. The Marianna land seller, a broker, already had a back-up buyer in the event we couldn't make it. He was happy. He agreed to finance our new land purchase once we found the new site.

We are actually going to build it!

Chapter 2

THE BIG QUESTION

by Jack Reed

As we look at our cities, our country, and our planet, we know what the challenges are. They are the problem buzzwords of our time: poverty, hunger, the economy, pollution, healthcare, crime, war, and the increasing destruction of our environment. Most of us are aware of the doom-and-gloom scenarios about what will happen by, say, the year 2020—when the population has grown to 8.2 billion or more, there isn't enough food to feed everyone, and we have altered and polluted the planet to such an extent that the environmental issues, such as global warming, have become by far the most significant issues of this millennia as they threaten all life on the planet.

Serious problems, right? But now ask yourself this: Since there are enough resources and manpower on this planet for ALL OF US to live not only abundantly but also in balance with nature, the big question is: WHAT THEN IS THE PROBLEM? Why are two of every five people in the world living in poverty? Why are there people who cannot get proper nutrition, sanitation, and medical care? Let's repeat the startling and simple truth that is the corner-stone for finding a solution:

IF WE CHOOSE TO MAKE LIFE WORK FOR EVERYONE, THERE ARE ENOUGH RESOURCES AND MANPOWER ON THIS PLANET FOR ALL OF US TO LIVE ABUNDANTLY!

Just now close your eyes and ponder that for a minute. Let it really sink in. Ask yourself why it isn't happening. Then, you may well ask yourself, "What can we do about it?" The forces at work that are causing the imbalances seem to be beyond our control. There are too many environmental, economic, political, and social causes and situations to correct that it's simply overwhelmingly impossible. At best, most solutions are a Band-Aid approach since everything is interconnected. For example, we can't address starvation in a given geographical area by simply providing food because there are usually political, economic, and environmental causal factors that are quite complex.

Part of the problem is the pervasive, long-standing attitude of againstness that we hold towards each other and towards others. This againstness probably stems from our need/addiction to control our lives. This often happens at the expense of another, and it permeates most of the interactions between one power broker and another, between one interested party and another, and even between one family member and another. This against-ness along with the unwillingness to go for a creative approach to collectively make our planetary situation truly work for everyone are roadblocks we must overcome. Given all the imbalances on the planet and the destruction of our environment, the sands are rapidly running through the hourglass for life as we know it on Earth. There is an answer, but it means that we must start making the planet work for all life on the planet. Stated simply:

IF WE'RE GOING TO CONTINUE TO HAVE A WORLD, WE'RE GOING TO HAVE TO START MAKING IT WORK FOR EVERYONE.

Given the connectedness of all things, we must go after the one thing that can address and include everything else, and that is HOW WE AS PEOPLE LIVE TOGETHER. Currently we live in what can best be described as an everyone-for-themselves world. That may look like every country for themselves or every family or every whatever grouping, but it all boils down to the everyone-for-themselves model. We do not have a "what would work for all of us" mentality and approach to life. The everyone-for-themselves approach to living and survival is so ingrained through thousands of years of practice that most people have never even conceived of an alternative approach—especially one that would include our entire planet. The piecemeal way our lives are set up, the way our cities are designed, and the way our economy runs all have the end result of isolating and separating us. They are set up for us to try to survive and get ahead on our own and to continue to intrude upon and disrupt our environment.

Therefore we need to move away from this individualistic model to one that really works for all of us and for all life. We have to start acting like one family where the needs of the one are the concern of everyone. This does not mean taking care of those who are thought of as not contributing, but it does mean setting up how we live together in a way that truly works for everyone. This is a total systems-approach—the systems-approach tells us that *all* things are interconnected and that to change a part, i.e. poverty or our ecology, we therefore need to change the entire system in order to really create effective changes. At this point in our history, nothing less is called for and nothing less will work for all of us. This new model has to be that we live on this planet in a way that is *for* THE HIGHEST GOOD OF ALL LIFE so that *we all* can experience more abundance, health, nurturing, loving, and fun.

Think about it, it's very simple to see the solution. In fact, it's so simple that that's why it's hard, because, in our fragmented approach to trying to understand and solve things, we're looking for something complicated to get us out of our present Earth predicament. We have so many thousands of years of programming in our power-based, everyone-for-themselves paradigm to overcome that it's difficult to perceive workable solutions for the planet as a whole. We have an endless history of againstness and conflict that get our minds focused and locked onto looking at life as a struggle for survival on our own as opposed to looking at life as a cooperative adventure that can work for all mankind and for all life on the planet.

We need to create a new model. All the "isms"—capitalism, communism, socialism, nationalism, racism, sexism, etc.—are not working for us, so we have no large-scale model of change to look at. However, CHANGE ON THE SCALE THAT IS NEEDED CAN ONLY BE BROUGHT ABOUT WHEN PEOPLE SEE AND EXPERIENCE A BETTER WAY.

Fortunately, the best way to show this is also the easiest for a group of people to bring to pass. The way we live together and relate together in Community is the basic building block that is needed to transform the planet. If we design Communities based on a Highest Good For Everyone model, we can live very, very abundant lifestyles that would appeal to almost everyone while simultaneously restoring our environment. This book, then, is about how we can live in Community for The Highest Good Of *All Life* and about the ultimate transformation of the planet, which will be caused by making life work for all of us.

As you continue reading, you'll keep hearing some form of this term, "For The Highest Good," over and over again. [I apologize if that term doesn't just roll off the tongue, but I don't know of any other term that fully encompasses the concept of making the world work for everyone and for the planet.] It includes both creating the outer form to work for all life and the consciousness which that choice requires, and it permeates every aspect of how we choose to live together on this planet. It's an internal commitment to all life on this earth, to wanting the best for all life on the planet, and it's putting that into action by fundamentally changing the form and consciousness of how we live together. It is the antithesis of the short-sighted everyone-for-themselves paradigm that has wrecked havoc on the earth and resulted in the physical, mental, emotional, and spiritual hardships and lack that touch all our lives in varying degrees.

Again, the simple truth—there are enough resources and manpower on this planet for all of us to live very abundantly and in harmony with ourselves, each other, and the environment if we change our model of living and our consciousness from everyone-for-themselves to a Highest Good For Everyone model. Drink this in, for this must be *Our Next Evolution.*

As you look at this idea, I invite you to expand your consciousness to include the welfare of the entire planet. Imagine that you are *all* people in *all* countries and in *all* situations. In many cases you would currently have basic human needs that are not being met, and you would be living on the very edge of survival. However, the solution is so simple that it has escaped us: let's make the planet work for everyone; let's choose to live *for* THE HIGHEST GOOD OF ALL LIFE.

As you continue reading, I invite you to toss out your reference points and to step outside the box of how you think life has to be. So hold onto your hat as I first point out the obvious in terms of current conditions on the planet, and then I offer a practical solution for not only saving the planet, but also making this Earth a more enjoyable place to hang out for *all* people and for *all* life.

FROM NEALE DONALD WALSH'S CONVERSATIONS WITH GOD, Book 2

GOD: *"In terms of geopolitics, why not work together as a world to meet the most basic needs of everyone?"*

AUTHOR: *"We're doing that or trying."*

GOD: *"After all these thousands of years of human history, that's the most you can say?*

"The fact is, you have barely evolved at all. You still operate in a primitive 'every person for himself' mentality.

"You plunder the Earth, rape her of her resources, exploit her people, and systematically disenfranchise those who disagree with you for doing all of this, calling them the 'radicals.'

"You do this for your own selfish purposes because you've developed a lifestyle that you cannot maintain any other way.

"You must cut down the millions of acres of trees each year or you won't be able to have your Sunday paper. You must destroy miles of the protective ozone which covers your planet or you cannot have your hair spray. You must pollute your rivers and streams beyond repair or you cannot have your industries to give you Bigger, Better, and More. And you must exploit the least among you—the least

advantaged, the least educated, the least aware—or you cannot live at the top of the human scale in unheard of [and unnecessary] luxury. Finally, you must deny that you are doing this, or you cannot live with yourself.

"You cannot find it in your heart to 'live simply, so that others may simply live.' That bumper sticker wisdom is too simple for you. It is too much to ask. Too much to give. After all, you've worked so hard for what you've got! You ain't giving up none of it! And if the rest of the human race—to say nothing of your own children's children—have to suffer for it, tough bananas, right? You did what you had to do to survive, to 'make it'—they can do the same! After all, it is every man for himself, is it not?"

AUTHOR: "Is there any way out of this mess?"

GOD: "Yes. Shall I say it again? A shift of consciousness.

"You cannot solve the problems which plague humankind through governmental action or political means. You have been trying that for thousands of years.

"The change must be made, can be made only in the hearts of man."

—Neale Donald Walsch, *Conversations With God book 2*, Hampton Roads Publishing Co., Inc., 1997, Charlottesville, VA, pages 172-173.

Chapter 3

FOR THE HIGHEST GOOD OF ALL LIFE

by Jack Reed

So, enough with the problems we're facing on so many different levels. Although you may have a different viewpoint on some of these problems, I think we can all agree that we must not be numb ourselves to the apparent overwhelming nature of our planetary plight, and that we must do something to make the planet work better for all of us. Because physical change initially comes about from a change in consciousness, the first step in that process must be moving into the consciousness that we, out of a heartfelt response, really want to make the planet work for all life. For all the reasons I gave in the second chapter, I call that consciousness "The Highest Good Of All." I now issue you a challenge to drop your reference points and assumptions about how we have set up life to work on this planet and to look at the world very differently than you may have up to this point. Then, with the consciousness of making it work for all of us, we'll start to look at how we can physically make the world work for The Highest Good Of All.

Let's start again with the basic truth: there is enough on the planet for all of us—there are enough resources and manpower for all of us to live not only abundantly but also in balance with nature. In fact, given an ideal utilization of those resources and manpower, we could create a model where everyone could essentially live like responsible millionaires on a pollution-free planet. Yet, in the midst of this potential for plenty, we constantly read that a lack of money is being used as the excuse for not doing—for not providing needed healthcare, for not cleaning up and taking better care of the environment, for not enabling retired people to live a more abundant life, for not providing better education, and so on.

HOW DID WE GET TO THIS PLACE?

As a starting point for looking at where we are now and what we can do about it, let's first journey back and look at where we've come from. In the ancient world, people would trade products such as grain for sheep or cows. Eventually, to avoid hauling around real sheep or real sacks of grain to make the deals, they started using tokens to represent the products. This trading system mutually benefited groups because it could improve their lifestyles over what they each could have alone.

This system continued to evolve through the centuries— sometimes peacefully and other times violently, as some groups would want more than just what they could obtain through barter. Several of these aggressive groups were the Western European Francs, Goths, Anglos and Saxons. These peoples, the descendants of barbarians whose histories were rooted in violence and centuries of fighting, would become the first people in history to spread their civilization across the entire planet. What they had in common was that they became the heirs of the Holy Roman Empire and came to believe themselves to be a chosen people.

But how was it that such small-scale countries and economics could end up dominating the world several hundred years later? India and China had all the inventions and many times the people. The answer is that the concept of individualism came out of the Western European countries. The West opted for individual (as opposed to collective) rights, the private ownership of property, and a free market economy. The ideas of individualism along with the world view that these people believed themselves to be the chosen people who could do what they wanted in the world, in the hands of the limited democracies—run by the property owners and the movers of money—were the basis of the phenomenal success and spread of the West through their conquests of others.

1492 marked the beginning of the systematic war waged against the native peoples of the world by Western arms, religion, and ideology. The conquest was accompanied by a genocide unparalleled in history. In the next century over two-thirds of the native population of the Americas died through violence or disease. Columbus wrote to Queen Isabella of Spain, "Our European civilization will bring Light to the natives in their darkness, but for ourselves we will gain gold and with gold we will be able to do what we want in the world." By this time gold was the token of choice for trading, and the West forcibly took it from the New World in exchange for death and religion. A strong case can be made that in pre-Columbian times, the lives of the natives of the Americas were better than they are now. Imagine the arrogance of the explorers who came to lands where people had no concept of private property. They simply planted flags and claimed lands—reaching far beyond where they could even see— for their monarchs. It didn't matter that there were already millions of people there who had lived there for thousands of years, people who viewed the land as sacred and not something that could be owned. This audacity came from the consciousness of superiority, and, thus, they viewed the natives as God-forsaken heathens. This action by the explorers, colonists and various financial exploiters was as presumptuous and audacious as people coming here in their spaceships from another planet, viewing us as inferior, and claiming whatever land they chose for their planet.

Yet, it was only in relatively recent times, during the enclosure movement in 15th century England, when common rights to land were abolished and individual title to land was established. As usual, power and the concentration of wealth in the hands of a few were the motives as 15,000 peasants were cleared off 794,000 acres in Scotland to create just 29 farms with 131,000 sheep. Each farm had only a single family and imported servants. This institutionalized ownership of land was deemed necessary to launch the wool industry, and, from that time on, land became something that could be bought and sold for whatever the market could bring and could be passed on from one generation to the next. It also spelled the end to the concept held by many cultures that the land was God's land, and it was inconceivable that it could be bought or sold. Individual ownership of land further set the stage for the exploitation of the peoples of the planet and the environment.

Starting in the 17th century, people given to exploitation to further their own ends misinterpreted the teachings of Francis Bacon, the founding father of modern science, and came up with the concept that we could detach ourselves from nature and manipulate it to advance our own human interests. Ignoring Bacon's warning—that nature, to be commanded, must be obeyed—from that point in time, the environment then became looked upon as something to be exploited for our own agenda. This misinterpretation of Bacon's philosophy and scientific method gave the expansion-minded Western civilizations the world view that it was their right to manipulate the environment in order to further their short-term goals and material interests on a scale never before imaginable.

Then, in the mid-18th century, the Industrial Revolution, born and developed in northwest Europe, changed the world economy forever. Western consumerism was born from mass production, and with it the expectation that it was a God-given right for them to have more of everything, and, after that, more again. So the money players kept their mass production going night and day, and scoured their environment for the resources they felt they had a scientific and moral right to take. But could it go on? Wouldn't they eventually run out of raw materials?

With the Industrial Revolution, the countries of northwest Europe had taken over the world's trade. The reason their manufacturing capitalism was able to continue was through the exploitation of the Third World. Other parts of the world had what the Westerners needed, so they colonized the Third World to get their hands on the raw materials to sustain the Industrial Revolution and consumerism. The Europeans had the means through military strength and steam power to make their wishes felt across the entire planet. Steam power allowed the Europeans to build railroads from the ports to the mines and plantations and to bring in all the equipment to secure the resources. However, they did not build railroads to anywhere else or train the locals to be managers. The net result was to wipe out the local economies and to install their own local administrations and transportation systems to suit their own businesses and to shape the countries to their needs. In almost every case that meant developing nothing else. We created copper republics, banana and tin republics, etc. These countries which were once self-sustaining then became dependent for survival on exporting one or two products and the success of these products in the Western marketplace.

Eventually the colonies gained independence, but they were anything but independent. While they imported from the West, they still could only export the raw resources, now hooked into world prices. The more well-to-do who controlled the countries also wanted Western products. But since the countries themselves had little money, they had to get loans from the West, which was willing as long as the Third World was willing to continually rip up their countries to continue to supply Western consumerism. By 1994, the Third World was $1.2 trillion in debt, with the interest alone being $50 billion/year. During the past decade the poorest countries paid $1.5 trillion to the richest countries and still their debt doubled. Because they can't even afford to pay the interest, the only thing they can do is to continually sell off their countries—i.e., the rain forests for cattle and crops that soon destroy the fragile topsoil, leaving the land useless for further growing—just to pay the interest on their debts.

A WORLD TRAPPED IN AN ECONOMIC BOX

Eventually there won't be enough left to sell off to pay the debts, and the Third World will become poorer and poorer in relationship to the wealthier countries. As an example, Mexico, a major exporter of food to the U.S., now is importing over five billion dollars in food crops—mostly for the wealthy who can afford it. Thirty years ago Mexico was self-sufficient in food. Now, though, most Mexicans fall well below the poverty line and earn less than a living wage. While exporting agriculture into the world market was supposed to build Mexico's economy, now most of the Mexican people really can't afford the food that Mexico grows. They are casualties of being hooked into the world economy, and this pattern is being replicated all across the planet. In a world in which the farmers still grow an abundance of food, the farmers go broke and millions go hungry.

Even within the U.S., as we stated earlier in the economics section, the gap between the rich and poor is growing, and more and more people are falling below the poverty line. At the same time, remember that the national debt, with its compound interest, is also growing rapidly. It's like being in a casino poker game where the dealer averages taking 10 percent of every deal. Eventually he has almost all the money, and the whole system breaks down because not enough people can play. Therefore the dealer creates more money a little at a time, loans it out at interest, and continues to have the world more and more in debt to him. The dealers have been the power elite and money brokers within the wealthy countries. There is unbelievable wealth concentrated in the hands of just a few people. Remember earlier when I asked who's got the money. Well, if our national debt of over 5.7 trillion is over 13 times greater than there is money in circulation to pay for it, then the only way we can keep operating is to keep borrowing from those that have accumulated the money. But even the dealers may have now lost control of the system because there may eventually not be enough people in the world who can afford to participate in consumerism, and, at that point, the factories and services close for lack of a market.

Most people have looked at what's happening in the economy as if we're in a stable post-Industrial Revolution system with some minor ups and downs, but we're not. Manufacturing capitalism was based on the exploitation of the Third World. However, the population explosions, environmental damage, and the creation of a massive debt system are causing the system to lapse into chaos while the system plays out to its conclusion. Historically, the current problems are the same as they were thousands of years ago. We still have archaic political institutions in which the few dominate the many, unequal distribution of the fruits of the earth between rich and poor, and grossly wasteful consumption of those resources by the rich. While most people viewed the shakeup of Eastern Europe as a triumph for freedom, we viewed it as primarily economically driven, and that situation continues. The Western countries may be a few years behind as the situation is played out to its logical conclusion—the Third World first, then the poorer developed countries, then us. All this is happening against a backdrop of pollution and environmental destruction that is threatening the continuation of life on the planet.

STUCK IN AN UNSUSTAINABLE ECONOMIC SYSTEM

Our economic system is based on a fantasy, the fantasy of unlimited resources and thus the potential for unlimited production. As we continue to alienate ourselves from nature by seeing it as a resource to use and abuse, we are now rapidly using up those resources in our non-sustainable economies. We are nearing the time when we have to face the reality that our economic system is doomed.

Since our plight was excellently stated in the Canadian Broadcasting Corporation's program, *Trading Futures, Living in the Global Economy*, I will quote from that show:

"All life on earth survives in the same way—making a living out of what that planet provides, and we are no exception. Everything that's vital to our survival comes from nature—air, water, soil, minerals—but the supply is finite, and somehow we've forgotten that. Yet, we believe that our economy can keep on growing forever, far beyond the limits of the natural world. We have come to think of nature as raw material—fuel for our industrial machine. The economic perspective sees nature as a resource for us to extract and use, instead of as the foundation for all life on Earth. That's what's carving up the world and denying us a sustainable future. We're stuck in an unsustainable economic system, and we're hitting the limits."

Hey, but if our GNP keeps increasing, how can we possibly be heading for economic disaster? Again, let me quote from *Trading Futures, Living in the Global Economy*:

"It [the GNP] records production, but it doesn't record depletion of resources or the damage we cause to air, water, and soil. Like governments around the world, we cook our books, excluding the real costs of our economy. With this type of bookkeeping, a country could exhaust its minerals, cut down its forests, erode its soils, pollute its aquifers, and hunt its fish to extinction, all without showing a drop in its GNP.

"This type of accounting turns negative costs into pluses. Cigarettes kill 35,000 Canadians each year, but the medical costs help keep the GNP healthy. The Exxon Valdez oil spill created jobs, sales, and demand for services. The cleanup was perversely a two billion dollar shot in the arm for Alaska's economy.

"Economists so far haven't found a way to put environmental costs on the balance sheet. This accounting system supports conventional economic analysis: when global resource depletion and environmental damage aren't counted, things look good."

But things don't look so good to Herman Daly, Senior Economist for the World Bank, who noted in the same program that, "We've moved from an era of economic growth into an era that we might call anti-economic growth. That means that expansion of the physical scale of the human economy now increases environmental costs faster than it increases production benefits. So, at the margin we're increasing costs faster than increasing benefits, this is making us poorer, not richer. I think in many ways it's not an exaggeration to say that we're living by an ideology of death. We're pushing into the capacity of the biosphere to support life."

Daly also notes the fallacy of the GNP as a measure of our financial status. Because the GNP does not indicate whether we are living off income or capital, interest or principle, it is misleading when we are using up our resources. This is because the depletion of resources is not considered any different than sustainable yield production, which is the only true income. But there is a substantial difference between the way economists look at GNP and that true income, for "... the value of a sawmill is zero without forests; the value of fishing boats is zero without fish ..."Since the time of the Industrial Revolution, we have been using up the resources that support all life on the planet. It's so insidious because it's happening slowly enough that we don't see the day-to-day effects of our folly, and, because most of the decision makers can still buy almost anything they want, they don't see that we're living by an ideology of death.

THE SORCERER'S APPRENTICE

The good news is that it's good news that the current economic system is in jeopardy. It's good news not only because we may be forced to do something about the threat to the environment but also because the system already is not working for growing numbers of people. At the risk of repetition, let me hammer the point once more—there are enough resources and manpower on this planet for all of us to live very abundantly. Given this reality, looking at what we are doing to ourselves, to others, and to the environment makes what we are doing seem really, really crazy!

Using money as the excuse for not providing basic human needs and needed services is REALLY CRAZY! Money is an artificial construct. You can't eat it or shelter yourself with it. It's basically an agreement. Even in the beginning, though, that concept was based on the "we-ness" and "they-ness" of groups of people and individuals within those groups, and that concept just doesn't make sense anymore in a world that now needs action taken to make the system work for the continuation of life on the planet.

As an example of the absurdity of our current economic model, a few days after the devastating 1994 earthquake in Kobe, Japan, the Los Angeles Times ran an article titled, "Major Rebuilding Effort Could Aid Economic Growth, Analysts Say." The article began, "The killer earthquake that hit western Japan on Tuesday caused immense damage likely to run into billions of dollars, but the reconstruction effort should give a boost to economic growth, analysts said." A half century ago the onset of World War Two helped lift the world out of a depression. What's wrong with this picture? Why do we have to have disasters to assist our economies? If a disaster can spark economic growth, why can't we pick any disaster—like pollution, environmental damage, health-care, billions of the world's people living on the edge of survival or the 40,000 children who starve to death every day—and do something about that? Is it just because we are numb to these daily disasters? If all those resources and manpower were there to be put into use, why can't we put them to use without a "disaster" and feed people who are starving, shelter people who are homeless, and restore the environment? Is the whole system we created to serve us, the everyone-for-themselves paradigm, now beyond anyone's control or was it just never designed to make the world work for everyone?

What has happened to us with this old exchange system is like what happened to the Sorcerer's Apprentice in Disney's movie Fantasia. The apprentice, needing to fill a large container with water, picked up the wizard's cap and created a broom with arms to haul buckets of water for him. The apprentice, pleased that success was being achieved with minimal effort, then dosed off and dreamt of his new-found power to control the universe. Just as he was dreaming that he could direct the rise and fall of the waters, he was awakened by the rising water level from the now out-of-control broom. As he tried to control his creation, he only succeeded in creating a rapidly escalating dilemma. By not being able to stop the legions of water-carrying brooms he'd set into motion, the waters threatened to completely inundate him. Only the wizard's reappearance saved him

At first the broom carrying the buckets of water (the money exchange system) seemed to make trade easier, but, as more players got involved and people thirsted for power positions, the system eventually got out of control and took over. It became a monster with a life of its own, burying the individual needs of most people. With that monster (which is really an illusion, because money is an artificial construct) still in control, now everyone thinks that they're at the mercy of the illusion. Yet we have so bought into that illusion that we now believe ourselves as people to be at the mercy of money and/or the lack of it. With the survival of the planet in the balance, let me say again that this really is crazy! However, the wizard represents the consciousness of the Highest Good For All Concerned. We need that wizard consciousness now.

The wizard would tell us that, in truth, economics is a philosophy, not a science. Our Federal Reserve can put into or take out of our economy as much or as little money as they want, whenever they want. Nowadays, a lot of money is not even tangible—it's electronic—and the Fed can just create it and put it wherever they want, or make it disappear. If a philanthropic wizard could create, without the Fed knowing, billions of dollars to provide housing, healthcare, education, and sustainable, income-producing businesses for those in need, this would have a negligible effect on our economy—except for helping those people.

Meanwhile, as was pointed out earlier, natural disasters become a boon to the economy. Again, this is crazy—we don't need these outside stimuli. We can do whatever we want—healthcare, education, restoring the environment—but, at this point, it's more politics than it is economics, and every one of the players has just agreed to play everyone-for-themselves economics the way we're doing it. Also, the U.S. and the big money interests can exert enough pressure on foreign countries to get them to play the same game. Therefore, it's only a political reason why we don't end suffering, hunger, and poverty. Again, economics is a philosophy, not a science. Why don't more of us question why we use "lack of money" as the excuse for not doing what is needed to save this planet.

As a result of our buying into the money illusion, the present economic, political, and social systems look like they were either created by a madman or maybe by just a few self-serving people around whom the rest of society has rotated since the days of the pharaohs, monarchs, and the landed wealthy and "nobility" from the feudal systems. In truth, capitalism eventually replaced feudalism, but control by the power/money elite has really usurped capitalism and democracy. Historically, we have just about always lived by the Golden Rule: he who has the gold, rules. This has resulted in our being so entrenched in thinking individualistically—trying to get by in this every-person-for-himself system—that we haven't stopped to think about what would really work for all of us and for the planet. We have been behaving like people in battle—we want to have more stuff and more power/control than the next person, even if it's at the expense of someone else. When we're not doing this individually, it's group against group or country against country with staggering amounts being spent on weaponry. Meanwhile, more than a billion people are undernourished and three billion in poverty—one-half of humanity excluded from the global marketplace due to the everyone-for-themselves economic system.

IT'S EVERY-PERSON-FOR-HIMSELF

I keep using the terminology "everyone-for-themselves." What does the term mean? Well, it literally means that everyone basically acts out of his or her own self interest. It means, therefore, that we don't get together and really explore how we can make a situation work for all of the parties involved. I mean really taking the time and care to thoroughly and creatively explore how we can positively make that situation work for everyone involved and everyone and everything that the solution would affect. Instead, the parties involved are generally preoccupied with what effect the outcome will have on their own positions. They are concerned that others do not get more or get a better deal than what they get, and they therefore are very watchful and suspicious of the others involved.

There's an interesting little exercise I use in the team-building work I do. The group pairs up and two people stand facing each other and grip hands shoulder high. I tell them that the object is to score as many points as possible in one minute and the way to score a point is to touch the other person's shoulder. It sort of looks like two people about to do standing arm wrestling. When I say go, that's exactly what most pairs proceed to do. At the end of one minute, some people have struggled mightily and have managed a standoff scoring no points. Other people have dominated their perceived opposition and earned a score of ten or whatever to their partner's zero. I never say to the group that the object is to defeat one's partner, yet, in our every-person-for-himself society, that's exactly what most people are predisposed to do. Others mildly cooperate and score a few points, and once in awhile I get a pair of people who get that they can accumulate the most number of points by really exercising their creativity in cooperating with one another. In a minute's time it is possible for those creatively cooperating pairs to score a combined 500 points. At the end of the exercise, those that entered into the everyone-for-themselves power struggle are tired and stressed, those that mildly cooperated are still experiencing some degree of isolation and being tuned out, and those who creatively cooperated feel elated and energized.

This exercise is a perfect metaphor for the everyone-for-themselves paradigm versus a Highest Good For All approach. The everyone-for-themselves paradigm has winners and losers vying for a perceived limited amount of resources, whereas the Highest Good approach has no such bounds, and we are limited only by our imaginations. In the above exercise, the power struggle produced small scores as compared to the cooperative approach producing scores several times higher. It's like when we use the lack of money as the excuse for not providing needed services for each other and for the planet. That's a very limiting approach. Of course we can provide adequate healthcare, nutrition, and an abundant standard of living for everyone while still protecting and healing the environment if we just choose to let go of this mass hypnosis that has gripped us for thousands of years. It's just like the exercise—in the competition based model, it isn't possible to do this, but we do not have to continue buying into this paradigm.

There has been a lot of brainwashing to convince us that cooperation on the scale of making life work for everyone is bad or won't work. We don't question the need for the everyone-for-themselves paradigm because, for thousands of years, variations of that system have been the only models presented for us to look at. More accurately, I should say that this is how history has been taught to us. Drawing on the work of the noted archeologist, Marija Gimbutas, Riane Eisler in her book, *The Chalice* and the Blade, gives us a remarkably different picture about peaceful and abundant cooperative societies that existed for thousands of years. Pick it up, it's worth reading. Conveniently though, we were not taught much about these alternative cultures, which generally were far more successful and long-lasting than the power-based models that now are the norm.

Well, you might say that it has to be this way because even in the human species it's survival of the fittest—the weak don't survive and flourish. In Darwin's *Origin of the Species*, evolution was defined in terms of adaptation in the continuous struggle to survive. The theory was immediately embraced by the power brokers of the last century in order to justify the squalid conditions at the onset of industrialization. Mankind was seen as not being exempt from the domination by the fittest, and this, supposedly, was all a natural process. However, Darwin never talked about "survival of the fittest," a concept often credited to him, but rather, he described those who survived as fittest for a specific ecological niche.

Yet, while Darwin's theory might explain some aspects of evolution, in it's nakedness it is a narrow approach. Cooperation has also played a huge role in creating our world. For example, flowers have evolved vivid colors and inviting scents to attract bees, which pollinate and, as a result, provide for the perpetuation of the species. In fact, the interdependence and cooperation among the species is the very backdrop of evolution. Among all the species, the choice is there for us, as humans, to fully embrace cooperation for the Highest Good rather than trying to dominate each other and the world's resources.

It's amazing that we unquestionably believe that competition and the survival of the fittest is how we have to do things in our capitalistic, democratic way of life. In his 1986 book, No Contest, sociologist Alfie Kohn analyzed hundreds of studies conducted over the last sixty years that compared cooperation with competition. His findings concluded that both, in business and in education, cooperation consistently outproduced competition. In the next section I'll give you a very graphic example of the cooperative synergy that is available to lift a whole group of people.

The everyone-for-themselves struggle for survival ideology is also a doomed approach for humankind because it does not take into account that the Earth is a closed system with finite resources. We can't just take and take and take for personal gain, it has to be balanced for all of us. Otherwise, we will be just like all the species that have disappeared because their habitat became depleted and no longer capable of supporting life.

A REVOLUTION—OR DO WE HAVE TO KEEP DOING THE OLD SYSTEM?

What if enough of us decided to change the rules of the game and throw out the limitations so that we can make life work for all of us? If we changed to "It's all right for you to have every bit as much as me, including equal power," then all the energy and resources being spent trying to perpetuate our economic and political caste systems could be used to enable every one of us on this planet to live very abundantly. And I'm not talking only material wealth but also in terms of addressing and healing the isolation and alienation that most people feel to some degree. In Chinese medicine, illness is the concentration of or lack of energy in one place. Too much wealth concentrated in too few hands and not enough in others creates an economic illness through the lack of flow. In our everyone-for-themselves world, the wealth of the planet has now been concentrated into the hands of so few, while millions starve and billions live in poverty, that our planet is indeed ill—in spirit as well as ecology.

There is a new movement happening in this country right now where some people are attempting to bring more balance into their lives by trading off time spent pursuing income for time to be more nurturing towards themselves. While a 1995 nationwide poll commissioned by the Merck Family Fund found that 82 percent of the respondents agreed that "most of us buy and consume far more than we need, it's wasteful," 28 percent are doing something about it by cutting down on their consumption to create more time for themselves. Of those, 90 percent are satisfied with the results. This trend, called the voluntary simplicity movement, is growing so rapidly that it is becoming recognized as a movement. The Washington Post reported on January 9, 1996, that, "This (voluntary simplicity movement) is a grassroots reaction to the fractured American Dream... Some experts say the turn toward the simplified lifestyle nationwide is starting to reach proportions that foretell a fundamental shift in American society and its consumer culture."

Joe Dominguez, a former Wall Street broker, and Vicki Robin in their book, *Your Money Or Your Life*, took it a step further. They outline a way to basically earn enough to invest and then live cooperatively in small units very cheaply off the income from the investments. Their book is aptly named as they have reclaimed their lives by not buying into the old system and now help others to do the same.

While the simplicity movement is certainly a step in the right direction in terms of people leading fuller, more balanced lives and alleviating some of the pressure on nature through reduced consumption, it still is not the revolution that is needed to rescue the entire planet. These people have admirably chosen to make a small difference, but the system as a whole needs to be changed to effectively rescue the planet from the monumental challenges that we face.

As an example of how a larger group of people can share and work together for The Highest Good Of All, the story of the Mondragon region in the Basque region of Spain comes to mind. This difficult area to live in was devastated by the Spanish Civil War and years of subsequent government persecution under Franco. Out of the ruins, Don Jose Maria Arizmendianieta, a Catholic priest who rejected laissez faire capitalism and the State collectivism of Karl Marx, guided five professional men in the village of Mondragon into starting their own manufacturing firm. They organized their firm as a cooperative in which the highest paid worker never earned more than three times what the lowest paid workers earned and where all workers owned one share of the co-op, earned an equal share of the profits, and could elect and be elected to the board of directors. (This income spread is a bit different than our system, where the average CEO in 1995 made 187 times the wage of the average factory worker, which was an increase from 1960 when the spread was 41 to 1.25).

The cooperative started in 1956 in the village of Mondragon, manufacturing two products with 24 workers. By 1959 they had jobs for one hundred people. Their firm was modeled after the successful 1844 Rochdale cooperative in England which flourished until it opened itself to more capital participants who outvoted the original group and took control. Within three years the Rochdale company then became an ordinary capitalist firm.

However, the Mondragon Co-op model proved to be so successful that, in less than 30 years, it grew from one cooperative with 25 workers to more than 100 worker cooperatives with 19,500 workers in the region. This was made possible by starting cooperative banks which mobilized small reserves enabling the local co-ops to be financed. Because the goal was for everyone to succeed, the banks would meet with prospective new co-ops and help them succeed. They would help find land, supplies, a market for the products, personnel, training, etc. They would also do feasibility studies, monitor progress, and make up one-third of the co-op's board of directors. The system proved so successful that only 3 of the 103 worker cooperatives created between 1956 and 1986 were shut down. Compare that with what we know about starting businesses in the everyone-for-themselves paradigm. Since only 20 percent of our new businesses survive even five years, Mondragon's survival rate of more than 97 percent across three decades indeed commands attention.

Since the cooperatives were worker owned, the Spanish government would not help with welfare, medical care, etc. No problem. The co-ops created their own co-op social security and healthcare. They even built a co-op hospital and a co-op university where the students also worked and produced products and owned the co-op. Many of the supermarkets and schools also became cooperatives. Because housing was expensive, they also built co-op housing owned by the tenants.

How successful are these worker-owned cooperatives? The productivity of the Mondragon Co-op workers is the highest in Spain, higher than the most successful capitalist firms, and the net profit on sales is twice as high as the most profitable capitalist firms. Also, the Basque region never received nor had to depend on outside investment capital to get started or to expand their businesses.

The reason for the success of the now prosperous Mondragon region is that the people decided to pool their resources and make it work for everyone. Because managers and workers both knew that they served each other's interests, they could move ahead boldly with an unusual degree of agreement. Also, since they lived in the same villages, no differences were perceived between managers and workers. They also limited the co-ops to 500 members (beyond which they split up and formed a new co-op) because they found that co-ops couldn't operate beyond that number. This also helped maintain a family feeling. The now prosperous Mondragon region is an example of people working together for the mutual benefit of all. Had the everyone-for-themselves paradigm been in effect instead, the result probably would have been that a few people gathered most of the money while the majority of the people would still be living in poverty in the region.

LET'S MAKE LIFE WORK FOR ALL OF US

What if we thought of ourselves as one family where the needs of one, whether it be a person, a group or a country, are the concern of everyone. Granted that to do this we would have to rein in our egos and sacrifice our selfishness, but what could we gain? What do we really want more of in our lives? Some immediate thoughts are more leisure time, more play, quality time with good friends, opportunities for creative expression, beauty in nature, etc. We'd all probably also opt for less stress, more peace, less pollution, and more healthiness.

So, again, in thinking of ourselves as one cooperative family, let's plan how we all could be living very abundantly on all levels. Let's let go of our notions of this everyone-for-themselves social, economic, political system. Let's start from scratch in terms of what we think has to happen to accomplish our goal, and let's just say that the environment and all life forms must be taken care of in the best way possible. These are the only requirements. Theoretically, let's also toss out all jobs and then start creating and, if necessary, putting back only those things that support our goal.

If we are truly cooperating as one family and we are taking care of all life, we find that we need only about 20 percent of the current jobs. Only 20 percent, and probably less, of the current jobs are essential! The other 80 percent plus are either there to protect and perpetuate our everyone-for-themselves economic caste system or they are what I call "nonsense jobs" which are created solely for the sake of providing a person or some people with money to survive in the current system. Falling into that category are an incredible number of products that are created, again, solely for peoples' incomes in our non-cooperative economic model. Just drive down any city street and see how many establishments wouldn't have to be there if the idea was for the system to really work for everyone.

As an example of the waste of mind power and creativity in our capitalistic system, I know of two very bright men who wanted to make big money with as little effort as possible. What they came up with was providing a bunch of cheap products for promotions, thus using manpower and resources for products that will soon take other jobs to haul them to diminishing landfill sites. They are making a lot of money, but it would be nice to put creative people to work doing something useful and not needlessly consuming our planet's resources. Many lawyers are very sharp too, but, in a cooperative society, few if any of them and the host of other jobs they support would need to exist.

All the jobs involved in the game of making money from money would also be gone. That means the banks, investment houses, and speculators. Dealing with the stock market is really like going to Las Vegas. There are the slots and the dealers who take the house share of the money. Meanwhile, some of the players win, some lose, and a bunch of non-essential and nonsense jobs are created. The interest game was also one of our system's really horrible ideas. Who invented this system-from-hell which basically enslaves individuals and paralyzes whole countries, while a few money brokers do very well? Jobs were created to make money off of money, and, now, as I related earlier, the whole economic system has grown into a monster-out-of-control that really is not working well for most people on the planet. If something needs to be done, we need to have a system where we can just bring our manpower and resources to bear on correcting the problems and just DO IT, and do it in a way that's in harmony with nature! Then we can start saving the planet.

The current economic system is one of consumerism, which aims towards more jobs, more production, a bigger GNP, and less sustainability. If we can create a system that will work for all of us while also eliminating those 80-plus percent of the jobs and the nonsense and unessential products and their accompanying manufacturing plants, storage facilities, and stores, then we could cut way back on our work week hours, do more leisure and creative activities, have more time communing with nature, and use the manpower to start restoring the planet. We could also use that manpower to start creating a better lifestyle for all of us.

Again, there are enough resources and manpower for every being on the planet to live abundantly. Not providing services and a good living environment for all life because there is "not enough money" is an illusion based on our lack of cooperation and creativity. But, what is not an illusion in our consumerist society is that the damage done to our environment has become the major issue of our time. Adding to this, our skyrocketing world population coupled with our rapidly decreasing ability to produce food with our ecological damage means that the quality of life in our everyone-for-themselves economic system will continue to decline. In fact, a Cornell University Team concluded in a 1994 study that the world can support only two billion people at the standard of living now enjoyed by industrialized nations.

We are at almost 6 billion now with 8 billion forecast for the year 2019. The National Resources Defense Council said that the 55 million people that will be born in the industrialized countries during the 1990's will pollute the planet more than the 895 million born in third world countries. Remember that the Worldwatch Institute reported that "As a result of our population size, consumption patterns, and technology choices, we have surpassed the planet's carrying capacity." That is RIGHT NOW! With our declining environment and a couple of billion more people, the situation will become much worse unless we choose to do something drastically different.

Yet, amazingly, the multinationals are pushing for globalization to open up new markets. This is really crazy because it will only hasten the environmental decline of the planet. The physicist/ecologist Vandana Shiva excellently discussed this concept:

"Development, to me, is a word that basically has extremely benign beginnings, in the biological domain, where a seed of the oak tree develops into the oak tree. It's something built into the seed. It's something built into the structure of self-evolution, self-organization. Development really comes from that biological sphere—a child develops into a grown-up, stays himself or herself, but becomes different. And that capacity of inner-generated evolution is where the word "development" really began. But the way it came out of the World Bank—and it did come out of the World Bank—development became, not internally generated, but externally imposed. Development was not something that happens with your resources, your abilities, the abilities of a society, an organism, a person; development becomes that for which you have to take loans and credits, and get indebted; and get enslaved—just the opposite of what development should really be.

"The narrow concept of development—and not just the narrow concept... the perverse concept of development, as it has guided the relationships between the North and South over the last five decades—is definitely anti-ecological. It's anti-ecological because it tries to globalize a pattern of production and consumption that is globally impossible! It tries to universalize the consumption of materials at the scales in which the affluent industrialized West does. We know that twenty percent of that tiny population of the West consumes eighty percent of the planet's resources. So if the development project really had to be achieved, it would need literally five planets to meet its objectives. It is therefore against the very logic, ecological logic of this planet's resources. We don't have five planets! We just have one.

"'Maldevelopment' is basically a development paradigm that destroys; does not build. Maldevelopment is development that does not build on peoples' capacities, it does not build on the limits which ecosystems put on human activity. It disrupts cultures. It violates ecological boundaries, and it just imposes a very, very narrow model of what a preferred human existence is on the entire world. In fact, when development started... and it started absolutely around 1948, where the rest of the world, of the Third World, which had been left poor because of colonization, was declared 'underdeveloped.' Suddenly, we were 'underdeveloped.' And development was a yardstick in which the only measures were how much paper you can consume and how much cement you can consume, how many chemicals you can consume, how much petrol and fossil fuel you can consume. Now quite clearly, subsistence societies did not consume any of that! They were not involved in the ravaging of the planet. And maldevelopment basically sucked them in with loans from the World Bank and bilateral aid. And made them feel that unless they could shift from organic fertilizer into chemical fertilizer they were 'underdeveloped.' Unless they could shift from their bullock carts to tractors, they were 'underdeveloped.' Unless they could shift from the hundreds of diverse housing materials that are used across the world according to what is available, what is the climate, how will people protect themselves and give themselves shelter? That diversity of housing was devastated by concrete and steel."

Indeed, we can have an abundant lifestyle for all the billions of people on the planet, but this cannot be achieved in an everyone-for-themselves paradigm based on the God of profit. It can only be done when we create a model where we can make the world work for all the people, and this means equitably sharing, conserving, and renewing resources. It also requires having the consciousness where we care enough to act for The Highest Good Of All.

Don't mess with Mother Nature! We're now finding out what happened to earlier societies that prospered and grew and then mysteriously abandoned their civilizations. With their farming practices along with their need for lumber, many cultures from Mesopotamia to the great pre-Columbian cultures of Central America ruined their environment to the point where it could no longer support them. Eerily we now are repeating this past mistake, only now it's on a worldwide scale, and, unlike previous civilizations, there is no new land to migrate to! When history looks back on us 50 years from now, the question will be asked, "Why didn't people of the 20th century see what they were doing and change it? This was madness."

We are now near the end of the line in our current way of relating with our environment. Those who don't believe that are still clinging to the attitude of subduing the environment to serve mankind's needs. In his book, *The Green Lifestyle Handbook*, Jeremy Rifkin described environmental relationships as being "similar to personal relationships. By attempting to subdue nature, by refusing to accept it on its own terms, by manipulating it to serve expedient short-term material ends, we have made our long-term relationship with the environment less secure and now face the prospect of a wholesale depreciation of the life-supporting processes of the planet."

To take care of ourselves and all life, we need to move into sustainability, which means a way of living on this Earth so that each generation passes on the Earth's natural resources intact to its children. We are facing an emergency and must make decisions that will be not only for our Highest Good today but also for the Highest Good for generations to come. While changing the way we live in order to preserve ourselves and our planet may be a big change, it can be accomplished with a workable plan. I call that plan "The Next Evolution: making the planet work for everyone," and I'll get into the details of that plan in the next chapter.

NEW DEFINITIONS

To keep our resources intact, we need to eliminate as many non-essential jobs and products as possible, and, acting as one family, we need to share our wealth and resources. We need to redefine wealth as USE and ACCESS rather than as POSSESSIONS and POWER. The everyone-for-themselves paradigm has used up our planet's resources by producing more materialism—for some, and only some, people, but not for the vast majority of the people on the planet. The majority would have far more if wealth were redefined as "use and access" and if we all acted according to that definition. We can live cooperatively with so much more abundance available to us. As a planet, we can no longer afford to have individual ownership of so many things when we can get by, and do even better, on much less when it is shared. For example, almost none of us have boats, but, with the Highest Good "use and access" approach, more people could enjoy boating and with far fewer boats (and thus the resources it takes to build and maintain them). In almost any marina, about 99 percent of the boats go unused most of the time. If we shared access, those boats would be in use rather than 99 percent docked. Just think of the possibilities if this were a "Use and Access" world—we would all have the freedom to do so much more.

Did you know that there are over 25,000 supermarket items, including two hundred kinds of cereal? There are also over 11,000 magazines, mostly filled with ads for more products. There is such a tremendous amount of stuff in stores and warehouses with more being produced all the time (and eventually hauled off to landfills). In fact, there may be as much in storage as there is being used. Much of it is also the art of selling us what we don't really need. Such is the nature of capitalism. Also, in the spirit of sharing, we need to look at quality of life more in terms of intangibles such as fun, shared creative activities, nurturing, loving, etc.—things that money really can't buy. I have reserved the next chapter to describe more in detail what that might look like in a creative model of living that would work for all of us.

The idea of great wealth at the expense of great poverty doesn't make sense any more when we must now do no further damage to our environment. Molly Olsen, a member of President Clinton's

Council on Sustainable Development, stated that "A society with a grossly disparate distribution of the fruits of development cannot possibly sustain itself in the long term." Take deforestation for example. Because most industrialized countries have already destroyed most of their own forests, most deforestation is now occurring in Third World countries where people are living on the edge of survival and need either more farming land and/or fuel to survive even this generation. Along with that, their debt-ridden governments think they must sacrifice their forests and resources looking for short-term profits to pay off their debt interest. We can't just ask Third World countries to stop cutting down their forests because the issue must be tied into improving the quality of their lives. We can't have people living in poverty trying to support a family because they will take from the environment what they have to in order just to survive.

But, as a reminder, the issues are not just environmental. We can't have people working at minimum wage trying to support and effectively raise a family. Put yourself in the place of those trapped by poverty, the lack of education and skills, and even the lack of positive role models. With that hopelessness it's easy to understand why people turn to drugs and crime.

So we must change the world on the level of how people live together. For this to happen, it requires a change of consciousness where we switch from the everyone-for-themselves paradigm and start acting for The Highest Good Of All. We must also consider the Earth as a partner in that change. Imagine the Earth as a living being—would we choose to continue to slowly poison it or choose to begin to heal it? To heal it, we have to start thinking about what we're doing every time we buy, use, or discard anything, and we need to creatively rethink how we can change the whole system that created our current patterns in the first place.

Unfortunately though, we haven't set up our lives so that we as a group can easily make Earth-healing choices. On the one hand, we have those trapped in poverty forced to use up the environment, and, on the other hand, we have consumerism producing unnecessary, and far too many, products with their accompanying packaging and disposal problems. Most of our cities' landfills are full and closed and are contaminating our ground water in addition to releasing methane gas into the atmosphere. We Americans have been throwing away enough "waste" each year to fill a convoy of ten ton garbage trucks that would reach over half way to the moon. The packaging for our consumeristic lifestyles contributes the largest percentage of that "waste" — 50 percent of all paper produced in the U.S. and 90 percent of all glass. We Americans also have the highest level of consumption in the world. With 6 percent of the world's population, we consume more than 30 percent of the planet's resources. In addition, we use twice as much energy per person than any other country and are responsible for more than one-fourth of the carbon dioxide and CFC emissions.

As a result of the Industrial Revolution and the resulting pollutants now being released into the environment, man now has the possibility to destroy the planet, even without a nuclear war. However, the fact that there may be no easy way out of the world economic dilemma, along with the now obvious environmental threat, may be a good thing. Ultimately it will push us in the direction of trying to act for The Highest Good Of All Concerned, of acting like one family, of taking care of each other in a more loving and nurturing way, and of addressing the quality of life for everyone on the planet.

WE NEED A WORKABLE NEW MODEL

So where do we start? There are so many imbalances, so many things that need to be corrected, and so many just causes that trying to do something about each little area of interest gets to be an overwhelming task. Save the dolphins, the whales, recycle, end political corruption, save the rain forests, do something about crime, reduce our drug use, eliminate domestic violence, etc., etc., etc. So much to do, and so little time left for the planet. Also, there's the problem that everything, as physics' Systems Theory tells us, is interrelated, so something like saving the rainforests is not as easy as it seems because it relates to so many factors including the quality of people's lives. Therefore, there must be a systems approach to rescue the planet, and it must include and address the quality of life for everyone on the planet. To do this requires two things: we need a different approach for how we as people live together, and share together and we need to move into the cooperative consciousness required to do this—the consciousness where we truly dedicate ourselves to living for The Highest Good Of All.

Because most of the people in the world would have no idea what it would look like if we chose to live together for The Highest Good Of All, the first step would be to create a MODEL COMMUNITY, based on the concept of making life work for all of us, to show the world how life could be very, very different. While "intentional" egalitarian communities are certainly not a new idea, with many small ones currently existing, none have been created with the intention and on the scale that is needed to arouse world-wide interest. We need to see an approach that not only could heal the planet but will also show a different way of living with a daily quality of life that would be more uplifting for almost anyone living on the planet.

The way we live together and relate together in community is the basic building block that is needed to change the world. The creation of a model Community that demonstrates living for The Highest Good Of All will enable others to see how we can all cooperate and enjoy a higher and happier standard of living. With the successful demonstration and media coverage of this model, people from all over the world will be able to see and hear about a lifestyle that they too can enjoy and how we can start by setting up life to work for everyone, for The Highest Good Of All.

Again, there are enough resources and manpower for all of us, all life on the planet, to live together very abundantly. We just haven't set it up that way yet because of the legacy of our everyone-for-themselves socio-economic-political approach. It is now time, so I invite you to expand your consciousness and open your heart as we describe a model that could work for everyone, that would stave off the dire predictions of what otherwise is in store for us.

Chapter 4

LIVING FOR THE HIGHEST GOOD IN COMMUNITY

by Jack Reed

THE WAY WE LIVE TOGETHER AND RELATE TOGETHER IN COMMUNITY IS THE BASIC BUILDING BLOCK THAT IS NEEDED TO CHANGE THE WORLD.
—*The Community Planet Foundation*

Utilizing the concept of living For The Highest Good Of All Life, how do we design our model living situation (Community) so that it will work for all of us? We must not only meet the needs of the planet by living sustainably, but we must also meet the needs of the people involved by optimizing the quality of life for ALL people. So the questions are:

1. Does being ecological mean that we have to suffer? and

2. Does sharing our resources mean that we all have less?

The answer to these questions is an emphatic NO! In fact, living in harmony with each other and the planet can be more fun, far more abundant, and much more satisfying than the lifestyles most of us are currently living. Given the Western society's penchant for consumption and indulgence, if we can't provide a more satisfying model for living, we won't change how we live until the decaying environment eventually forces us as a society to change our consumption patterns. But we don't have to let it get to that point because doing the best for the planet will also optimize the quality of life for all of us if we choose to live together in a way that can truly work for all of us. So open your mind and your heart to the possibility of how we could be living, and, if there's something that we may leave out of our description or that you may wish to alter somewhat, just put that in because you would be a part of this model too and your needs are important.

HOW HAVE WE DESIGNED OUR TOWNS AND CITIES?

As a starting point let's look at how traditional towns and communities get started. How did your town or city end up looking and operating as it does? Chances are that it started out with a single home or two—possibly even farms—located on some fairly flat land. Then there were probably more homes built as people moved into the area, and they were followed by some businesses. When the cluster grew big enough, government and service buildings were added until there was an unplanned and unintegrated hodgepodge of structures and streets. Also, because of the everyone-for-themselves economic model, most of the space under roofs and most of the concrete laid down to cover the earth ended up robbing people of their connection with each other and with nature, which eventually got pushed out of their lives.

With the advent of cars, we started paving streets, driveways, parking lots, walkways, and freeways until an astounding amount of land was covered with asphalt and concrete. Since it was easier to build on the lowlands and flatlands, we forced the farms further and further out from the cities and, with suburban sprawl, further out still—eventually even leading to the demise of the small farmer. Then, as the cities overcrowded, those who could moved away from the town centers dreaming of the good life with a home in suburbia. They moved into their large suburban homes, which now don't even reflect the current living/relationship patterns. But, with the need for the everyone-for-themselves income, we often have to jump back onto the freeways and spend a lot of time in congested rush hour travel. We also have to get back into our cars to go and do almost anything—shopping, recreation, errands, meetings with friends, etc.

So, before anyone ever stopped to do an environmental or sociological impact study, we created havoc for both our immediate environment and our lifestyles. We pushed out nature. We pushed out fresh food grown on the best farmland. We tied up our lives in traveling and depersonalization to the point that many of us now get minimal exercise (we are now a nation of overweight and obese people largely because of this factor), minimal playtime, and, most importantly, minimal quality time spent with good friends and family. Chances are, for many of us, the jobs we have to do to support ourselves take up—and sometimes become— most of our lives, and many of us spend 99+ percent of our time with concrete between us and the earth.

CAN WE DESIGN LIVING IN HARMONY?

When I give my presentations on the Community Planet vision, I ask the audience the question, "What if we, the people in this room, had the power to have the world work for everyone? Imagine that we are the decision makers and are not bound by the in-the-box current economic/political system. Could we transform our planet so that it works for everyone and for all life on the planet? Could we do it???" Well, we met almost weekly for three years and created that vision, a vision that has the powerr to absolutely transform our planet.

The population of the Community would be between 400 and 500. That size would be large enough so that the Community could have the kinds of amenities and opportunities for a variety of recreational and creative expressions, yet not so large that it would preclude each person from taking an active role in the decision-making process in the Community. Cooperative communities have existed for years, but none based on the Highest Good For All model on the scale that would have more universal appeal such that people not living there would say, "Yeah, this Community's lifestyle is much better than my own. I'd like to live there!" Most are too small to have the amenities and the diversity that would appeal to people used to certain oppor-tunities of urban living.

Critical to the design of the Community is what I call the fun factor. Communities have stagnated and ultimately failed because they weren't fun, and people lost interest. But, if people are having fun, others are drawn in. Thus, for the Community model to be viable, fun and pleasure must be interwoven into every facet of the Community. In fact, a Highest Good approach mandates that fun, joy and loving be the essences in our daily lives, because they are so essential to our individual and collective well-being. People need to know that we can have a society where we're really connecting with each other and having a lot of pleasure. Most people now have grown up thinking that fun is having control over others, being self-indulging, being greedy, being lustful, and competing with and having enjoyment at the expense of others. People need to rediscover in a deeper way what fun is for them, and a Community designed for The Highest Good Of All will provide the ideal stage for this rediscovery. The tremendous potential of the "use and access" principle I described earlier is an integral part of this.

IT'S IMPORTANT WHAT QUESTIONS WE ASK

Not only is it important that we ask questions about how we live together, but it's important to ask the right questions. Any community is only going to be as good as the fundamental questions it asks and is willing to take on. The questions determine the outcomes, so it all starts with the questions. In 18th century America we once asked the question, "How can we live with more freedom, equality, and harmony?" It was, at the time, revolutionary in the world. Even today, everywhere in the world, people know of Washington, Jefferson, and Franklin. But we've stagnated and largely forgotten that noble question that was the foundation for our country, and it's now time to take freedom and equality to the next level. In fact, with what we've done to the planet, it's needed for our very survival.

Any good idea, or good question, is always subject to corruption if it is not constantly and creatively explored and energized. Right now it's obvious that the power brokers and money interests in our everyone-for-themselves paradigm have exploited the once noble question our founding fathers asked. The planet isn't going to survive in an everyone-for-themselves paradigm with the questions that the power-based system asks: "How can we get control and shape people's lives?"; "How can we gather for ourselves as much wealth as possible?"; and "How can we disempower and numb people out so they don't overthrow the system and we lose control?" While the last question may not be absolutely conscious, the big players absolutely have a huge stake in maintaining the status quo. Remember the Nicola Tesla story earlier, well that's just one of a million examples.

Because of the stagnation and narrowness in the questions we currently ask, that's why we, in our Community Planet Community description, decided we had to be really expansive in the questions we chose to ask about how we live together in Community. While we could have just described areas like economics, agriculture, education, recreation, etc., we chose to focus on more expansive questions involving how people live together:

1. How do we share our abundance?

2. How do we interact with our environment?

3. How do we reach consensus?

4. How do we beautify our environment?

5. How do we enjoy ourselves?

6. How do we enrich ourselves?

7. How do we coordinate what we live to do?

8. How do we nourish ourselves?

9. How do we vitalize ourselves.?

10. How do we communicate?

11. How do we bring forth inner wisdom?

12. How do we expand our Community?

For example, the question we asked about how we govern ourselves—"How do we reach consensus?"—stands in stark contrast with the current ideology of how does everyone try to get their way and how do the power brokers manipulate and control the masses. If we were to ask "How do we reach consensus?" in all our decision-making, the question is so expansive and all encompassing that we would eventually come up with a decision-making system that includes The Highest Good For All. As part of that question, we would take on the more fundamental question I've posed, "Given that there are enough resources and manpower on the planet for all of us to live abundantly and in harmony with our environment, what is the problem?" As long as we have the imbalances on the planet that we currently have, we need to passionately keep asking that question and start acting upon it. Eventually we would end up with a model that would work for all life on the planet and for future generations.

Again, it all boils down to what questions we ask and are willing to take on, and I think most societies have been asking very limiting questions, at best. For example, the Puritan culture, which still has an influence on us today, asked very controlling questions: "How can we get people to behave out of fear?"; "How can we punish people to keep them in line?"; "How can we show that suffering is good?"; "How can we keep women in their place?"; and "How do we repress people and get them to keep their feelings to themselves?" At this time in history we need to ask very different questions, the kinds of questions that we asked in our Community description of how we would live together more successfully and more abundantly. Underlying all the questions is our foundational, fundamental question, *"HOW CAN WE LIVE TOGETHER FOR THE HIGHEST GOOD OF ALL CONCERNED?"*

HOW DO WE SHARE OUR ABUNDANCE?

One of the first questions a group of people living in any community needs to ask is how to define their financial interrelationships. This question gets answered by default in our current world economy because we just continue the old everyone-for-themselves paradigm without exploring other possibilities. Also, wealth is typically defined as a person's net worth. But isn't wealth so much more than that? An ailing and/or depressed billionaire would probably give all his or her material wealth in exchange for health and happiness. Recognizing that abundance in our lives means far more than material wealth, in our question concerning how we interrelate with respect to "wealth," we chose to ask how we can ALL live together abundantly. This planet could be a paradise for ALL of us to share. It's a very abundant place to live, if we would just make that choice.

As I stated in the previous chapter on the Highest Good, sharing resources has incredible advantages. We can have so much, much more when we pool our resources. We currently tie up so much of our wealth in individual possessions that we individually use. If we can redefine wealth as use and access rather than as possessions, then we can really cut down on our consumerism while at the same time having access to much, much more than we would individually have. We don't need to each own a lawnmower, a complete set of tools, laundry appliances, vacuum cleaners, etc.—we only need easy access to these things. Although there is nothing comparable in scope to the model Communities we're proposing, the 60 members of the Twin Oaks community were living on only $250 per month each in 1986, and the 14 members of Alpha Farm in Oregon were living comfortably on $140 per month each. Through sharing resources, we can not only have use and access of far more things than we normally would, but we would be using far less of our own financial resources, not to mention using far less of the planet's resources. We also don't need as many people laboring to produce the quantity of material goods that we consume.

Because we see ourselves as one family, we decided that, "The land, structures, and communally-used or provided resources belong to and are the responsibility of all residents." As we look at the damage we've done to the planet, in retrospect it looks truly crazy that people have been able to do whatever they wanted to the environment regardless of The Highest Good Of All. When individual interests can do what they want with the land, water, and air as opposed to planning as a group with the welfare of generations to come taken into consideration from the start, then we have a recipe for the life-threatening environmental problems we now face. Instead, we need to design land usage to work for everyone; we need to again think of and act towards land and nature as being sacred. If we don't do this, housing and cities get stuffed together, nature and productive land upon which to grow food disappears, pollution becomes a major problem, and concrete spreads like a seal over the land while walking disappears. This is OUR WORLD, *IT BELONGS TO ALL OF US*, including future generations, and we need to plan and share it and its resources with ultimate care for all life in order to keep it intact for our children and our children's children.

In regards to housing, group ownership becomes a very freeing concept. As the system is now, people can become stuck in housing situations due to finances. Many have moved to suburbia with long commutes and the necessity of jumping into a car to do almost anything. We usually also have no idea who our neighbors are and no real connection to them as people. Because buying and selling is at the mercy of the ebb and flow of the market, people get trapped in locations, sometimes for years, while their lives get progressively more isolated. Then, because they need their 9-to-5 jobs to continue their lifestyle, they get trapped on the treadmill of life.

Our model Highest Good Community would provide basic human needs to all residents. These benefits include food, shelter, health needs, recreational and creative equipment and supplies, communication systems, educational opportunities, and transportation. However, if a person chose to work outside the Community and the person earned more than the average cost per resident cost of living, the resident would only be obligated to contribute ten percent of that excess amount to the Community. Likewise, residents working within the Community and making money outside (i.e. through outside investments) would contribute ten percent of their outside income. With the above system, we felt that all residents would have a baseline lifestyle at a very high level, and the people who want even more could not only still have that, but also their increased riches would benefit the whole Community as well.

*A century and a half ago Thoreau wrote about situations where
people get trapped by their housing. This description in*
Walden *could just as easily be about the entrapment many
people feel today.*

"*And when the farmer has got his house, he may not be the
richer but the poorer for it, and it may be the house that has got
him ... I know one or two families, at least, in this town, who,
for nearly a generation, have been wishing to sell their houses
in the outskirts and move into the village, but have not been
able to accomplish it, and only death will set them free.*"[4]

—*Thoreau, Henry David,* Walden

As I wrote earlier in the "Highest Good" chapter, the now prosperous Mondragon area of Spain is an example of people working together for the benefit of all. Another example of the value of cooperation is the kibbutzim in Israel. With less than four percent of the population living on about 250 kibbutzim, they still produce forty percent of Israel's agriculture and seven percent of Israel's industrial exports. At the same time, they provide all the food and housing for their members as well as the medical needs, education, and entertainment, and recreation. With an entire Community planned from the beginning to be in harmony with all life, with the sharing of resources, and with our renewed sharing with nature and with each other, we can do even better in our model Community in terms of the abundance of our lives on all levels.

Interestingly, while our consumption has increased 45 percent since 1970, the Index of Social Health reports that, during this same time, the quality of our lives has dropped 51 percent. Consumption and materialism do not equate with abundance and often are the antithesis of what abundance truly is. A 1995 Merck Family Fund survey indicated that Americans would be happier with lifestyles based on gratifying personal relationships rather than on consumption. According to a *U.S News and World Report* poll, 51 percent "would rather have more free time, even if it means less money."

One downside of what we typically think of as wealth is that most of us get stuck on the treadmill of having to slave to perpet-uate our lifestyles, and that really drains the life out of most people. We've been chasing a concept of freedom that we've thought of as having enough money to do what we want, when we want, to the extent that we want. The trouble is that in an everyone-for-themselves model this isn't possible for the vast majority of people. If there's not even enough money in circulation to pay the national debt, then there is a finite amount of what people think of as wealth, thus producing the haves and the have-nots. We've bought into having lots of possessions because we think they create freedom through security. However, freedom is anything but being stuck on the treadmill, and wealth is really so much more than money or material goods.

HOW DO WE INTERACT WITH OUR ENVIRONMENT?

Remember that, since the time of Francis Bacon in the 17th century, the question that our culture has asked about our environment has been, "How can we detach ourselves from nature and manipulate it to advance our own human interests?" This question has led us to our current environmental crisis. Utilizing the concept of The Highest Good of All Life, the question we must ask is, "How do we design a physical situation that will work for *all* of us and *all* life on the planet?" We know that we must meet the needs of the planet by practicing sustainability. We must also meet the needs of the people involved by optimizing the standard of living for all people.

Because of the cooperative nature of the Community, one of the immediate design improvements we can make would be to design it to be a pedestrian Community. We could bring walking back into our lives, and, when needed, use the Community solar rechargeable electric carts. Because most people would work within the Community, we could also cut way back on the use of cars (which would be parked on the outskirts of the Community). For a Community of 500 people, we may only need 50 or so cars, probably even less. With the amount of resources most of us tie up in our cars, just think of the savings we can have in transportation. Also many, if not all, of these cars could be run with non-polluting energy. In addition, just picture a living situation without fences and without all that concrete and space we use for roadways and parking areas.

According to the USDA, we're losing over 3 million acres per year of agricultural land to development.[13] That's almost three times the size of Delaware, much of it being put under concrete, every year! Almost all of this is due to the lack of cooperation in our current system. When we all finally start living For The Highest Good, there are machines that eat concrete and turn it into sand. Then we can reverse our current course and instead start eliminating millions of acres of concrete every year. In addition, the buildings would be designed from the beginning to be multi-use and multipurpose structures. In the current everyone-for-themselves paradigm, most private and even civic structures go unused a great portion of the time. In a cooperative Community, we would need to have fewer structures while, at the same time, having far more facilities for all of us to use.

Using existing technology, we can generate all of our own energy—through solar power and other options, depending on location. As examples, there are six thousand villages in India that are running on photovoltaic and the story of the Gaviotas village in Colombia provides us with an incredible model of energy self-sufficiency in the most challenging of environments. Also, when designing from scratch rather than trying to retrofit, we can save a huge amount of energy by designing and building in energy efficiency in the first place instead of coming along later and trying to correct past mistakes. It's interesting that ancient cultures even knew how to save energy in their designs, but we blindly build for convenience and try to muscle in, by use of fossil fuel, things like heating and cooling. Technologically, this Community would in many ways be like a Disney World Epcot Center built along the lines of sustainability. The Community would be a living demonstration of a future that is not grim, foreboding, and poverty stricken, but rather a future that is both sustainable and very desirable. Built with local, non-polluting building materials, the Community would also be a showcase for positive design, technology, and building materials.

Designing a Community to work for everyone will look different in different environments. However, in every environment, we can improve the quality of all life by designing and building cooperatively. For example, in areas with a lot of snow, we can build domes over the living and working areas, just like they put domes over stadiums. This will enable the residents to enjoy the winter while at the same time being able to walk around and play without the burden and expense that snow and ice and cold impose.

The promise of technology in our age was that it was supposed to improve our lives by lifting us above the whims of nature. While science and technology have largely delivered on that promise, it has often come at a price—the earth has been monumentally damaged, and there is now the threat of irreversible damage not only to the environment but also to the future quality of ALL life on the planet.

Technology was meant to be our servant, not our master, and we are now left with the task of trying to figure out how to correct the damage that we've done. This task is made even more difficult because we don't want to sacrifice any of the Western consumerism to which we've become accustomed. Creating a positive model for future development is the key to returning technology to its role as a servant to humankind. Fortunately, we currently have the science and technology to rectify most of the problems facing us, especially given that we can change the way that we live together to make it work for all of us. However, it is obvious that we first need a revolution of consciousness. As Einstein said, "It has become appallingly clear that our technology has surpassed our humanity."

HOW DO WE REACH CONSENSUS?

When we were meeting to generate the Community Planet description, we realized right away that perhaps the most important question to consider in designing a Community in harmony with the principle of The Highest Good of All is "How are we going to govern ourselves?" The age-old, supposedly politically correct model is democracy's "majority rules" system. Unfortunately, this is the very system that has swept across the planet, resulting in the mess in which we currently find ourselves. So what were the alternatives? Through the centuries, many groups like some of the Native American cultures and the Quakers have successfully used consensus decision-making. Right away we loved the idea because a Community of people living together really do need to be living in harmony with one another, while still providing for individual needs and considerations.

Popularly, consensus is thought of as decision via compromise in which everyone loses something. So you don't get confused with how politicians use the term, we described consensus as "differing with other forms of decision-making because it stresses the cooperative development of a decision with people working with each other rather than competing against each other. Everyone has a chance to be heard and come into harmony with the decision. Thus a decision is reached that is acceptable to all, a decision that everyone can say 'yes' to. There is no voting, and therefore no losing minority. Because the essence of consensus is creativity and accessing The Highest Good of All Concerned, there also isn't the need for compromise."

So, in the spirit of The Highest Good of All, the question of how we not only govern ourselves but also do our decision-making in the Community became, "How do we reach consensus?' Meeting weekly for months, we brainstormed, explored, and sometimes argued about how we could do consensus decision-making in a Community of up to 500 people and still have it work. It was a monumental, yet fun endeavor which finally paid off in the very unique design which you will read about in the "Guidelines" section. Through the whole process, we, ourselves, adopted the consensus process, and every decision we made after that point was always done by the process of consensus.

When we ask "How do we reach consensus?," the question stands in stark contrast to the fundamental question that the governments run by the power brokers have asked through the centuries. Their question has basically been "How can we impose our will over the greatest number of people with the most efficiency and the least resistance in order to further our own self interests, and how can we get it past people so they either don't notice or don't object?" Make no mistake about it, this has been the basic agenda on the part of the forces that have controlled governments. Also, whether it's decision-making in businesses, organizations, or groups of all types, the most powerful and outspoken have always had a disproportionate influence over these decisions that affect our lives. The everyone-for-themselves approach has been characterized by a very definite lack of true consensus. It's time that we start asking how we can make decisions on all levels that work for and include everyone. To do that we need to consider the deeper questions we keep asking: "Given that there are enough resources and manpower for all of us to live abundantly, what is the problem?" And, "How can we live together for The Highest Good of *All* Life on the planet?" This takes creativity, it takes challenging our assumptions about how we have to live together, and it takes respecting and valuing each other and all life on the planet. We can do this, and we must.

A consensus decision-making system is only workable when there is the commitment and consciousness to go for The Highest Good of All. However, as I said before, if we're going to continue to have a world, we're going to have to start making it work for everyone. This first model Community will require that consciousness of committing to go for The Highest Good of All. Then, when people see how much more freedom and abundance they can have through cooperation, that will probably be the most significant thing the Community will contribute to changing the world. As McLaughlin and Davidson wrote in *Builders of the Dawn* about the Philadelphia Life Center (Movement For A New Society), "They see consensus as a concrete example of the real healing work that is needed in the world, the elimination of power relationships between people and the celebration of our mutual humanity. It teaches people to open up on a more spiritual level, on an interactive and intuitive level with others."

Majority rule is a competitive, win/lose approach. You win when you get the most votes, and you lose when you don't. Because you're trying to prove that you're right and the opposition is wrong, there is often much divisive arguing. Also, people listen to the arguments not really out of concern for the needs of others but to try to develop counter arguments. Historically we've voted for so many issues and for so many people that have lost that none of us really feel that we are represented politically and that our needs are being met. The majority rules system has resulted in all of us, except the power brokers, feeling that we are a minority group. As a result we usually vote for the lesser of two evils; we vote against someone or something rather than voting for someone or something in an election. That's why most election commercials focus on trying to give us reasons to vote against the opposition because they're so terrible. They do this negative electioneering because it works. In our "democracy" we also see partisan politics every time any hi-profile issue comes up—the other party almost always takes the opposite side. They do this just to be against whatever decision is made, and they do it purely in an attempt to try to discredit the other side and try to win the "againstness" vote.

As we all have experienced, there is a hierarchy of power in majority rule groups where the opinions of leaders, money interests, and outspoken players carry a vastly disproportionate influence over the rest of the group. People outside of the power game who may be shy in speaking out or have difficulty putting their ideas into words may be ignored even though their ideas may be better. Also, because whoever the minority is in the moment can so easily be dispensed with by just outvoting them, the notion that everyone can participate in a democratic system is not really accurate.

With so many people and their input being left out of the process, the quality of majority rule decisions is also diminished. The process often boils down to voting between two positions proposed by the main factions. Innovative and creative approaches and solutions are often not considered, and systems-approach solutions are virtually never considered. Supposedly this is to expedite the process, but instead this causes monumental inefficiency as the sub-quality decisions negatively impact our lives. Those decisions then have to be redecided again and again through the years because they either don't work or are short-sighted in the long run. Also, because people are left out of the process, they may easily feel justified in feeling resentful and not supporting and/or sabotaging any given decision.

In true consensus decision-making, everyone has a chance to participate and be heard. The softer voices and the more unique approaches all have the opportunity to be responded to by the group. Also, not just logic but feelings and intuition are valued as well. Consensus has an advantage over majority rules because the best thinking of the entire group is included, and the synergy of the group creates even more than the sum of the parts.

In *true* consensus decision-making, the process of creating a decision that works for everyone brings in the element of *creativity* as well as the qualities of caring and concern for others. We really have to listen to and respond to the needs and concerns of others. In that process of going for The Highest Good of All, innovative, high-quality solutions are reached, and the support of the group in implementing those decisions is assured. While this may sound too good to be true, keep in mind that a prerequisite for living in this Community must be that a resident is committed to going for The Highest Good of All. This does not at all mean giving up individuality, but it does mean not imposing one's ego-position on the group. Consensus is not "group consciousness," but rather it requires people to be honest and mature and to express what their needs are, where they're at, and what will work for them. While the final decision may not always be everyone's personal first choice, it will be one that serves The Highest Good of All Concerned, one that everyone feels that they can support. As opposed to the disempowerment in our current "democratic society," it will be exciting for people to become reinvolved with the decisions that affect our lives.

Because individuality and individual self-interest are so highly valued in our culture, it's time to clarify how individual needs interface with a Highest Good For All model of living. Does making life work for everyone mean that we have to sacrifice our self-expression and individual needs? Not at all, in fact, with more support and less stress and pressures from life, people will have much more of an opportunity for expression and for getting their needs met. Sure, people are responsible for their own self-interests, but, to have a quality life, what we must understand is that getting our needs met in a truly optimal way means having happy, healthy and abundant people and a healthy environment around us.

Getting individual needs met means considering the big picture, considering the whole context within which we live. Self indulgence at the expense of others ends up sabotaging the very self-interest we're after. The immediate wins that people go after are often really not in one's self-interest in the long run if those wins come at the expense of the planet or any of its people. It is not a rich life with rich and happy surroundings when those around us have to struggle to try to get ahead and are stressed out and not having a lot of fun in their lives. It really limits our opportunities when our neighbors have no time or energy to share with us.

In a Highest Good approach to living together, we can create abundance for all. Then our self-interest is achieved with having happy people around us who can really share and appreciate our successes. We must expose the myth that cooperation means compromising our own self-interests. Remember that the Systems Theory tells us that all things are interconnected. We can either choose to continue to go for the immediate gratification, which later can work against all of us, or choose to lift everyone. We call this latter approach "enlightened self-interest" because it encompasses the fact that we are all interrelated and it is the only approach which will even work for us individually over time.

With everyone having input into the process, you might think that it may take too long to make decisions. While that may be true at times, the long-term benefit is that time is actually saved by making much higher quality decisions instead of having to continuously work to correct poor quality decisions that didn't include the needs of everyone and the environment. As people gain trust in and experience with consensus, the process gets faster and faster without loss of quality. Also, because of the participatory nature of consensus, it's difficult to work consensus with more than twelve people in a group. Therefore, for our Community to work consensus in a group of up to 500 residents required an innovative approach.

As an epilogue to this consensus section, perhaps the biggest export of our model Community will be this concept of going for the Highest Good, and consensus decision-making will be a major key ingredient in that. It is unreasonable to expect most people to begin to work consensus right now. It really does require the commitment to go for The Highest Good of All Concerned. However, as people see and hear about the benefits of working consensus in a Community setting, people will become interested in getting training in how to work the consensus process. Consensus can have a transformational effect on relationships at every level.

I'd like to conclude this section that relates to how we govern ourselves by saying something about rules. I think that we'll find that the fewer rules we have, the better we'll function. A lot of rules reduce freedom and responsibility. I think we've noticed that the more we try to enforce rules, the more resistant people become. Laws create outlaws. With people gaining the consciousness of the Highest Good and acting accordingly, we will have need of far fewer rules.

In this country, people's lives have been virtually enslaved by being at the mercy of over-regulation and over-regimentation and the complications of laws and rules that people are at the mercy of. We have more and more reporting, i.e. income tax is a major annual ordeal, and the government wants more and more information on all of us and where our assets are, etc. People live in fear of and obsession about laws, taxes, bills, and balancing their own personal finances while trying to save for an uncertain future (especially given what the government is doing and how many services will still be around). Then if we want to do something or if we need to protect ourselves from someone wanting to do something to us, we often, because the rules are so complicated, have to hire a lawyer for $200 plus per hour to represent us. In fact, our judicial system is now really a throwback to the old trial by combat. You hire your mercenary (lawyer) and they hire theirs. Usually the outcome has more to do with who has paid for the best combatant rather than anything having to do with truth or fairness.

In a consensus decision-making system, we don't need to live with the outside control that has preoccupied so much of people's time and life-force. Solutions arrived at where everyone is heard and all needs are considered have the effect of simplifying our lives and causing us to relax, knowing that we don't have to protect ourselves from others. Our life-force needs to be spent with personal growth, making a contribution, service, pleasure, and having fun.

HOW DO WE BEAUTIFY OUR ENVIRONMENT?

Boy, how did we come up with this question for the subject of architecture and Community design? Again, it's important that we ask questions and what questions we ask, and we struggled with what the question was for this area. Traditionally, nature has not been considered in the design of towns, cities, and even an individual's use of land. It seems that the question our culture has asked is "How we can remove a few more trees, cover more land with concrete, and add a few shopping centers and malls so that we can get people out shopping so we can make money without the objections from these damned environmentalists?" Because we need to restore the environment rather than keep imposing on it,

when we considered what we would design, we always came back
to the question of how we would beautify our environment. The
architectural design then comes out of that. But we have to start
with considering the whole, the impact that anything would have
on the whole area and its use, and not just consider the buildings
and the architecture in isolation. Living in a beautiful place that is
in harmony with nature also has the effect of greatly enriching our
lives, and that resource is a major part of how we can all live
abundantly.

One of the problems of the American housing industry is that
living situations are generally not being designed and built for the
needs of the people. The building industry still builds homes as if
most of us are married people with children. Also, even if most of
us were in that status, our housing needs change during our lives.
We would go from being single to being married to having
children to the children growing up and leaving home. These
stages all require different housing, and this is hindered by the
current economics of buying and selling and moving.

The Community will offer a whole new concept in housing
where flexibility is the key. With the Community as a whole, and not
individuals, owning the housing, and with resource sharing, we will
be able to create innovative designs to provide different options to
people in different stages of life and with differing needs. We will
demonstrate cheaper housing with the option for shared spaces and
the opportunities for more social interaction. However, there will
also be the opportunity for and respect for private space both within
one's living space and in outdoor sanctuaries.

Designing a Community as a whole before anything is built,
such that the Community would be in harmony not only with our
lives but also in harmony with nature, would be an eco-architect's
dream. The structures would be designed for energy efficiency, be
built with natural, non-toxic materials, be earthquake proof, and
would even capture and store rainwater. The innovations in this
area are already here and being built on an individual basis, but
the creation of an entire cooperative Community built for The
Highest Good of All residents and nature would truly be a thing of
wonder—like the Epcot Center idea I described in "How Do We
Interact With our Environment?"

In thinking about having less personal space within your walls than you would have in a conventional house, some of you may think that that's a lot to give up in going for the Highest Good. However, remember that the entire Community with all its amenities and opportunities for recreation and creative expression is now yours. Also, some interesting information comes from the co-housing movement. Co-housing residents are people who have decided to live together usually with less personal space (which is individually owned) and with some shared areas such as a dining/meeting room big enough for all residents, possibly some multi-use rooms, and outdoor areas. The individual co-housing homes normally have a kitchenette, small living room, bedroom(s), and bathroom(s). Interestingly, after some years of living in this experience, what the residents almost universally say they would do differently, if they were to redesign their co-housing, is to build their individual areas smaller and create more and larger group areas.

HOW DO WE ENJOY OURSELVES?

Most towns and cities have a parks and recreation department, theaters, museums, events to partake in the arts, and various other opportunities for leisure time activities. For us, though, we thought that we needed to ask a broader question. Our lives don't have to be so compartmentalized that we don't build enjoyment into every fabric of our lives. We need to do that, we need to start designing our lives so that they are a living affirmation of self-actualization, learning, and enjoyment. Too often the question our society has asked us is how we can get people more regulated, squeeze more time and money from them, and get them to bear down harder and produce more and have less free time (and spend money with the free time that is available). While our society is suspicious of free time, our Community will focus on bringing joy and creativity into every aspect of our lives.

In our largely urban society, we spend hours in our cars commuting to work, shopping, running errands, and driving to where we can play, be in nature, and exercise. As a result we are increasingly losing time in our lives for family, friends, and recreation. According to a Harris poll, we have one-third less leisure time than in 1973. This is having an adverse effect on both our physical and emotional well-being. Depression is now our fastest growing medical problem. Remember when we were younger and recreation and play were very much a part of our lives? Not being burdened with responsibilities and having other young people around us ready to play, recreation with family and friends was readily available.

Now, for many of us, play and recreation have become something we yearn for and struggle to build into our lives. But often people come home from work with so little available time and energy in our isolated and alienated lives that reaching out to others is not even an option. It's so much easier to just ease into a recliner or lie on the sofa and watch the box. Also, quite often exercise has become going to a gym and exercising by ourselves as opposed to the group sports and activities we used to enjoy. A large part of the problem is that we have such divergent lifestyles. If we try scheduling fun on a regular basis among friends, we bring out our planning books only to find that our schedules don't match up. Maybe there's a Tuesday next month on the 17th when we can meet in the evening, but not too late because we have to drive home and get up early to get back on the treadmill. How did we ever get so caught up in our lives? Remember high school days? It was always possible to get people together on a regular basis to play.

Most adults have forgotten how to have fun. It's been so absent from their lives that they actually become frightened of it. Instead, they just make adjustments to the reality of having less and less fun and don't want to be pressured with the thought of anything more. Just as people adapt to oppression, diminished opportunity, stress, and poverty, people also have adapted to a world of little fun.

Do you know what our national pastime is now? It's no longer baseball, football, or any other sport—it's now gambling. Far more people spend their time in casinos than in any other recreational venues.[30] Also, the net $50.9 billion lost on gambling in 1997 exceeded the amount we spent on movies, sporting events, theme parks, and recorded music combined! This is just another sign of the isolation, alienation and economic stresses that characterize our lives at the start of the 21st century. As a result, the increasing number of people addicted to gambling is one of the fastest growing addictions. We've got to wake up, folks. When our lives are being eroded with concrete, over-regulation, stress, isolation, and alienation, it's no wonder that people are turning to a desperate attempt to try to buy some freedom or, at the very least, to try to beat the system. Also, I thank God that I was not raised with video games because I have seen so many people get hooked on the ease and isolation of playing alone vs. the joy of participating with others. Instead, I had my support network of friends to go out and play ball. This may be unpopular to say, but all the people I know who have visited Cuba were struck by how happy the children were. Without all the trappings of consumerism, the children get together to play with whatever resources they have.

Most of us yearn for more fun and more time for fun in our lives. To me that's what will be one of the most transformational things about the Community. This Community will be a really great place to have fun.

Living with nurturing and loving friends, a "family," we will design recreation and creative opportunities back into our daily lives. Just think about it—if you're into music, there are people who get together to jam and to dance; if you've ever wanted to act, there's a community acting group. When was the last time you played basketball or volleyball or softball? Well, the Community would have days and evenings with all sorts of organized recreational and creative opportunities. Bridge, anyone? Whatever you want, we can build into our lives on a regular basis. Also, we will not only have a host of high quality friends to participate with, but it will all happen within easy walking distance. Plus, in a world where recreation and creative pursuits can be expensive, the residents of the Community have access to far more opportunities through resource sharing. And, because our usual mode of transportation within our pedestrian Community is walking, exercise becomes a normal part of our daily lives, and, in addition, we have access to walking in nature.

With the increased social/recreational interaction, we will be able to see and study the effects that breaking down barriers between people will have and the effects that creating more connecting and bonding will have on our mental and physical health. The Community will also have a really good recreational therapist, a sort of Minister of Fun position, who can enter into the Community work situations and show how people can work and have fun at the same time. Having a good time working increases the quality of our lives and also results in increased production.

Part of the essence of freedom is having fun and pleasure, and living in our Community will be incredibly fun and rewarding on all levels as we heal the alienation and isolation that have characterized our civilization, and we move into being nurtured by nature and by each other. That really is our divine heritage.

WE'RE GOING TO HAVE TO LEARN TO START LIVING WITH MORE FUN IN OUR LIVES.
—Commuity Planet Foundation

HOW DO WE ENRICH OURSELVES?

In our everyone-for-themselves world, the question here has usually been "How can we get enough money to be able to survive or to do what we want in the world?" When we consider ourselves as one family, it gives us a certain basis of support and freedom to look at the bigger picture of what freedom and wealth is. We don't have to live with the pressure we all individually experience when it comes to finances. As we relax into that realization, we start to get the bigger picture of what wealth in the quality of our lives really is, and how much more wealthy we can be by living in a Community based on the Highest Good For All. We start to look in a holistic way at how we can truly enrich ourselves.

Still, to be successful, this prototype Community must have the capacity to financially support itself. Although there will be a tremendous savings in the cost of living (through both the sharing of resources and correctly designing a Community, in the first place, for efficiency), a Community still needs to be able to provide goods and services to markets outside of the Community in order for it to be financially viable. These products and/or services could be almost anything, so there is no need here to get into specifics. However, in keeping with the sustainability of the planet, whatever is produced must be of positive value to the planet and must be totally recyclable.

Ideally, much like the Mondragon model, these businesses would be owned by the Community as a whole, although several variations are possible and would be limited only by our creativity and keeping in mind The Highest Good of All. Also, existing businesses, realizing that we must start making life work for everyone, may wish to relocate into an intentional Community setting.

HOW DO WE COORDINATE WHAT WE LOVE TO DO?

Who does what job? Those who have been in control for thousands of years have asked how they can get people to do the jobs they don't want to do. The rest of the people have dealt with what they have to do in order to survive. In our society, a multitude of people work in jobs where their health is severely at risk. Others just work in uninspiring jobs that basically suck the life out of them. We need to do better than that; we need, in fact, to enjoy what we do. If that takes overhauling how we do things, then that's what we must do. The question of work, therefore, needs to become, "How do we coordinate what we love to do?"

This area concerns the work that people do. All work would fall within the 12 focus areas, and this focus Hub would coordinate that work. Two key elements of doing the work are focusing on the spirit in which the work is being done and using a creative approach to that work which people may not want to do. We tend to think of undesirable work as inevitable—"It's a dirty job, but someone's got to do it." But we'd like to approach that differently and ask how can we change things so that we can either make the task more enjoyable or perhaps eliminate it altogether by redesigning what we're doing. Whereas it's very difficult to do that with the economic forces at work in the everyone-for-themselves model, the creativity inherent in the Highest Good approach will enable us to redesign and/or eliminate tasks, and, with the elimination of stress-related illnesses and boredom, it's also more cost-effective.

Remember, most of our current jobs based on the everyone-for-themselves economic model are also unnecessary—especially the most tedious ones like accounting for what's mine and what's yours and the sitting or standing around trying to sell you something. The 8-to-5 workday would be a thing of the past unless one so chooses. With the elimination of unnecessary jobs and unnecessary work, there would be opportunities during the day for personal time for rejuvenation through play, retreat, creative pursuits or whatever one chooses.

Through sharing work and resources related to childcare, parenting can also be a much different experience in the Community both for the parents and for the children. Because the Community as a whole becomes the support system for families (if they so choose), the parents are freed up to have time to be involved with many nurturing and re-energizing pursuits. As a result, the parents and other residents get to interact with children more when they want to than when they have to. Think of how that can increase the quality of adult/child relationships. Existing intentional communities have been experiencing these benefits for years, resulting in the maturing of confident, responsible, well-adjusted young people into adulthood.

In physically designing the Community, the architects will include designs that are not only safe for children, but also child-friendly. This means that most of the areas will be safe for the child to explore without an adult having to say, "NO! Get out of there, NOW!" We all have been a little scarred (and scared) from that "No" word and the power struggle which that set up inside ourselves. Designing things to support all of us in the first place is just such a logical thing to do to support us all, to go for The Highest Good of All.

In our society we have also often not considered the needs of older people. We put them aside when they retire, and because so many retire dependent on the meager amounts from the government, they often end up in facilities where they are grouped with other people waiting to die. Yet we have many examples of older people who continue to be vibrant because they continue to make a contribution. In a Community with common ownership, an opportunity to participate with diverse people of all ages, and a wealth of opportunities to be involved, we would expect people to be more active, live longer and healthier lives, and make a valuable contribution to all. We can do better than abandoning people to a fate of isolation and alienation.

HOW DO WE NOURISH OURSELVES?

How we feed ourselves has been a constant part of the history and prehistory of man. In fact, the quest for food is obviously essential for all physical life. As population has proliferated and densified into areas that can no longer support it, the food industries' question has become, "How can we subjugate and manipulate our environment to make a profit growing food on huge tracts of land?" and "How can we produce all kinds of essentially junk food with no real food value, but which will generate a big profit?" When we consider the question of nourishing ourselves, rather than just feeding ourselves, we again have to look at the bigger picture. To really nurture ourselves, we need to look at how we relate to the land and to all the life on the land. We also need to look at how we can put the best possible nourishment, on all levels, into our bodies.

Current agricultural practices are depleting and polluting our groundwater, our topsoil, and our forests, and providing us with food having toxic levels of pesticides and preservatives. As towns and cities have been built in the good bottom lands and as population growth has squeezed us together, this trend has also squeezed agriculture further and further away from population centers. This, combined with economic pressures, has resulted in fewer and fewer small farmers and concentrated farming in huge tracts with the resultant harm to the environment. The average produce, often picked unripe and treated with preservatives to keep it from rotting before being sold, now travels over 1500 miles to market in the U.S. The clearing of huge tracts of land for farming has brought chemicals to the forefront in the past half century as the natural predators of the pests have been eliminated and superbugs resistant to the chemicals have emerged. The process of hybridization for large-scale agriculture, resulting in our now having a lack of variety within plant groups, has also left our produce vulnerable to insects and disease as well as decreasing the food value. In fact, we have lost most of the strains of our plants and seeds, and we must reverse this through local, smaller scale growing.

Noting the problems associated with the recent growth of large-scale intensified agriculture, Dr. David Tillman of the University of Minnesota concluded, "A hallmark of modern agriculture is its use of monocultures grown on fertilized soils. Ecological principles suggest that such monocultures will be relatively unstable, will have high leaching loss of nutrients, will be susceptible to invasion by weedy species, and will have high incidences of diseases and pests—all of which do occur. The tradition in agriculture has been to maximize production and minimize the cost of food with little regard to impact on the environment and the services it provides to society." Dr. Tillman also observed that, "... greater diversity leads to greater productivity in plant communities, greater nutrient retention in ecosystems, and greater ecosystem stability. (Studies have shown that) each halving of the number of plant species within a plot leads to a 10-20% loss of productivity. An average plot containing one plant species is less than half as productive as an average plot containing 24-32 species." Therefore, as opposed to the traditional monoculture agriculture, growing a diverse crop of plants within the Community will not only replenish and sustain the soil, but will also result in increased productivity and fewer pests.

Perhaps the most distressing aspect of current agricultural practices is that the toxic chemicals have now spread to our waters where they are genetically altering animals, birds, fish, and reptiles, rendering them unable to reproduce. Likewise, our own immune systems are being damaged as our consumption of the chemicals takes a steady gradual toll on us. We are inadvertently involved in a gigantic genetic experiment because of our agricultural and other pollutive practices. For our own health and the health of the planet, we need to demonstrate non-toxic agricultural systems that are in harmony with the environment.

When we plan our food as a whole Community, we have the resources to produce most of our own food—vine ripened and without pesticides and preservatives. Using edible landscaping, permaculture, natural pest control, composting, hydroponics, aquaculture, crop rotation, and other proven natural methods, the Community will show how people can locally take care of most of their food needs without disrupting the environment. This will not only cut down on transportation costs and pollution but will also provide an important model for urban planning and for addressing poverty and hunger both here and abroad. This model of food production will also preserve the environment, replenish our topsoil, and return many devastated areas back to nature.

Mass production of food is costing us too much in terms of our environment and people's health—both farm workers' and consumers.' In the cooperative Community, many people can participate in the growing and harvesting of organic food. This even offers a therapeutic opportunity for those of us who love to participate in gardening, but whose current lifestyles preclude that.

The Community will have one or more restaurants where people will have the opportunity to eat (at no additional cost) every meal if they so desire. Of course, most of the living units would also have a kitchenette for those who choose to make any or all of their own meals. In any case, the Community will provide a variety of great fresh and natural food, which will have a very positive effect on both our health and longevity. It will also have a positive effect on the environment as we buy in bulk that which we can't produce ourselves, and thus we cut the waste from our consumption of food packaging materials by 99 percent.

HOW DO WE VITALIZE OURSELVES?

What to do about health care, now there's an ongoing quandary. With the financial limitations of the everyone-for-themselves paradigm, the questions that are now asked by our society are, "How can we pay for health coverage?" and "How can we cut back what health services are covered so that the government, businesses, families, and individuals can afford to have coverage?" These are very limiting questions and have caused much suffering on the part of people who need cared for physically, mentally, and emotionally. Again, using money as an excuse for not providing needed services just means that we continue to have an illusion control us. Besides, I think we all deserve far more than just basic services. I think that every one of us deserves the opportunity for maximum health on all levels, and that means the mental and emotional levels as well as the physical. Thus, we ask the question, "How can we vitalize ourselves?" which is to say, how can we have the most vibrant lives and vitality that we can possibly have? We have the manpower and the resources to provide excellent holistic health coverage for everyone, and, in cooperative Communities, we can demonstrate this reality.

The preventative approach to health is now at the leading edge of medicine. The old model was to approach health in a piecemeal fashion and go to doctors to fix the pieces instead of looking at the big picture of what may truly be causing our dis-ease. The Community will provide a full array of optional workshops, classes, and individual consultation on this preventative approach—i.e., proper breathing, nutrition, developing inner knowing on how to take care of oneself, keeping clear and balanced with ourselves and each other, the importance of and opportunities for exercise and fun, etc.

The Community will therefore be an observational haven for researchers looking at the impact of proper foods, emotional health, belonging rather than isolation and alienation, a joyful approach to life, a nurturing family/support system, etc. Seldom before has there been the opportunity to study the effects that a vastly different lifestyle has on health. The Community will truly be a living laboratory for preventative medicine. Its lifestyle will be contrasted against our current model of waking up to go someplace to be unhappy while being on the treadmill earning money based on ticks of the clock. We can't wait to leave so we can commute home, try to recover, and get ready to do it again tomorrow. Imagine instead being able to get great exercise everyday in fresh air, eat the most nutritional food, and even get regular massages—all at no cost. We all deserve them in a Highest Good For All Community.

If most of us had to choose between health and money, we'd choose health because the wealth of feeling healthy and being able to have fun with a healthy body is more than money can buy. Living and playing in natural surroundings with great people will be very vitalizing to the health of the Community residents. Being intimately involved with the Community, people will be able to live much longer and healthier lives. The process of living will be very stimulating as opposed to the isolation and alienation that most older people (as well as people of all ages) now experience.

From the above description, I hope you get the picture that we can have vitality in our lives. We need to realize that we don't have to live with all the stress and the environmental and chemical threats that currently have such a tremendous effect on our well-being. In fact, if we're not experiencing joy and pleasure and growth in our lives, we really need to address that. When we do, we find that the key is how we choose to live together on this planet.

HOW DO WE COMMUNICATE?

How do we relate with each other in this society? The first thing that may come to mind is that this is the information age and we are technologically improving our communications systems all the time. We also have the media, which now, unfortunately, feeds us short bursts of sensationalized stories. But how are we relating with one another on a personal level? That question goes largely unaddressed except as it is played out in our everyone-for-themselves paradigm. We know, for instance, that there are laws that govern how we relate with others, and stepping out of line can have consequences (unless you can afford to hire a really good lawyer). We also know that there are rules of etiquette with certain social consequences if those rules are broken. Some of us were raised to be nice and not say anything if we can't say something nice (so we became passive-aggressive instead), and some of us were raised to express ourselves regardless of the effect (and damage) that may have on others. Our different backgrounds and styles in communicating make for some often volatile relation-ships, be it with friends or strangers. Yet no one really takes on the question of communication for society as a whole, and we are left to sort out this most important component of the quality of our lives by ourselves or, much more rarely, by seeking counseling.

We need to learn to live without acting against others and taking from others. We must reeducate ourselves and teach our children not to return harsh words for harsh words or a fist for a fist, but instead to act in kindness and loving, and to hold the consciousness of going for The Highest Good of All Concerned. In my experience, many people do not really know how to make friends or even how to get in touch with how they are really feeling inside. In a supportive, nurturing Community, there will be abundant opportunities for close friendships, and clear, loving communication. It will be almost impossible to experience the isolation and alienation that typify our society. I believe that the ability to get in touch with and connect with one's self and with other people has more to do with success and happiness than any academic skill.

The second part of communication involves the information/technology highway of which most of us are now a part. This technology will play a major role in the Community both in terms of accessing information within the Community and interfacing with information outside the Community. Communication technology enables consensus decision-making to be practical on a Community-wide basis. With everyone having the capacity to communicate with each other at any given time, this will also increase the closeness and Community-wide connections that are the cornerstone for cooperative living.

When we asked the question, "How do we communicate?," we intentionally chose to marry the technology of communicating with the quality and essence of our interpersonal and Community communications. We believe that these are two parts of the bigger picture, and, when we are creating a Community of several hundred people, we are going to have to be both responsible and creative in our communication so that we can successfully and joyfully live together. So far, though, it's a very unequal marriage in our society where technology has far outstripped the level of our interpersonal and media communications, which often display our individual and collective immaturity. Essentially our question gets back to how we can communicate For The Highest Good of All Concerned. Again, at this point in our planet's history, we can't settle for anything less. Peace and Loving need to be at the core of all our communicating, and, in doing this, we will find that our lives become incredibly richer.

HOW DO WE BRING FORTH
INNER WISDOM?

Education has been a hot political issue. But what questions has our society asked about education? Society has generally asked us to learn what they want us to learn, complete with proficiency tests. Our society has even asked us to learn history from an incredibly one-sided point of view, the point of view of the Western civilization that has subjugated the planet. What we have essentially been asked to learn is how to be good and obedient citizens to support the status quo of the everyone-for-themselves paradigm. Creativity is allowed, but only within that framework, and we are taught that stepping outside that box is to be ungodly.

Whereas the process of education traditionally has been pouring information into us, we believe that true education involves bringing forth the best of what is already inside all of us, and this applies to every one of us no matter what our age is. We all have a vast storehouse of inner wisdom that transcends anything that can be stuffed into us from the outside. Sure, learning information is often important, but it must be the servant to our inner wisdom and not the master. Communication is a major aspect of that, and in our present society the ability to effectively communicate probably has, as I previously wrote, more to do with success than any other single factor.

I've heard it said that one of the values of school is that it taught us to be bored so that we had practice for eventually working. How many of us have dreamed of revamping the educational process to make it more relevant, more interactive, and more interesting? We can do that in a Community where people have access to participating in every aspect of the Community and all its businesses, services, and enterprises. The totality of life needs to be our stage for learning rather than just depending on what we can learn within the walls of crowded classrooms with often uninspiring curriculum. That curriculum has become even more uninspiring recently as more and more of our creative classes that would enrich us have been eliminated due to financial constraints, even though we can spend billions on weaponry.

Recognizing that the roots of learning and communication start early, the children of the Community will find many nurturing people of all ages to learn from and participate with in all aspects of Community life. But education is not just for our youth—we believe that it is a life-long process in which we all need to be participating. Stagnation is often the first sign that it's time for changes. As opposed to the very limited way that our society approaches education, I feel that we have a format for making it a joyful, life-long experience when we approach it as life itself being our canvas and our entire Community being the educational support system.

HOW DO WE EXPAND OUR COMMUNITY?

When I first started thinking about an intentional Community that could provide the model to transform the planet, I read many books on actual and fictional utopian societies. It seemed obvious to me that in order to have a so-called utopian society, what was needed first were utopian people. At this stage in our planet's history, with the survival of the planet and the prospect of an adequate life for everyone and anyone now at risk, we must replace the old everyone-for-themselves model that has led us to the precipice of being engulfed by our ignorance concerning the balance of nature. Now, perhaps more than ever, people seem to be willing to embrace the concept of going for The Highest Good of All Life. Teaching people this concept is the essence of what the people in this Hub group would be doing, for we must expand the Highest Good approach to include all life on the planet.

In order for the Community to be able to make decisions by consensus, it will take residents who both have a real commitment to what the Community is and have the consciousness to work consensus. There are, of course, skills that one can learn to better be able to work consensus, but still there has to be the absolute choice to commit to working consensus and going for the Highest Good, rather than running one's personal stuff at the expense of others.

For us to successfully live together, we must know ourselves; we must seek self-awareness and realize our collective oneness. Without that, we cannot move forward to making the planet work for everyone. But, with a Community of people demonstrating the Highest Good consciousness along with abundance on all levels (including fun), then people will be inspired to realizing our collective oneness as taught by all the great spiritual teachers. More than anything else, the Community will show the world the value of people willing to go for The Highest Good of All.

Therefore, for this model to succeed, we will have a very comprehensive (but also fun and interesting) screening process. The residents who pass this process and come into the Community will have the commitment, ability, and support necessary to work consensus. If not, persons not yet ready to come into the Community will come out with solid feedback on what to work on if they wish to reapply. This is not an againstness process, it's just that for this model to succeed we must be able to be successful and to show people the value of choosing to go for The Highest Good of All. Historically, cooperative communities were not good at screening members, and this later usually led to their demise. I can't stress enough the importance of people willing to go for The Highest Good of All, for it is time to change the basic paradigm of human interaction. There is just too much at stake for the future of the planet to do otherwise. Those who are "cooperation challenged" will have to wait and learn the value of a different approach before trying to inflict their out-of-date ways onto others in this New Age of cooperation we are entering.

Some people, upon first hearing some very basic information about this Community concept, have said that this would be a great thing for homeless people. But that's not what this project is. Instead, the initial model Community will have rather exceptional and successful people as residents because it is extraordinarily important that the Community be able to demonstrate both an abundance of lifestyle (that would appeal to almost everyone) and the Highest Good consciousness that will teach others what is necessary to create other Communities around the planet.

This demonstration Community will be a revolutionary model, and, as such, will be a mecca for both research and for media coverage. Besides screening for new residents, this Hub also has the job of communicating to the world what we are doing. Because the everyone-for-themselves model has been so entrenched in our consciousness, for many people the only way they can perceive of a way that we can all live for The Highest Good of All Life and live more abundantly and happily at the same time is to actually see a model that demonstrates the concept. This Hub group will make sure that people all over the world get an opportunity to see, through the various forms of media, the Community and how it operates.

LIVING IN COMMUNITY/FREE AT LAST

Many years after I first realized that, in order to heal the planet, we had to redefine how we lived together on the planet, it dawned on me that I had an idealized, yet fuzzy picture of what living in this prototype Community would be like. It therefore seemed that one of the first necessary steps to creating the Community was to create a written description of what the Community was like and how it would operate. To accomplish this, I formed a class that I thought would meet weekly for 10 weeks, at the end of which time we would have a finished descriptive product. Well, as soon as we really started questioning the assumptions that our society has made regarding how we have to live together and started to really think creatively, our timeline started stretching. To create the description, we met weekly for about two years. Each week was an adventure in massaging each of the questions in order to ascertain exactly what we wanted to say. The process, with its laughter along with occasional harsh words and stuckness, was incredible. As my fuzzy picture merged with the collective wisdom and intuition of the group, we came into a descriptive reality that far exceeded anything that I had imagined. I think that my friend, Mike Feeney, best described our journey with the "preface" that he wrote for our Community Planet description:

"The class met with the purpose of planning a New Age Community where people live and learn in peace and harmony with themselves, each other, and their environment. After the class members realized how strong our collective vision was, we dedicated ourselves to seeing it becoming a reality.

"Our first challenge as a class was how to merge all our individual visions into one. Although we shared pretty much the same larger vision, we often differed greatly when it came to

B.C.

details. Our solution was CONSENSUS. We saw the process of consensus being one where everyone is encouraged and given an opportunity to express themselves, and then an elucidation is found that all can agree upon and come into harmony with.

"Everything that was produced by the class, including this write-up, was done through the process of consensus. We started every class by each member taking time to share what was going on in their lives. We discovered that this helped us come into harmony with each other and to reach consensus. It also helped us to remain loving friends when reaching agreement was difficult. Out of these sharings sprang the idea of Hubs, which are the modular units that make up the Community. Each Community member would belong to one or more of these Hubs, small groups of people meeting together for support and decision-making.

"As a beginning exercise, the class started by imagining that we were all from a planet named 'Kungawungajungo,' a word we coined to represent all the positive qualities we wanted in our Community. On our 'home planet' we consider everyone in our world as family and the needs of the one are the responsibility of everyone. In our native language there are no such words as lack or poverty, which are comparative words that describe some people as having less than others, a condition unknown on our planet. The dual purpose of our adventure was to create a home where we could live in peace and prosperity and also to create a Community that would serve as a model of successful cooperative living for those on earth.

"Our first task was to observe the way the people of earth did things, to take note of where they excelled, and to observe where their actions did not serve them. From these observations, plus the vision we held coming into the class, we formed the ideas that became the Community Planet."

While we realized that our description was probably not complete (and it wasn't intended to be), we aimed for it to be readable in a few pages rather than a several hundred page document. You may be able to see some difficulties or holes, but I can testify that people getting together and looking at an issue via the process of consensus can come up with some amazingly creative solutions. The current crises our planet faces demand nothing less. Truly, if wise beings from another planet were to visit us, they would wonder how we created such a mess out of a place where everyone could be living abundantly and in harmony with all life.

Every focus area we looked at includes how we can attain more peace and harmony in our lives. People, all people, need to be free and supported—with time, opportunity, Loving, and nurturing—to fulfill their individual destinies, missions, and creative expressions here on the planet. We need to realize that each and every person is important and has something to contribute. But, the support is not there in our everyone-for-themselves paradigm. Right now we're living as victims of the structure of our society rather than being able to create fully positive choices. The structure of our lives is way too controlled by society and the hoops that an uncooperative system makes us jump through. Instead of giving us freedom, that system has sucked up our time, resources, and creativity as well as damaging all life on the planet. If we want to have more vital and more fun lives, we must unburden ourselves from the over-regulation that has fragmented our lives. Our living paradigms need to be set up to have a lot more peace and harmony so that people's energy can go to creativity, growth, and fun rather than survival and oppression.

ANOTHER PIECE TO THE PUZZLE

In the twenty years I've been involved in teambuilding training, rarely have I ever seen groups—whether they be corporate, educational, or civic—model effective teamwork. Recently I was working with a group that was comprised of the very best thinkers and innovators from a major international automobile/jet engine manufacturing company. Our lead facilitator cautioned our facilitators that we might have to really challenge these people because of how sharp they were. Well, they were just a little worse than the average group I work with in accomplishing the challenges. It's not that they didn't have the information available in the group to do the task, it's just that they had difficulty in effectively communicating as a group.

During the next few days I wondered about that—how a very hi-functioning group of individuals could be so bad working as a group. In observing hundreds of challenge-based teambuilding trainings, I've seldom ever seen a team truly model excellent communication and leadership. I've seen groups get "in sync" somehow and do really well on the group challenges, but usually they just did it without really knowing how it happened. Therefore, it would be uncertain as to whether they could move into a cooperative place were they to be given a new and different set of challenges.

Then it dawned on me, as I was out walking at night and was observing cars drive down concrete streets lined with dark, empty stores, that my community and society itself had been created haphazardly—because people had a very limited concept of how to work together in groups. People coming together to live in the same place did not know how to effectively work together. Thus, not possessing either the skills or the consciousness of how to work together for The Highest Good of All, we accommodate by taking the path of least resistance and making decisions individually and/or haphazardly. As well-intentioned as they might be, politicians, business and civic leaders—you name it—they all didn't have any more ability to effectively work together than all the groups I've seen for the past twenty years. So, everything in society evolved pretty much individually and not with a consensus and a spirit of oneness from a highly-functioning team approach. Therefore, with most people feeling powerless to work effectively in a group, what typically happens is that power is usurped by those who want power over others or power to get what they want—often at the expense of others. This is the everyone-for-themselves legacy that we have been doing for so many thousands of years that our very cultural pattern became the mindset that we think alone rather than being able to think as a group.

But wait, weren't there examples of hi-functioning teams that have accomplished great things. Militaries have sometimes gotten miraculous things done. For that matter, so have some regimes throughout the ages. But these are top-down, autocratic forms of leadership which both do not usually gather the collective wisdom of all involved, and their goals are almost always accomplished at the expense of others, rather than being for the benefit of all. For instance, if we were truly thinking of The Highest Good of All militarily, we would have put our resources and our trillions to work sending people and technology out to improve the lives of people throughout the world who are on the edge of survival. That act of goodwill would have protected our security far more than any military act. People often fight both because of limited resources and because they, like the rest of us, also do not have the experience of how to work together as a group.

But what of sports teams that have accomplished great things? Though these teams may have worked well together, they have done so within a win/lose, us vs. them, competitive system. Look at the bigger picture—everybody didn't win, there were far more losers than winners. Yet, this competitive model is virtually all that is presented in the media in sports and any other achievement. Who is the best? We must show or prove that we are better, and it starts subtle or sometimes outright wars between people.

We live with this consciousness of scarcity and lack—that there isn't enough for everyone to win—and this comes into play with people participating in groups. Thus, people either cooperate out of greed or get very competitive for perceived limited resources or opt out of the decision-making process altogether. We have been so ingrained by our limited cooperative abilities that we don't hold the consciousness of how we can make something work in the most expansive way possible for everyone. Instead, we go to our survival response.

Because we haven't been able to function well working in groups, we've put together our world by a combination of haphazard or autocratic, win/lose decisions. People have remarked to me, "Wouldn't consensus decision-making take too much time?" Well, yes, it might take more time as people educate themselves to tap into the consciousness of the Highest Good instead of the simple legacy of againstness. But, once that is done, it becomes easier, and the decisions that are made are more creative, long-sighted, save time in the long run, and work for all life.

We are not wrong for not knowing how to work coopera-tively—few have been trained both in how to access that consciousness and how to implement it. Most of us still have to deal with the underlying everyone-for-themselves issues we still hold. We have trouble even in groups of two where 50 percent of our marriages result in divorce and where many of the remaining 50 percent have learned how to accommodate their partner rather than absolutely going for creating the best, most dynamic relation-ship that they can possibly have. The same is true in families. It just seems easier to take the path of least resistance, rather than to learn and apply the skills.

We will change only when we see a better model of relating. With the consciousness of the Highest Good being the key along with the skill of how to work together as a group, Communities— based on this principle of the Highest Good For All—will be what transforms the world. People must see that there is an alternative

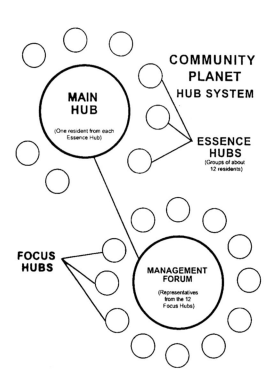

way to succeed or else they will continue to survive at the expense of others or by making others wrong.

Indeed, if we were truly to grapple with virtually any decision from the consciousness of the Highest Good, it would necessitate being creative, thinking out-of-the-box, and ultimately changing the way we live together. Let's take recycling and trash as an example. It is possible to recycle 100 percent of what we create, but the recycling itself is just part of the issue. How trash is created—by packaging, overconsumption, making products purely from the self-interest of the maker, designed obsolescence, etc.—must be addressed hand-in-hand with how to recycle. Thus, as I wrote earlier, we have to look at not creating or supporting anything that can't be reused or recycled. But, even beyond that, we have to look at anything that even wastes people's time and life-force due to lack of cooperation. We have to look at all the paper and office products that are created for an everyone-for-themselves society and all the hours that are spent supporting that system. If one Community of four to five hundred people could demonstrate this, then a cluster of Communities demonstrating the value of living together for The Highest Good of All could really show what is possible through consensus-based cooperation as opposed to our current haphazard approach to living together.

> *"THE WORLD IS NOW TOO DANGEROUS FOR ANYTHING LESS THAN UTOPIA."*
>
> —*Buckminister Fuller*

> *"It is possible that the next Buddha*
> *will not take the form of an individual.*
> *The next Buddha may take the form*
> *of a community;*
> *a community practicing understanding*
> *and loving kindness,*
> *a community practicing mindful living.*
> *This may be the most important thing*
> *we can do for the survival of the Earth."*
>
> —*Thich Nhat Hanh*

Chapter 5

THE PLAN

by Jim Costa

"Be the change you wish to see."

Mahatma Gandhi

Co-op Village is a community where we can cooperate in helping each other, get out of the "rat race" and get happy and healthy again.

It's maddening to think your finances, marriage and health can survive purchasing a house with a thirty year mortgage based on a three year a job.

WHAT IS IT?

A Co-operative Village is a non-profit built community with owner built low cost, affordable homes, whose 500 inhabitants pool their resources to become an extended family, to the degree they choose, while maintaining their own privacy and independence. Its purpose is to allow the residents, through cooperation not competition, the opportunity to live comfortably and independently by working part-time or not at all, ultimately bringing themselves to better health by reducing stress. Relationships and caring for each other is of prime importance. From inception to execution, **no one makes a profit on another**. The village would be earth friendly.

WHY IS IT NEEDED?

We have been trained by culture to be maximum consumers of goods and to look out for ourselves only. During this process we have become separate from each other, selfish, alienated, financially overextended spenders forced to remain discontented on the treadmill of employment. In truth we're gambling by trying to pay-off a thirty-year mortgage with a job that at best will last three years. Our current process has instilled in us insecurity, loneliness and ill health.

Co-op villages will reconnect us to caring neighbors, reduce our consuming and need for cash flow, give us control of our community lives, and allow us to focus on being unique, creative, free individuals. Here we could express who we wish to be instead of who we have been forced to be by economics.

WHAT IT IS NOT

It is not a commune, nor expensive gated community, nor retirement community, nor a cult or religious congregation. It is not a place with a lot of rules.

WHO IS IT FOR?

<u>Young Persons</u>: The community can help these persons by providing a means of home ownership in three to four years, help with child care, experienced advice and training, lower cost of living, security in the event of unemployment, dinners prepared during busy evenings, possible financial assistance, access to unaffordable assets, and dignity while starting a family and career.

<u>Middle Aged Persons</u>: The community can help these persons by providing a network of caring relationships, opportunity to reduce working hours, lower cost of living, daily adventure and an opportunity to serve others.

<u>Retired Persons</u>: The community can help these persons by providing caring relationships, opportunity to serve others and use their skills, home security while traveling, lower cost of living,

daily adventure and caring assisted living when they need it. It can also make you less reliant on dwindling pensions.

Children: The community can help these persons by providing help with child care / rearing, caring relationships, stability, transportation, advice, experience in maintaining unselfish relationships, community involvement, and learning cooperation instead of competition.

Elderly and Physically Handicapped Persons: The community can help these persons by providing caring relationships, involvement, dignity, concern and attention, transportation, physical work and assistance, repairs, lower cost of independent living, protection and need for their advice and knowledge.

Homeless Persons: The community can help these persons by assisting in financing of home ownership, job training if necessary, providing jobs, low cost of living, transportation, dignity, caring relationships and access to unaffordable assets.

ADVANTAGES OF CO-OPERATIVE VILLAGE LIVING

School does not teach us all the skills we need to know to survive easily and as young adults we do not have the time to learn these skills quickly enough to benefit ourselves. Instead we were simply taught to be consumers. In community we will be surrounded by others who have learned these skills and are eager to share with us for free. Thus there could be diet, cooking and dieting experts, exercise and holistic/herbal healing experts and nursing, massage therapists, family counselors, legal, financial and tax experts, automotive and home repair experts, tutors, etc.

Healthy organic food could be raised by those that choose to do so. Meals would be prepared by those that choose to do so. When you are faced by a crisis, the community would be there to help you through it.

It is said that 80% of our medical problems are stress related. Community living would greatly reduce the economic burden we each face thus freeing us from stress. We each would have security and a support system, freeing us from stress. We would never be concerned about becoming homeless. More of our time would be spent doing that which we choose and enjoy doing, a place where work and leisure become one. We would be able to work less on a job and spend more time on ourselves and our families. This is any doctor's prescription to a healthy and long life!

HOW WILL IT WORK?

Residents would build with assistance from neighbors. Time expended by neighbors would be charged to the owner's account, with a later payback from the owner hour per hour. The owner would have several years to payback the community at large by performing services he himself selects. Thus residents would be doing what they enjoy doing in their spare time anyway, not laboring.

Residents would be exchanging their trash for treasures. Older persons have too much unused time and talent but little energy. Younger persons have energy but little time or talent. Trash for treasure.

Older persons have cash that could be invested into the community to finance younger residents who have little cash. The younger residents would be available to provide assisted living to the older residents later if needed. Trash for treasure.

By dining together periodically we would all know each other enough to offer assistance if needed, and to discover when someone needs an offer of assistance. If I learned you have car trouble and I happen to enjoy working on cars I would offer to help make the repairs if you purchase the parts. It would be fun for me. We each have special talents needed by others. Thus trash for treasure.

Most of your serious problems could be problems of the community as a whole, thus you could choose to utilize networking at its best.

CONSTRUCTION COST SAVINGS?

To build a conventional $150,000 home financed at 7% for thirty years requires gross earnings of $450,000 to payoff the debt. Under the Village method gross earnings of $50,000 would payoff a similar home in about four years!

The savings would occur from free labor as well as a much cheaper exterior, as you would no longer be trying to impress your neighbors. Most of your investment will be going into the interior instead.

Features

Each site will contain:

Individual homes, all low cost, energy efficient structures. Housing would be closely clustered, central parking lots, nature preserved as much as possible.

Provide housing for approximately 500 persons.

There will be a common hobby shop, tool room, workshops and laundry rooms. It will contain only one set of tools, garden equipment, washer & dryer facilities, etc., minimizing the need for excess purchasing by all residents.

Several dining halls will be used for daily or semi-weekly community dinners. The meals will be prepared in the attached kitchen by the residents who wish to do so. The rest of the day it would be used as a lounge and coffee shop.

One utility bill for the entire site, with costs of utilities and community dinners divided by the families.

A large garden which will be maintained by those who wish to do so.

Central computer to monitor apartment fire alarms and fire sprinkler systems, control parking gates, telephone switching and internal activity communications. Each house would have a computer for better village communication.

One fence surrounding the entire site.

Jacuzzi, water garden and playground.

Guest lodge, eliminating the need of each home having a guest bedroom and bath.

Apartments

Apartments might be provided as a means of offering assisted living or nursing home environments. This might allow family members to live upstairs to give more support.

Houses

Houses would be small and of low cost construction. The focus will be on the inside rather than the exterior. Most of the construction would be done by the community.

Dwellings will be closely clustered without fencing.

Maintenance

All maintenance will be done on a volunteer or barter basis by the residents. Any additions or improvements will benefit all villagers.

Organization

The community will be run as a cooperative governed by consensus. As such, there will be few rules.

No one person or persons would lead the community. Leadership positions will be on a timed rotation method with each resident being offered that position in time.

All residents would be a member of a management team as well as a work team(s). Thus a resident would be their own boss (i.e. A resident could be on the plumbers' management team and be a plumber at the same time.)

Teams would focus on the following twelve areas as outlined in *The Next Evolution* by Jack Reed. Each of the following teams would assure that that the community serves the residents as they wish:

How do we share our abundance?

How do we interact with the environment?

How do we reach consensus?

How do we beautify our environment?

How do we enjoy ourselves?

How do we enrich ourselves?

How do we coordinate what we live to do?

How do we nourish ourselves?

How do we vitalize ourselves?

How do we communicate?

How do we bring forth inner wisdom?

How do we expand our Community?

Repurchase Agreement
The community will repurchase your investment in the community by refunding all money paid towards your share.

Growth Potential
Each village can be linked with others.

Businesses can be created utilizing the available talent and manpower. These businesses would have no employees but would be co-owned by all those involved in it. These short-term businesses would be exempt from most taxes.

Once enough families are involved, other buildings could be added, such as a learning center, guest cottages, computer rooms, child care facilities, clubs, health facilities, sport facilities, lounges, etc.

Ownership
The land and all buildings will be held by a corporation (Community Land Trust) owned by the Self Funding contributors. Their money will be used to finance new residents. This would be similar to a bank holding a mortgage on your property. When the collective residents pay off the debt this corporation will then be owned by the owner residents. In the meantime, the residents will have tenant rights to the property with all major maintenance done by the group.

Utilities, Food & Health Insurance
All basic utilities, food and health insurance would be provided by the community.

Economy
With a large enough population the village will have its own cashless economy. It has been estimated that 80% of current jobs would not be needed in a cashless cooperative society. Some examples of unneeded jobs are cashiers, sales persons, managers,

receptionists, advertisers, delivery persons, insurers & security services, bankers and bookkeepers. This means that each resident might work 8 hours a week doing only work that truly produces a better way of life for the village. The rest of the week would be spent doing what the resident enjoys doing. Because the cost of living would be so low there would not be a need for conventional 40 hour per week outside employment, unless the resident wished to work.

Education

Home schooling will be available to those that choose it. Cooperation will be stressed more than competition. Advanced education would be a problem for the community to provide the solution to, with the primary concern being to provide education in the skills that would perpetuate the community well being.

Education costs would be much less than in conventional society because in a cashless cooperative environment state education requirements through licensing would not apply. Thus some classes could be taught by the community, some being taken at college, and some could be avoided completely. Each student would be free to choose because the knowledge would be desired more than the certificate.

This would facilitate the changing of careers during a lifetime. If one tired of being a refrigerator repairman, she would simply have to train another to perform those duties and then would be free to study whatever she desired for her new life, be it vocational or higher academic studies. This would certainly take the pressure off young persons to hurriedly choose a lifelong career path costing their parents a hundred thousand dollars in the process.

FINANCING

Problems Anticipated from Banks and HUD

The land and most of the buildings will be owned by a Cooperative or Community Land Trust, not individuals. Therefore banks may be reluctant to lend money as they are not individual conventional homes.

Community Land Trusts have only been around for 20 years and historically have been unable to receive government grant assistance. However, now HUD will give financial assistance to land trusts if they provide affordable housing.

Most of the construction will be done by the residents, not building contractors. Therefore banks may not lend money as they are not conventional homes.

Because of the layout and lack of a contractor, it may be difficult to obtain insurance at a reasonable price. Without insurance, banks will not finance them.

Banks may be reluctant to lend to a Cooperative instead of individuals. Cooperatives are somewhat new to them.

Self Financing Fund

Members with cash reserves can invest in the Co-op with a return of X% over prime secured by a first mortgage on all land and buildings.

Rate: This rate will be much higher than conventional CD's pay but less than successful high risk stock investments.

Control: Although an individual could possibly make more profit in the stock market, self investment would be better for the investor's future. The investor would have more control over the future benefits generated by his investment and would not be investing in pollution, higher food or merchandise costs, etc. passed on by uncontrolled corporations. By self investing you are truly investing in your self interest exclusively in that you yourself control what is done with the money.

Withdrawal: The investor retains the right to sell his shares to others or withdraw it subject to certain rules.

Liability: Two co-ops would be formed: one to own/hold the land and buildings, the second to operate and manage the property. The holding company would then lease the property to the management company which in turn would lease to the individual "tenants". Therefore, if any lawsuits should arise as a result of accidents, they would be against the management company, not the holding company which owns the assets. Therefore, the holding company is for the most part insulated from lawsuits, leaving the investment secure.

Home Material Costs

Residents would be expected to provide cash for building costs (not including village labor). This should be in the area of $25,000.

Short term loans from the Self Financing Fund would be available where needed. Payback would be over about a five year period, making payments what one would normally pay for rent in their current life. Thus after the loan is paid out, the owner is out of the housing market.

Home Construction Village-Labor Costs

Time worked by other residents building a new home would be recorded. All labor would be valued the same: $10 per hour.

The benefiting owner would then be indebted to the village for that dollar amount or that number of man-hours.

The owner would have the option of paying cash and be debt free, or work off the debt at $10 per hour. If he chooses to work off the debt, he could work on other community construction projects, work in the kitchen, perform maintenance work, make cabinets, sew curtains, childcare, etc.

If the owner is physically unable to perform work, he might bring in others to work in his stead (grown children).

Community Buildings

Community buildings material costs would be financed by the Self Financing Fund.

Labor hours would be assessed to all members. Members would then work on that project or any other community project ongoing in order to liquidate the debt.

Cash Revenue Projects

Some members might perform outside work to raise cash for community projects.

Members not working on the Revenue project would then be taxed an equal amount of man-hours to be worked off on other community projects.

Chapter 6

VILLAGE LIFE —
NEW ECONOMICS

by Jim Costa

RAT SUMMATION

When I think of rats in a maze, I always visualize them seeking cheese (not unlike we do). Until recently I believed that whenever such a rat traversed a dead-end corridor in the maze, he made a "false" or "bad" decision. However, now I understand that in order for the rat to truly master the maze, he must journey down all of the corridors. This is especially true if he was fortunate enough to locate the cheese on an early foray—how else will he know if the cheese is all there is?

Most books or articles that purport to offer a new method or insight into an existing problem devote 20 to 40 percent of their pages just to outlining the problem. In trying to lay out in my mind a way to describe what a Co-op Village is, I stumbled across some interesting questions. Why is a restatement of the preexisting problem required at all? Is it really necessary to make readers uncomfortable, fearful, and maybe a little guilty by reminding them about the economic system we have created and live by today? Is it possible to cut out this step and still get the point across—that is, that the right time for Co-op Villages is now?

In our legal system, there is a rule of evidence known as "res ipsa loquitur," Latin for "a thing speaks for itself." It is applied when a thing is so obvious that it need not be debated but rather can be assumed to be a fact. Under this rule, the driver of an automobile, not someone else, is assumed to be in control of the car's movement. Accordingly, an injured party doesn't have to prove that it was the driver who ran over him, not the back-seat driver. To invoke this rule, the injured party simply says "res ipsa loquitur," and then the burden of proof shifts to the driver to prove that it was the back-seat driver's fault.

So what does this have to do with the Co-op Village? What does this all add up to—the final summation? I think it is entirely possible that 10,000 years ago we made a wrong turn in the maze in building an unsustainable economic system and a way of life that have led us to where we are today. That is to say, we have hit the wall. Our social, economic, and environmental problems are so obvious that we can now simply rise and shout from the rooftop: "Res ipsa loquitur!"

What we are attempting to do here at The Co-op Village Foundation is to offer mankind a new form of economics, an option out of the existing system. Maybe it will work, maybe it won't; but at least it is an alternative to continuing to bang our heads against that infernal wall and pretending all is progressing quite well (that is, 3 percent more people are hitting the wall over last year).

SERVE THE SERVING SHIP

As a teenager, I remember reading sea stories of the great square-rigged sailing ships and being enamored with them. What impressed me the most was the utter simplicity of the relationship between the seamen and their ship. The crew served the ship and the ship served its crew. If the relationship ever got badly out of balance, both ship and crew were inevitably lost at sea. It was quite simple.

Using the terminology of today's business world, what we are embarking on here at The Co-op Village Foundation is to take the essence of a corporation to a new level. Traditionally, corporations are crewed by three classes of people: the investors, management, and line workers. What we are attempting to do is make all three classes the same persons. And on top of that, we need to make the corporation serve that one class totally in all areas of life and forever!

I am not aware of this ever having been done. We are creating a business whose only purpose is to provide wealth, security, and leisure to all involved with it. Instead of how it pays cash dividends, it would be judged by the amount of happiness it pays out.

I recall reading two historical books that dealt with the D-Day invasion: *The Invasion of Northern Europe* and *The Longest Day*. They both chronicled the extraordinary amount of detailed planning that went into the assault. The thought that kept occurring to me throughout the reading was this: If this same amount of planning went into living instead of killing, how much better off the world would be! Why don't we do this kind of "planning for the living"?

The Co-op Village is an attempt to create a corporation whose business is to mind our own business. This corporation would balance our collective checkbook, prepare our budget and manage it, shop for us, monitor our maintenance schedules, help educate our children, research our legal problems, look out for our well-being, etc. We, the members, would use our collective skills to ensure everyone's welfare instead of each of us managing our own personal affairs, as we are now inadequately prepared to do in some areas and are suffering accordingly.

The traditional view of a corporation dictates that it squeeze the maximum production out of the line workers in order to reward the investors. When an employee can no longer produce at maximum level, he is laid off and is left to fend for himself. Under our new vision of a corporation, the interest of all concerned would be the deciding factor. This is because the members are both the employees and the investors. In this scenario, that same employee would still be laid off, but the corporation would then have to find another suitable position for him; otherwise it would be failing in its mission to provide wealth (in the form of well-being, security, and leisure) to all involved.

The traditional view of a corporation also dictates that it grow X percent each year. If it doesn't, it and its management are deemed failures. This pushes corporations to a higher degree of risk each year—and closer to bankruptcy. For what? Forcing a corporation towards its ultimate doom seems a reckless business plan. Under our new vision of a corporation, growth is unnecessary. Security and leisure would be the driving motivators, not growth.

The traditional view of a corporation dictates that it discard an employee who produces at a slower rate. To retain him is to reward him—in effect, to pay him more for underachieving. For example, if it takes him two hours to perform a one-hour job, he draws twice the pay per job of other employees who perform efficiently! Therefore, he must go.

The Village is a cashless environment. The employee, as a member, does not draw pay, but instead receives dividends in the form of well-being, security, and leisure. This system recognizes that not everybody produces at the same rate. It allows the employee to take as long as he needs to complete the assigned job. He is not penalizing the investors (including himself) if he takes longer. Here everybody gets what they want and the job gets done.

The traditional view dictates that businesses run at around 80 percent capacity. When events cause production to increase closer to 100 percent, companies begin to get into trouble. Our new view allows the Village, as a business, to run at around 30-40 percent capacity, leaving plenty of safe fumble room.

To return to the sailing ship analogy, this "new-vision" corporation will serve all collectively to the degree that it is served. Simple as that. It's in the best interest of both the Village and its members for everyone to serve this "serving ship" to the best of their ability.

LIFE SYSTEMS CO-OPERATIVE

We are creating something new to the business world: a Life Systems Co-operative. It is essentially a corporation owned by, managed by, worked by, and for the benefit of the residents only. Its sole purpose is to provide all life support systems to maintain a decent, secure, worry-free life for all residents and their offspring for life. The dividends: Happiness!

MASLOW ECONOMICS

What would happen if you took the best of communism and combined it with the best that capitalism has to offer, and in the process dropped the negatives associated with each of them? This might produce a system that guarantees life necessities such as food, shelter, heath benefits, pensions, etc., to ensure a dignified living. It would also offer luxuries to those who are willing to work harder for them if they so choose.

Currently, the United States attempts this to a degree, but it is not working all that well. One problem is that money is given to some persons to create parity, such as social security. It gets intermingled with luxuries as well as providing for others who do not qualify for benefits. What is suggested here is to provide a house; provide medical coverage; and guarantee meals every day to all persons. Simple as that. If you want more than "just a house," then work towards a fancier one. But in the meantime there is no suffering.

WARM FUZZY

The new corporate economic system created by the Village will not be cash hungry like its outside cousin corporations. Nor will it be burdened by wages, taxes, workers' compensation insurance, and large overhead. It will be a lean, mean non-cash-hungry machine that can cherry-pick the profitable business contracts and take them away from the large established businesses. It will be like genetically creating a new small, warm, fuzzy animal similar to a rabbit to be released into the jungle. It will not be very hungry. It will just sit in the bushes. But when it does get hungry, it will be able to easily devour any lion it chooses.

REVERSE ENGINEERING

In the early 1980s, as mainframe computers began to drop below $250,000 in cost, reverse engineering came into vogue. Knowing that the current computer technology would be obsolete in just three years, manufacturers decided not to patent the machines. Schematic drawings were required in order to file a patent. A competitor only had to review the drawing now made public, make a minor change, apply for his own patent, and compete in the marketplace. Manufacturers realized that if they didn't file a patent for protection, their competitor would be the first to purchase a new machine. But the reasoning was that it would take competing engineers at least two years to disassemble the machine, understand it, and copy it, which was longer than the one year to copy it if they had the drawings. We are reverse-engineering an existing village economy system to work in our time and location.

If we assume that there is intelligent life in space, and some of it is probably much more advanced than we are, then some of it must be at a higher level of evolution than we are. If that is the case, then we must also have to believe that they would surely have worked past the inequalities and sufferings our current culture visits upon millions of people in the form of famine and ill health, the result of poverty.

What we are trying to do is to imagine that system of living that a far more advanced race would have in place and to reproduce it to fit us here and now. We intend to build such a system. By reverse engineering, we are free of all of our preconceived notions of how things should be, free of discriminations, biases, and cultural demands. We are free to start anew to once and for all eliminate poverty.

JOBS

Because the Village is a cashless society, 80 percent of the jobs typically found in an economy will no longer be needed. Such unfilled jobs might include cashiers, sales, marketing, truck drivers, advertising, security, payroll clerks, bankers, bookkeepers, etc. The Village must fill only those jobs that directly benefit the Village, such as constructing and maintaining buildings, raising and preparing food, and providing healthcare. With fewer jobs (only 20 percent of the usual number), the need for the standard forty-hour workweek will be eliminated. Assuming most members want to have Village jobs, a typical member might work twenty hours per week or less. Job sharing would be the rule rather than the exception.

Training for some jobs might be provided through on-the-job training received from those already skilled. It might also require some additional classroom time, in the Village or at a local vocational school, with the costs borne by the Village. Because members might not sell their trained services outside the Village, typical certifications might not be required. With this in mind, many requirements could be ignored, such as a plumber having to take a general education class in order to obtain certification.

Some members might choose to keep their outside jobs. The Village would support them in this endeavor by maintaining those constants in their home life such as home repairs, preparing meals, babysitting, and maintaining the car and lawn. In exchange, the Village might receive an agreed-upon percentage of the employee's wages. All would be happier and less stressed.

RESTRUCTURED JOBS

Jobs in America are plagued with the polar problems of either consuming too much time (up to sixty hours a week) or having no jobs available to others. What if you restructured the jobs so that there were far fewer jobs, but they would be able to be worked by almost everybody, paying the same rate to all, with a maximum workweek of twenty hours?

This is doable! By going to an internal cashless society, 80 percent of most jobs are eliminated. This would then create the above situation in which job sharing is the rule. Because there would be no competition for jobs, those with the skills would be most eager to share their knowledge and skills with the untrained so that the twenty-hour maximum is not exceeded; the pay is the same.

CABALLERO

The Spanish word for gentleman is "caballero," from the root word "caballo" (meaning horse). Thus, a gentleman is a man with a horse, a nobleman who can afford a horse and mobility, much the opposite of a peasant.

Wouldn't it be more honest if the English language had such a word for a high-classed single parent? Such a word would differentiate him or her from a peasant single parent, that being one with no car or an undependable car; no permanent dependable baby sitter; no ready supply of cash or gas for commuting to work—and therefore, one without the possibility of ever having a steady job. Maybe it's time that we can be honest about the hell our current economic system puts some people through. Let's call it what it is.

SLAP AROUND

During the time of the great square-sailed ships, sailors of the British Navy took joy in playing a game I've dubbed "slap around." Their huge warships carried 500 men and a dozen or two young cabin boys. Invariably on each voyage there were at least half a dozen new boys around the age of nine venturing to sea for the first time. Once at sea, the sailors would get bored and would initiate those first-timers.

A short piece of rope was tied to each boy's left wrist with the other end being lashed to the mast, placing the boys in a circle facing each other's back. Their right hand held a board. The rules were simple: When you were tapped by the boy behind you, you had to tap the one before you. You could hit as hard or as soft as you wanted; you were free to choose.

After several rounds of slightly tapping each other, someone would always feel that they had been tapped too hard and would accelerate his blows. Before long the sailors would be roaring with laughter at the sight of the boys beating the hell out of each other. What was so funny (or sad) was that all that was needed was for one boy to choose to go back to tapping, but they couldn't comprehend that what they did was a delayed version of what was coming back around to them. All they had to do was simply stop!

We are playing in an economic game of slap around that is also torturing us. All we have to do is simply choose to stop playing it.

LIES

In his book *Looking Backward*, written in 1863, Edward Bellamy describes the current economic system as one in which everyone is forced to lie in order to survive. To sell our product or services, we must hype them as superior to all others, not reveal weaknesses and defects, obscure competitors' benefits, and make recommendations which we know might not be in the buyer's best interest. Bellamy goes on to say that lying to survive is so rampant that if an angel came to earth and decided to stay and raise a family here, he would have to join our economic system, a system that "would even perverse an angel."

Michael Lerner goes even further in his book *The Politics of Meaning* in detailing the lies we must tell. He describes a culture based on so many lies that we come to expect them from everybody all of the time. We look each other straight in the face and no longer question the fact that we have just been lied to—as if it should not bother us in the slightest. We've come to expect it. In fact, it would be considered rude to call someone on it. And thus our whole culture is based on lies and untruths.

What a terrifying way to base a life on.

Co-op Village life should change this as there would be nothing to lie about. No one is trying to sell anything. No one is being forced to take advantage of another. There is nothing to conceal; no money or power shifting. There is only the truth for all to share. Surely creating a culture based on truth is a turn in the right direction. No lie!

TRANSPARENT CORPORATIONS

Many corporate histories reveal common practices of self-serving back-room deals, discrimination, and acts that are beneficial only to the corporation and its people while not exactly good for mankind. Although there may be little actual board room discussion on these subjects, many corporate decisions are indeed flavored this way.

Several hundred years ago, when corporations were first chartered, a reserved right of the chartering government was to recall that charter if the corporation no longer served the common good. Somehow we have lost sight of that reservation. It is now accepted that a chartered corporation lives forever no matter how it serves, or fails to serve, humanity. We seem to have willingly given up the right to recall them.

The Village will require and own several corporations to run itself. Some will be charged with running the Village itself, while others will be created to provide outside jobs and income for those that choose it. To ensure that the Village corporations serve the good of all the residents, the corporations must be both transparent and ever watchful of losing their chartered purpose—that being to serve the best interest of all concerned. Transparency means that all decisions, transactions, activity, and risks, both current and future, are actively disclosed to all residents. This implies not only that the records are readable and available, but that all residents need to have been trained to review and understand those records. To ensure equality and justice, all residents would need to be trained as auditors and board members.

Nontypical disclosure might include listing of the names, benefits received, rate of pay, and time worked of each person associated with the corporation, as well as the overall benefits to the community at large. All residents would then know who benefits from those activities.

These disclosure tools would then make it easy for the residents of the Village to understand the benefits of the community supporting that particular endeavor and to continually evaluate the risks involved with it. This would also be used to determine if the corporation has gotten out of hand and perhaps needs to be reined in, personnel changed, or the corporation be closed down as it may no longer serve the greater good of all concerned.

This is how corporations were originally intended to be run. The only difference is that this was originally the power of kings but now will be the power of all concerned.

DREADED "D'S"

The village economy would provide a lifetime shield from the financial impact of the dreaded "D's"—downsizing, divorce, death of a partner, disease, disability, dementia, and delinquent utility bills.

DIVORCE

So how might divorce be handled within the Co-op Village? First of all divorce might not be as traumatic in the village because the economic stinger would be removed. There would not be any doubt about how the family would survive economically. For them the economics would remain the same. No one would be homeless. No one would lose their job, be in turmoil over child care, have to leave town, or move in with family. There would be no near bankruptcy currently associated with divorce. No one in the family would worry about their next meal. What would remain the same is the emotional turmoil of "I'm not loved." But that should be a lot easier to deal with insulated from the economic upheaval of traditional divorce.

What would change is that one party would move to another home on the other side of the village. If the spouses worked together, one may choose another work group. But in the meantime, both parents would be there for the children. The spouses might only see each other at the softball field, and that would be at their choosing.

The big twist might occur regarding court-ordered child support. If both parents continue to work within the Village, the Village might decide to pay the child support on behalf of the paying spouse. This would be done with the expectation that the Village would be paid that support check back from the receiving spouse each month. Thus it would merely be a sham to keep the paying spouse from having to work outside the Village for wages. These payments would continue as long as both spouses continue to reside in the Village. This might even force the spouses to be more cooperative in the breakup so as to not drive the other party out of the Village from loss of dignity. Because the work output and well-being of each resident is of importance to the entire village, all residents close to the divorcing couple would probably assist in the healing and recovery process and help each retain their dignity.

COURTING

Young single persons and divorced persons might wish to meet and date outsiders. This might be accomplished by providing transportation for outside schooling or employment. That person also would have the benefit of seeing the outside world in more detail so that they could decide for themselves which culture to live in. The Village might even provide housing in the nearest town for these people for a year or two.

Genealogy records would be maintained on all residents so that eighty years down the road, inbreeding could be prevented.

REQUIRED WORK AND PERSONAL INCOME

Of great concern to residents are the questions: "How much time would I have to work?" "Will everyone have to work the same amount of time?" "Would I have to share my pension?" and "What happens if someone refuses to work?"

These issues would be decided by the entire community itself through three of its twelve focus groups:

1. How will we share our abundance?

2. How will we enrich ourselves?

3. How will we coordinate what we enjoy doing?

But in the meantime, simple answers are offered here as to how the focus groups might resolve these issues in the early startup stage. However, before these questions can be answered, residents would need to understand several factors about Village economics—that being:

Factor #1. Transition Periods: It will take time to get residents to go from an "each man for himself" mode of thinking to a "what's in the best interest of all concerned?" mindset. It will take time to go from the current cash culture to a self-sustained cashless culture. It will also take perhaps ten years for startup, that being financing the construction and land acquisition and then to payoff that financing, before the Village is truly running as envisioned.

Factor #2. Cash Requirements: At startup, a great amount of cash will be required to purchase land and building materials. Success of the Village will always be at risk as long as outside parties (banks) have a mortgage on the property. Therefore, it would be wise to raise as much cash as possible from the residents and at the same time prioritize paying off any third-party financing as soon as possible, ensuring that the community land trust will be free to manage the property for hundreds of years, as envisioned. After startup, a small amount of cash will be required for some utilities and other outside services the community simply cannot provide for itself.

Factor #3. Limited Pensions: Some residents will come into the community receiving pensions, annuities, social security, or passive business income. It is probable that in thirty years, no resident would have these income streams.

Factor #4. Room and Board: Each resident would be expected to provide the cash or cash equivalent to pay for their share of the land, infrastructure, and house. Each resident would also be expected to provide the cash or cash equivalent (labor) for their living expenses.

Factor #5. Timecards: Initially an accounting office would track payments made and time worked by residents. After all property has been paid for and the Village has shifted its mindset successfully, this function might cease.

Factor #6. The Focus Group: "How do we coordinate what we enjoy doing" would attempt to assign jobs in accordance with our personal likes; thus we would enjoy the tasks assigned and not feel like we were working. This focus group would also do all it could to coax residents to socialize and at the same time perform additional efforts on behalf of the community that only outsiders might consider work.

In addition, a few possible solutions to some of these factors are:

Possible Solution #1. Purchase Money: The first issue would deal with the "purchase money" needed to pay for a resident's share of the land, house, and infrastructure. Cash would be needed to pay outside vendors for the land and materials. Village companies could be formed so that residents without the up-front cash could perform outside work. This job might be, for example, for twenty hours a week for three or four years until the debt is paid.

Possible Solution #2. Living Expenses: Each resident would have to contribute for his or her share of food, utilities, property taxes, etc. Because cash would be needed mainly in the formative years, those with cash incomes might be able to provide cash, at a predetermined rate, instead of performing work. Those without an income would be required to work a Village job, internal or external, for perhaps twenty hours a week, forever. This might be in addition to the temporary "purchase money" job some would hold.

Please note that in a short period of time, the "purchase money" job would be eliminated. Also note that in time, those with outside cash incomes would die off so that eventually no one would be in a position to cash himself out of performing work.

Some residents may be exempted from work due to inability to perform any type of work. The Village may allow an elderly family member to reside there who is unable to work, as we all may be in time. However, even physically disabled residents might be able to answer phones or snap peas. Again, all of these issues would be decided by the community through its focus groups.

> *Possible Solution #3. Personal Income:* If a resident has cash income of more than his share of living expenses, he should be allowed to keep that excess. Remember that in time, this disparity will go away through attrition.

> *Possible Solution #4. Refusal to Work:* In the event that the focus groups cannot get a resident to perform his required work, then the community could decide to refund his purchase money and perhaps provide additional help to get him established to live elsewhere. The refund amount would be as predefined in the Community Land Trust Bylaws. This would not be an act of ill-will towards that resident, but rather a recognition that some persons might not adjust to this way of life and would be happier elsewhere.

HOW WILL THE VILLAGE FINANCE ITSELF?

Before this question can be answered, the reader must first read the prior section on "Required Work and Personal Income," paying close attention to the economic factors discussed.

Working under the economic factors mentioned above, Village construction and maintenance financing might be achieved utilizing a combination of the following methods:

> *1. Resident Entrance Fees:* A nominal fee (say, $1,000) might be required from each resident so that he will be considered seriously.

2. Resident Full Payment: Residents with the means to pay their share of housing and village costs up front would be expected to do so.

3. Resident Investment: Those residents with excess cash or investments could invest funds into Financing, Inc. This corporation would hold a mortgage on the land and buildings and would pay interest to the investors at a rate more than CD rates at a typical bank but less than the typical return on stock investments. The stockholders of this corporation would be only the investor residents. As soon as these funds are repaid, this corporation would be dissolved, leaving the land free and clear.

4. HUD Financing: Up to 70 percent of the finished market value of the land and buildings might be borrowed from the Federal government at a low rate for up to forty years.

5. Creation of Outside Jobs: Outside businesses and jobs as well as Village industries could be created so that those without the up-front full payment could earn the cash needed for their share of buying into the Village. After the mortgage is paid off, some of these jobs could still be filled so that some cash continues to flow into the Village for outside purchases.

6. Entitlement Revenue: Some residents might qualify for HUD Section Eight rent assistance based on low income; others might qualify for Medicare home nursing assistance, family housing assistance, or some other government assistance that might go towards "rent".

7. Pensions and Passive Incomes: Those residents with pensions, social security, or passive incomes might wish to share some of that income with the Village either as a gift or instead of performing labor.

8. Grants: Grants will be applied for whenever possible.

9. Deferred Options: A fraction of the land needed might be purchased with options to purchase the remaining fractions at later intervals. This would lower cash requirements until the Village is prepared for its next expansion.

Most of the above would be managed by the focus group "How do we enrich ourselves?"

FINDING 500 MEMBERS

The following suggested ad might be run in the Sunday newspaper once a month in order to spark younger membership when we are ready to build. The ad would be in the General Employment section.

Now Hiring—All Trades
No Experience Necessary

Long-term employment, 300 positions

Health benefits/retirement benefits

Family housing provided

Free child care

Free job training

Single-parent families welcomed

Personal transportation not required or needed

No relocation from this area; located in Santa Rosa County

Nonprofit organization

Contact: www.co-opvillagefoundation.org

The ad is a tongue-in-cheek demonstration to the individual who recently posed the reasonable question of "How are we ever going to find 500 people locally who wish to live in the village?" It is not hard to imagine that we would find ourselves flooded with applicants—far more than we could possibly accept. Please remember that one of the twelve focus groups, "How do we expand our community?" would be charged with the task of membership screening.

KNOW YOUR NEIGHBORS

No, you will probably not know all 500 of your neighbors. A resident will be extremely close to about thirty members of his Cluster, though, sharing breakfasts together and participating in work parties. A resident will also be somewhat close to the 100 members of his Neighborhood (three Clusters), coming into contact with them at nightly dinners. However, little contact would occur with the remaining 400 Village residents unless you work with some of them or share a hobby. These 400 will nonetheless be concerned with your well-being, the same as you will be with theirs. If later you decide to make a change in your life, you are free to move to another Cluster at no cost. This would afford you an opportunity to begin life anew as you choose.

THE HUMAN ELEMENT

We realize that adjusting to the "greatest good for all" concept will take some readjustment in thinking for most folks as they join the Village. So, all prospective residents will take free classes on consensus thinking, personalities, and meditation, and will be assigned a mentor to aid in their six-month transition into the Village. After that transition time, all of their needs will be supplied for life—shelter, food, utilities, education, job training, family, security, etc.

The other concept that may be difficult to grasp is decision making on a scale necessary to cover 500 residents in the Village. But if the Village has its basic needs for economic and social security met, the smaller Hubs should be able to handle the rest of the internal decisions necessary to govern themselves by consensus.

HOMELESS TO ALIENS

Yesterday I attended a workshop regarding the lack of affordable housing for persons with disabilities and the homeless. As I sat there, I noticed that half of the participants were professionals employed as social workers, attorneys specializing in discrimination litigation, etc., and the rest were referred to as their "consumers." I listened as they all agreed that there just were not any affordable homes available, period. Just this week the city of Pensacola, by its actions, implied that affordable housing was new homes in the \$175,000 to \$200,000 range. It appeared that nothing at all was accomplished by the workshop except for a little venting, and a few consumers learned to fight harder for one of the remaining affordable houses.

During the workshop Albert Einstein's statement, "The enormous problems we face today cannot be solved by the same frame of mind that created them," kept going through my head. Maybe we are looking at the problem too closely. I wondered how an alien, unfamiliar with our culture and economics, would have assessed yesterday's workshop and addressed the housing problem? I think possibly the following:

• This is a long-term problem that has been occurring for many, many years. If the goal is to make the problem disappear permanently, it is futile to solve the long-term problem with a short-term solution.

• Based on 10,000 years of history, it is obvious that governments have no intent of permanently resolving this problem. Therefore, it might be concluded that in the scheme of our social economic system, the "problem" is beneficial in some way and is not a problem to the whole. Or perhaps it is just a small flaw of our system that we tolerate.

• The problem may have been sliced and analyzed too thinly. Litigators view it from a litigation viewpoint only. They are paid to do that, so they must close their eyes to other viewpoints. Social workers do the same. Landlords do the same. These persons are not paid to resolve the problem for the whole.

• If the problem could be permanently resolved in one day, would the above-mentioned persons elect to do so? Probably not; they themselves would be without a job and be subject to homelessness. This is the culture we live in.

• A short-term solution is to put economic underachievers in a home and then leave them. In our suburbia culture, lacking transportation, medical assistance, community support, and livable-wage jobs, most of these placed persons will rejoin the homeless.

• It is assumed that because most of these persons cannot locate a forty-hour-a-week job in the want ads, they are unemployable and thus will always be nonproductive to the community.

• There are two money problems in our culture: the lack of money and too much money. The problem with too much money is that we use it for security, and if you lose your money, there goes your security. Oddly, the more money you have, the more insecure you become!

• Earlier in our history it appears that we systematically destroyed tribal communities. Perhaps this was done so that we could control them with money. Until the arrival of our culture, the tribe was a member's security, so he had no need for money.

• It appears that the current culture dictates that any activity undertaken must be taxed by supplying a living to others around it. This need not be so.

Possible Solution

Perhaps it is time that we establish villages or communities small and large enough to house both moneyless and the wealthy, providing security for all. Only affordable housing costing around $40,000 per unit would be constructed. The community would not be dependent on transportation as most jobs would be provided to all who wish to work there. This would be a place that would be internally sustainable forever. This would be a place where the professionals who would work themselves out of a job would rather be at, anyway. From start to finish, no one would make a profit on the venture.

Fighting over the few remaining affordable houses is not the long-term solution. Building a surplus of affordable houses is.

DISCRIMINATION

To an alien it would appear that practically all "civilized" cultures, as defined by historians, had and still have homeless and poverty-level people. All "civilized" cultures had and still have second-class citizens and discrimination. It can be deduced that this is to balance out the economic system and allow those in control to profit on the unfortunate lower class. If it were not profitable, it would not continue.

Because this is too hard to admit, over generations humans have replaced the real reason with bogus reasons that make no sense at all, but allow those in power to live with themselves as they continue to profit.

Aliens might conclude that the root basis for all of this is humanity's fear that "there is not enough to go around." Oddly enough, though, "uncivilized" cultures on earth (indigenous tribes) do not have second-class citizens, homelessness, poverty, or discrimination. Nor do they share the belief that "there is not enough to go around."

One of the founding principles of the Village is that there is more than enough to go around; therefore, no one would be able to profit from discrimination—social, racial, economic, religious, or any other type—and all of the Village would suffer if any one member was discriminated against.

FACTORIES

Just because the Village is small doesn't mean that all created jobs would be low-tech. The Village might construct a factory or lease one off site, employing both residents and nonresidents, with the resident employees being bused.

The factory might manufacture a product that doesn't have a steady demand, such as composting toilets. Or it might be a seasonal business that capitalizes on its ability to lay off its workforce without harming it and then to rehire it when demand is up. Two or more villages might cooperate in establishing a small clinic or hospital in the region, and could supply some of the labor.

REDUNDANT PENSIONS

One of the biggest problems facing Americans today is the continuing loss of pensions and retirement benefits and the probable shrinking of social security benefits. One's entire security system could be wiped out by the actions of one bankruptcy attorney or the vote of congressmen. This scenario is not hard to imagine as it is repeated over and over again.

But imagine an economic system in which you earn a 100 percent vested interest in your entire pension benefits package the first year on the job. Now imagine that you control that pension plan totally—not outside investors, not bankruptcy attorneys, but you. You decide if the benefits should increase or decrease.

This would make current pensions that we sell our soul for obsolete, redundant! Imagine the impact that would have on this nation. Now imagine the Co-op Village . . .

STORED WEALTH

In order for one person to profit from gaining power over another and taking wealth from them, the taker must be able to store the wealth gained. Early in our history the storage method was most likely grain or precious metals, whereas our current storage medium is cash. However, in a cashless society, such as the Village, there is no storage medium. Because food and utilities are given equally to all, not even those can be used for wealth storage. Therefore, unless someone was willing to eat more than their share of beans for dinner that night, it would not be profitable to gain power over another.

MISSED MARK

The first few Co-op Villages constructed may miss the mark in some areas of environmental sustainability. Why? Tremendous effort has to be focused on that first giant step—creating community. It entails getting 500 people to "check their guns at the door" and take on 499 other persons as their main concern. This is a huge undertaking for people. It could safely be said that building a caring, committed community represents 70 percent of what it takes to get a Co-op Village going. Being environmentally responsible is the other 30 percent.

Therefore, trying to do both at the outset may be too much. In the minds of many prospective new members, we could be seen as "environmental nuts," extremists who eat rice cakes and live in homes made of Budweiser bottles. It might be better, therefore, in the planning stages, to focus initially on the 70 percent (community building) by shooting for less-extreme environmental goals: a smaller environmental footprint, less materialism, less waste, and less consumption. Then, with further education and by consensus, gradually more comprehensive, responsive sustainability goals could be implemented. However, I can see some excellent potential members being offended by this suggestion.

What we are undertaking is similar to building a railroad spur. In our endeavor to divert the train off the main line, we will be offering the option to turn. If the turn is too abrupt or steep, the train will derail. To be successful, the turn has to be a comfortable, inviting one. Once the turn is made, our train can continue in any direction we, the members, choose—but over time.

$30,000 PER HOUSE?

How can the Village build a house for $30,000 when developers can't build one for less than $200,000? Our biggest savings is that all labor costs and profits are cut out entirely because the Village will provide all labor. Another savings is that the buildings are smaller than what developers are offering.

A tremendous advantage of the Village is that by having a Community Land Trust own all of the land, it will not need to be broken up into individual lots for each house. This allows the land to remain zoned as agricultural and avoids the costly fights to get the property rezoned as residential. It also avoids being classified as a residential neighborhood development. This allows the Village to escape county requirements for road systems, sidewalks, expensive stormwater holding ponds and drainage systems, twice the number of septic tanks, underground utilities, street lights, etc. The only major county jurisdiction over the Village is the building code requirements. This is a developer's dream come true!

All of these advantages are things that for-profit developers can never have. This assures us that where a Village is being built, it will never have to fear competition from developers moving into our price range. They can't touch it.

WHY VILLAGES?

After the first Village is built, hundreds of others will pop up around the country as this will be the only viable option that millions of people will have to live in dignity. This will transform the country. These villages will provide what our culture and governments promise but cannot deliver.

This is probably the only current viable option for mankind to mitigate the disasters that lay ahead globally, both financially and environmentally. Cowboys know that you can turn a bull's body simply by turning its head; so, too, can the world be turned if the U. S. culture can be turned. This is a means to accomplish that quickly before governments can stop it. Currently we are just silently marching towards a cliff. But when enough villages are built, society will then have an option to choose how it will create its future.

We have designed a village for which there is a strong demand; it is a sound business investment, blueprinted so that it can be replicated anywhere, and it economically dovetails nicely with our current capitalistic system. All that remains to be done is to build it.

UN-CHECKMATE

As a result of globalization, the United States now has two principal industries: war as a result of the military industrial complex, and the looting of the rest of the world through its multi-national corporations.

During the past fifty years, our democratic form of government has been hijacked by the lobbyists of that military industrial complex and those multinational corporations. We have now arrived at the point that the direction our country takes is dictated by those lobbyists. The voiced opinions of the common citizens no longer matter, contrary to the wishes of our founding fathers. How could this have occurred?

Many of us as children wondered how Hitler could have remained in power. We pondered how the citizens of Germany could have allowed their government to cause a world war killing 20 million people. How could they have stood by and allowed this horror to unfold? And now we know—one day at a time, because it was profitable.

In our political situation, we too find ourselves frozen for that same reason. We wage war and arm other countries because it is profitable to our businesses. This is also why we export our jobs, quit manufacturing and instead import, escape our pension debts, etc.

So why do we do it to the peril of the common citizen? Why don't we stop this madness before it goes further? Why don't we simply change what we are doing? I suggest it is because we can't. We are in checkmate; we are powerless to move from our current position. What is ironic, however, is that we willingly allowed ourselves to be placed in checkmate!

We allowed ourselves to be maneuvered into the corner by believing we all deserved to live as the wealthy. Madison Avenue convinced us of it. Advertisers proved we couldn't live without it. Our 401(k) plans dared us to demand maximum returns on investments in multinationals. The military industrial complex scattered itself over all fifty states to ensure that we would fight for its growth. Our multinationals leave just enough jobs behind to secure our support. All in all, we allowed ourselves to be bought out. We have no alternatives—no other jobs; no place else to go. And yet our personal investments are tied up in the very machines that are destroying our way of life! We have the proverbial tiger by the tail.

The reason no one has stepped forward until now to offer a comprehensive solution solving most of our problems is that we are in checkmate because of those investments and the fear of losing our few remaining jobs—we can't see ourselves letting go of the tiger. So we continue moving closer to that catastrophic cliff.

Our option out is to reduce support for the runaway industries by moving displaced workers into Co-op villages, returning to them more than they forfeited by letting go. In effect, this gives a citizen the option of unchecking himself. When enough citizens have unchecked themselves, those industries will have been deflated enough to where they can now be brought back under control, yet still remain in business. This is the only way out of the mess. We have to offer lifeboats to remove enough people so the overcrowded pleasure boat can stabilize itself before it capsizes.

Carl Sagan

"I had an experience I can't prove. I can't even explain it, but everything that I know as a human being, everything that I am tells that it was real. I was part of something wonderful, something that changed me forever, a vision of the universe that tells us undeniably how tiny, and insignificant, and how rare and precious we all are. A vision that tells us we belong to something that is greater than ourselves. That we are not, that none of us, are alone. I wish that I could share that, I wish that everyone, even for one moment, could feel that awe, the humility and the hope. . . ."

—Ellie Arroway in Dr. Carl Sagan's novel, Contact

Chapter 7

C L U S T E R   B U I L D I N G S

by Jim Costa

Each Cluster will contain approximately fifteen homes and will house about thirty to thirty-five persons. Three Clusters combined will be considered a Neighborhood and will be isolated from other Neighborhoods both visually and by a ten-minute walk. Each Neighborhood will have a dining hall feeding a maximum of 100 residents. One hundred is the maximum because the social dynamics change when you exceed the hundred mark. The Village will contain five Neighborhoods for a total of fifteen Clusters, housing about 500 residents.

Each Cluster will contain the following features:

- Fifteen homes

- Meeting hall

- Garage and workshop

- Laundry and exercise room

- Gazebo

- Lodge

- Playground

- Minimal parking only for those that absolutely need their cars daily.

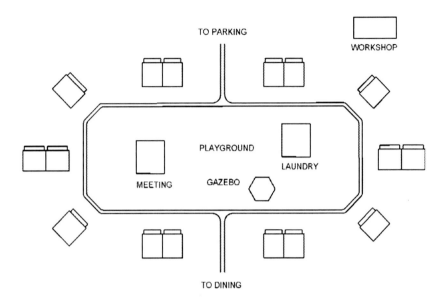

Figure 1. Cluster housing thirty people.

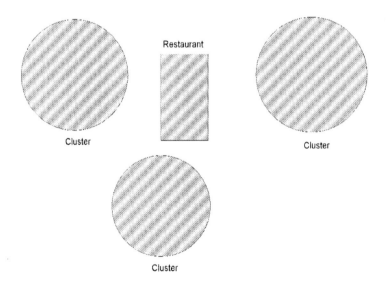

Figure 2. Neighborhood housing 90-100 people.

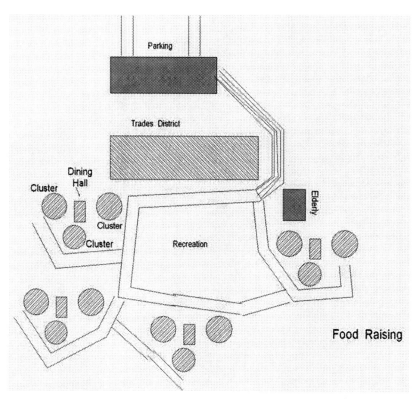

Figure 3. Village layout.

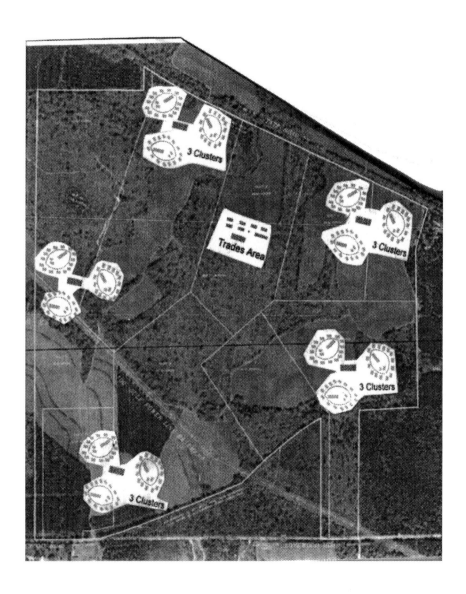

Figure 4. Land footprint.

EVOLVING HOUSE

The Evolving House was designed under the following design requirements:

Location: To be situated in Florida, which has a mild winter with no snow; a heat problem nine months of the year; and extreme humidity year-round, all of which makes it unbearable to live without air conditioning.

Rapid construction: The Village will probably need to be completed within two years, which will require that ten homes be completed per month in order to provide the approximately 255 homes needed. This means that materials must be readily available, and construction techniques must be used that are standard, simple, and not strenuous so that the entire population can provide the labor.

Acceptable by permitting authorities: The materials and construction methods should be readily approved by authorities

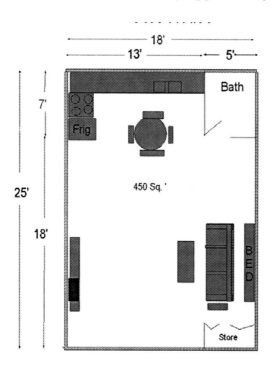

Figure 5. Evolving house—healthy single person.

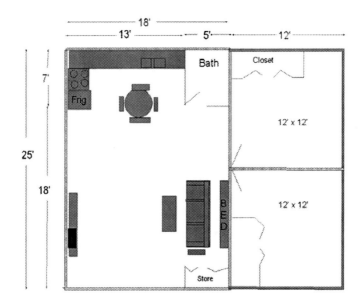

Figure 6. Evolving house—two bedrooms.

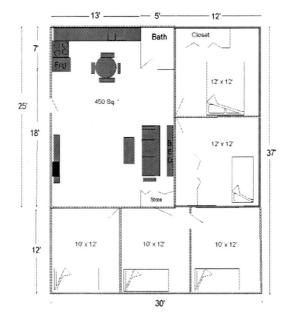

Figure 7. Evolving house—five bedrooms.

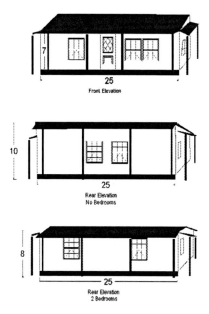

Figure 8. Evolving house—front elevation.

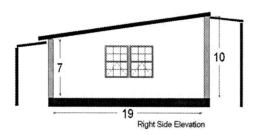

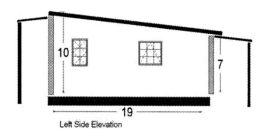

Figure 9. Evolving house—healthy single person—side elevation.

so that costly engineering battles, time delays, and building destruction and reconstruction are avoided.

Low energy demand: Each house must have an energy demand as low as possible to eventually be self-sustaining while still providing enough comfort to entice residents.

Built-in bedding: With the utilization of Murphy beds, roll-out beds, built-in beds, lean-to room housing a full-sized bed, or trundle beds, a bedroom can be eliminated for a healthy single person, or made smaller for families, thus cutting down on construction costs and energy requirements.

Small, expandable footprint: A basic single-room core house of approximately 450 square feet could be provided for a healthy single person. Upon marriage, two bedrooms could simply be added, as they will be planned for. With the arrival of children, three more rooms could be added. The key to simplicity is to have the walls raised on the core house so that a "shed roof" can be installed, which would slip next to the existing roof line without modifications to the original roof.

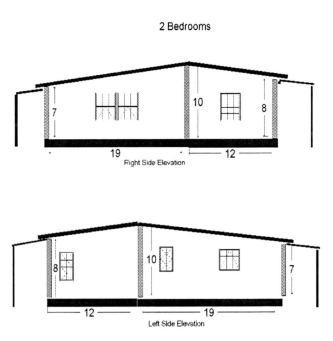

Figure 10. Evolving house—two bedrooms—side elevation.

Wall Detail   Roof Panel Detail

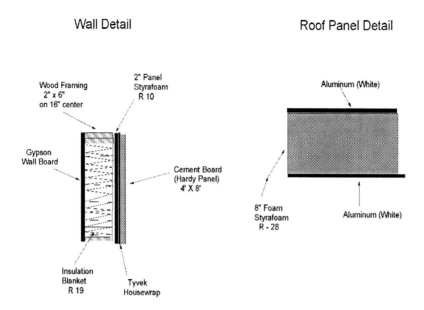

Figure 11. Wall construction details.

CONCRETE DOME HOMES

Concrete dome homes are being looked at. We believe that we can purchase the equipment for about $50,000. We can then send residents to school to learn the construction technology.

These homes can be constructed by us for about $30,000 each, which is comparable to the stick houses planned. They have high insulation properties, have lifespans of up to 100 years, and are maintenance-free.

The problems with building dome homes are:

• We are unfamiliar with the technology,

• Errors can be unforgiving,

• We do not know whom to train,

• Skilled workers will be required.

Because of these problems, it might be best to build the first fifty homes with conventional stick framing that novices can learn quickly. Then a few select residents can be sent to school in order to gradually shift over to dome homes as training and equipment allow.

MEETING HALL

Each Cluster will have a meeting hall, which might have the following features:

- Large open area with tables that fold up into the wall. This would be a great place for the kids to play on rainy days.

- Kitchen capable of feeding thirty people. This could be used to prepare breakfasts, especially on school days.

- Office space to be used by cluster residents.

- Conference table.

- Garage and workshop

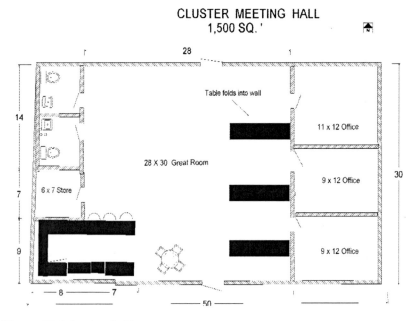

Figure 12. Meeting hall.

Each Cluster will have a garage and a workshop, which might have the following features:

- A double-car garage space to serve as a tool room and for use as a storage area. It could have the following:

- A typical garage door

- The ability to service an automobile

- Workbenches, any tools needed by the Cluster, and perhaps wood-working equipment.

- White metal roof so that it would not become an oven.

- Bathroom

- Telephone.

There also would be a large air-conditioned workshop with tables and benches. It could be used for sewing, electronics, arts and crafts, or perhaps as a training area.

There also would be a second double-car garage space that could be used for storage. This would not be for long-term storage, but rather for those items residents anticipate using during the

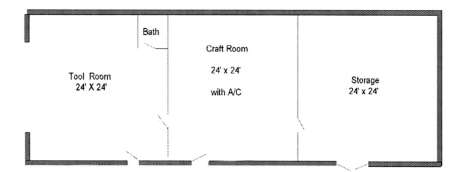

Figure 13. Garage/hobby shop/storage area.

year, such as luggage, sporting or hobby equipment, winter clothes, etc.

Construction Phase

- Interior walls would be left out and both ends would be framed for double garage doors. This would yield a 75' × 25' fabrication shop and warehouse with box fans at either end. House wall sections, trusses, and cabinets could be assembled here.

Laundry and Exercise Room

Each Cluster will have a laundry and an exercise room as outlined below:

- Two commercial-grade energy and water-efficient washers.

- Soap and chemicals that will not render the waste water unusable.

- Two commercial-grade dryers. Houses also would have access to clotheslines.

- Exercise room housing exercise equipment.

- Closet containing vacuum, carpet cleaner, etc.

- Shed containing toys and outdoor equipment, accessible from the outside.

- An optional freezer bank could be added to the laundry room if it was widened. Each household might have access to one shelf. Three households would share a key.

Gazebo

The gazebo in each Cluster might have the following features: It would be 20' × 20' in size.

- The gazebo would be screened in.

- The flooring would be cob or concrete.

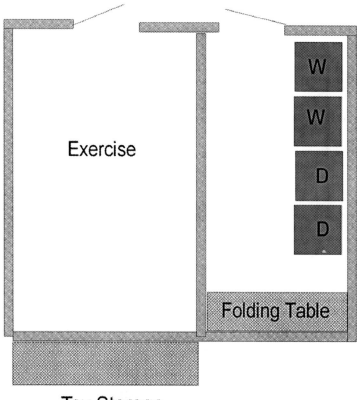

Figure 14. Laundry/exercise room.

- Roof of white metal so that the temperature underneath is the same as outside air.

- Have three-foot awnings on all sides for additional shade. These awnings could be lowered during winter. They might have clear panels built in for winter viewing.

- Have two hinged walls, each two feet high, that can be raised during the winter.

- Pot-belly stove.

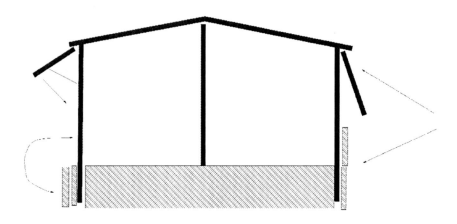

Figure 15. Gazebo with folding awnings.

Figure 16. Gazebo.

- Built-in center table and benches.

- Electricity.

Guest Lodge

The guest lodge would serve as a mini-motel and can house three families and sleep ten people. The total floor space is only 750 square feet, with the following features:

- Two main bedrooms, each 12′ ×12′ with built-in beds, a closet, and an alcove housing a desk or table and a storage locker. Each main bedroom sleeps four people.

- The exterior wall of the two main bedrooms would have a 5′ tall window on each side of a single French door which steps out into a private covered Japanese garden. This not only gives a private entrance but also brings the outside in, making the quarters appear larger.

- Each main room would have a desk (with a lamp over it) that pulls out into a table seating five people. It would have two legs on one side and would rest on a track on the wall side. It can be raised only one inch when pulling it out, thus preventing spillage of top contents. A trunk would be built into the alcove under the desk for storage of bedding, etc. The alcove would also house folding chairs for the table.

- Pull-up canvas curtains could be used for privacy while still bringing in light.

- Skylights could also be used in main rooms, kitchen, and baths.

- A television set would be installed on upper wall over bed and would be viewable with headsets.

- Pull-down bed would be located above the couch, with a built-in ladder which allows the couch to be slept upon.

- Two bathrooms, one wheelchair accessible.

- Small shared kitchenette.

- Open TV room, equipped with headsets, that can also sleep two people. This area could have a three-foot high wall separating it from the kitchen while leaving the space open. A drop-down curtain would then turn it into a bedroom.

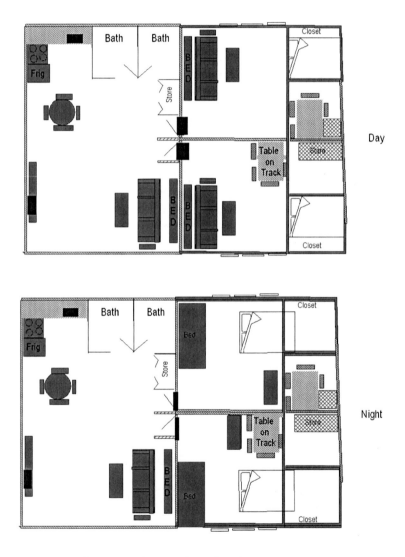

Figure 17. Guest lodge can house three families.

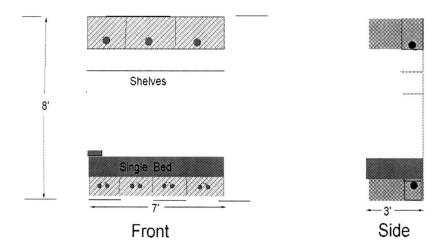

8'

Shelves

Single Bed

7'

Front

3'

Side

Figure 18. Single bed.

Built-in Beds

Built-in bedding can be utilized in order to reduce the size of bedrooms or even to eliminate the need for a bedroom altogether.

Single Bed

This bed unit would take up 7' × 3' of floor space. The system could be either free-standing or built into the wall. It would be similar to a captain's bed with drawers underneath and storage and shelves over it. Note that it has four feet of sitting space between the bed and upper cabinet. It could even have a pull-around curtain for those that sleep in the daytime or those not able to make the bed each day.

Bed over Couch

This unit is similar to a sideways Murphy bed. It would stick out about eighteen inches from the wall, but it would be positioned over a couch so that no floor-space is lost. At bedtime, the unit would simply drop down and the built-in ladder would be extended. The couch would also be available for sleeping on.

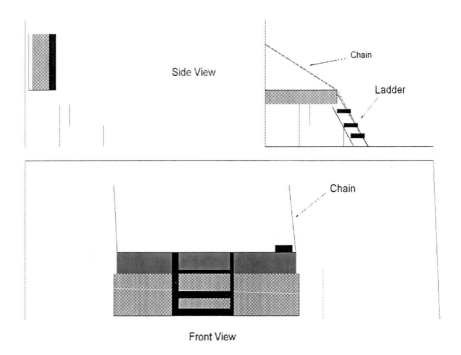

Figure 19. Bed over couch.

Full Bed Pull-Out

This full-sized bed unit would appear to be built into an exterior wall. Actually, the exterior wall is extended out seven feet and slopes down at a 45 degree angle to end at a height of three feet. This cavity then holds the bed on wheels and a rail so that it can be pulled out at night. The cavity above the bed would hold pull-out drawers and would have a storage cabinet above the drawers. The entire unit would be concealed behind sliding doors during the day. This unit drastically reduces cubic feet traditionally devoted to a full bed and accompanying furniture.

Dining Hall

The Village would have about five dining halls configured as follows:

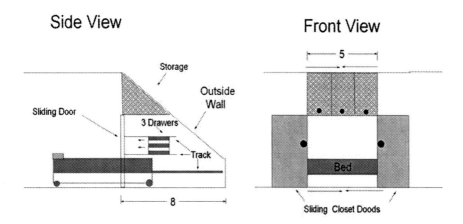

Figure 20. Full bed pull-out.

- There would be one dining hall for every neighborhood (three Clusters).

- Each would serve 90–100 persons, a crowd small enough to remain on a personal basis.

- Each dining hall would prepare its own menu and meals, staffed by the Clusters it serves.

- Fifty persons could be served for meals, or sixty-four persons could sit auditorium-style. Early seating might be by online reservation only.

- Probably only dinner would be served daily.

- A lounge or coffeehouse could be located at one end. Diners wishing to linger could move there, freeing up their table.

- During the day, the space could be used for meetings, child care, etc.

- A walk-in freezer might have a movable wall so that during certain seasons, empty space would not be cooled.

- The kitchen would have a separate air conditioning system and would be able to run off electricity or gas. Generators would be available if needed.

- A stove and a sink would be located on the covered porch for steaming, grilling, or baking outside.

- Menus would be posted online. Residents could dine at other dining halls if they so desire.

- Some tables would fold into the wall, making it easy for one person to clear the floor.

- Booths would be available for a more intimate setting. They could be reserved online.

- A mud room would be available for pedestrians' umbrellas and rain gear.

CONSTRUCTION FLOW

- Pre-construction Phase

- Have basic prints reviewed by an architect; incorporate suggestions into other designs; finalize prints.

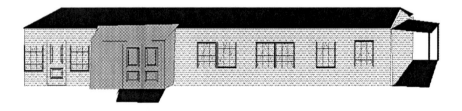

Figure 21. Dining hall—front view.

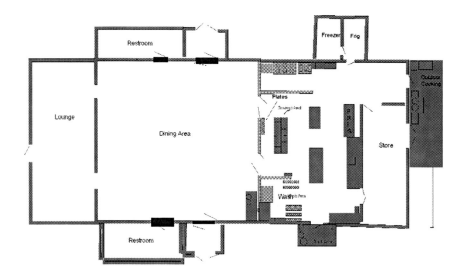

Figure 22. Dining Hall layout.

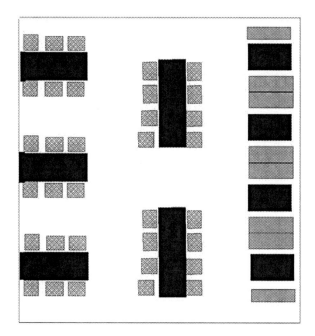

Figure 23. Dining hall with tables.

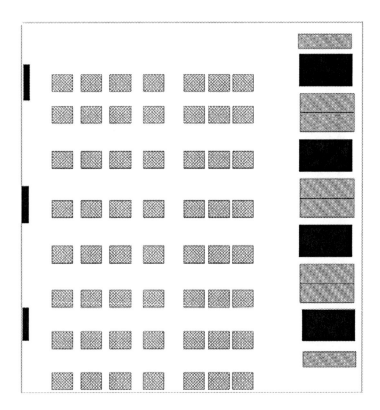

Figure 24. Dining hall with chairs only.

- Secure general contractor, master electrician, and master plumber. If necessary, train persons in the above fields to obtain licenses to work under.

- Purchase hand-held navigational equipment and perform civil engineering surveys ourselves to produce topographical maps for internal use only.

- Lay out construction sites and roads on maps. Layout on-site.

- Begin clearing land.

- Install basic infrastructure:

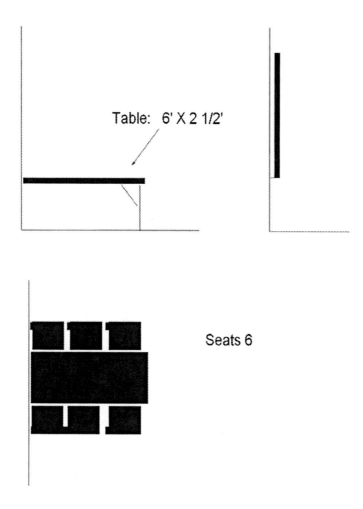

Figure 25. Wall-mounted folding dining table.

- Construct roads.

- Order electric power mains.

- Install water wells.

- Install central septic tanks.

- Install construction shack with phone service.

- Construct or secure warehouse for bulk purchases.

Construction Phase, per Cluster

- Construct Cluster garage, campground, gazebo, bathrooms (in place of washroom), meeting room, temporary construction trailers.

- Pour slabs. Install power poles where necessary.

- Frame walls and joists, prewire panels. This can be done inside garage during extreme weather.

- Assemble walls; install trusses and/or roof system.

Chapter 8

T R A D E S   A R E A   B U I L D I N G S

by Jim Costa

The following trades will be needed to service the Village:

1. Automotive shop/stable

2. Barber shop/beauty salon

3. Business office

4. Central operations

5. Chapel

6. Child care

7. Communications

8. Electricians/HVAC/plumbers

9. Farm

10. Fabrication shop—metal and wood

11. Focus group support

12. Gym

13. Health building

14. Library

15. Maintenance

16. Pet center

17. Retreat area (lodge, seminar, "no-tell" motel)

18. Sanitation

19. Schools

20. Social services

21. Warehouse

22. Welding shop.

ACTIVITIES, BY AREA OF TRADE

Activities are listed as they would be housed together.

Central Operations

- Visitor manager

- Guest lodges, campground, and retreat management

- Transportation coordinator

- Phone receptionist

- Central dispatch

- Post office

- Shipping

- Security

- Community organizer.

Business Office

- Accountant

- Auditor

- Bookkeeper

- Budget analyst

- Health benefits accountant

- Legal

- Small-business advisor.

Health Complex

- First responders

- Nurses and aides

- Alternative medicine

- Dieticians

- Assisted living coordination.

Gym/Exercise Room

- Physical fitness trainers

- Physical therapists

- Sports coaches

- Massage therapists.

Social Services

- Recruitment

- Human resources

- Social worker

- Counseling

- Legal

- Entitlement advisor

- Risk management

- Safety

- Education advisor.

Communications

- Media (cable/closed circuit TV/LAN communications)

- Computer techs

- Writers

- Journalists

- Photographers

- Graphic artists

- SCADA System operators

- Programmers.

Library

- Librarian

- Researcher.

Education

- Child care specialists

- Home school teachers

- Vocational teachers.

Fabrication

- Cabinet makers

- Cabinet painters and finishers

- Welders

- Metal workers.

Repair

- Auto garage

- Small-engine garage

- Appliance repair

- Heating/air conditioning repair

- Electrical

- Electronics

- Grounds maintenance

- Plumbing

- Painting

- Carpentry

- Pest control

- Building maintenance.

Warehouse

- Supply

- Inventory

- Purchasers

- Shoppers

- Store clerks

- Truck drivers.

Food Raising

- Farming

Chapel

SPACE REQUIREMENTS FOR TRADES
Barber Shop/Beauty Salon

- Construction phase

  - Workspace required: Portable chairs and sinks could be used in cluster meeting rooms or garage workshop.

  -Staffing: A part-time barber could be hired until resident barbers join or are trained.

- Post-construction phase

  - Workspace required: Shop housing four chairs and supporting equipment.

  - Staffing: Barbers and beauticians might need to be trained such that each person works only X hours per week, in line with other workers.

Automotive Shop/Stable

Trades: Auto mechanics, small-engine mechanics, electric-cart mechanics.

- Post-construction phase

  - Workspace required: Shop housing three bays and supporting equipment.

  - Repair to golf carts might be done here as well.

  - Shop needs to be stand-alone building for fire safety.

  - Staffing: Mechanics might need to be trained so that each person works only X hours per week, in line with other workers. Repair priorities would be for community transportation vehicles, trades vehicles, and vehicles used by those working off-site. Shop might be available for hobbyists on weekends. Some of these smaller repairs can be done in cluster garages.

Metal Fabrication

Trades: Welders, metal workers.

- Construction phase

  - Workspace required: Cluster garages including storage areas. Upon cluster occupation, workspace would be moved to next cluster.

- Post-construction phase

  - Workspace required: Shop needs to be stand-alone building for fire safety and noise factors. A covered awning would be needed for outside fabrication.

  - Staffing: Minimal. After construction, this would be more of a hobby shop.

Wood Fabrication

Trades: Cabinet makers.

- Construction phase

  - Workspace required: Cluster garages including storage areas. Upon cluster occupation, workspace would be moved to next cluster.

- Post-construction phase

  - Workspace required: Shop needs to be stand-alone building for fire safety and noise factors. Shop would have to be divided into two sections: fabrication and finish/painting.

  - Staffing: Minimal. After construction, this would be more of a hobby shop.

General Repair

Trades: Appliance repair, HVAC, electronics, computer techs, telephone/cable installers.

- Post-construction phase

  - Workspace required: Medium. Air-conditioned room for benchwork. Storage for spare appliances and parts.

  - Staffing: Medium.

Maintenance

Trades: Building maintenance, painters, pest control, carpentry, grounds maintenance.

- Post-construction phase

  - Workspace required: Storage only. Most storage could be dispersed to clusters.

  - Staffing: Medium.

Communications

Trades: Media (cable/closed circuit TV, LAN managers), writers, journalists, graphic artists, photographers, SCADA operators, programmers.

- Post-construction phase

  - Workspace required: Recording studio, offices.

  - Staffing: High.

Social Services

Trades: Recruitment, human resources, social worker, counseling, legal, entitlement manager, risk management, safety, education advisor.

- Post-construction phase

  - Workspace required: Private offices.

  - Staffing: High.

Central Operations Office

Trades: Visitor manager, guest lodge/retreat/campground manager, transportation coordinator, phone receptionist, central dispatch, shipping, post office, security, community organizer.

- Post-construction phase

  - Workspace required: Private offices and cubicles.

  - Staffing: High.

Business Office

Trades: Accounting, budget analysts, health benefits accounting, legal, small-business advisor, auditor.

- Post-construction phase

  - Workspace required: Cubicles.

  - Staffing: High.

Warehouses

Trades: Supply, purchasing, shoppers, inventory, general store clerk.

- Post-construction phase

  - Workspace required: Warehouses, cubicles.

  - Staffing: Medium.

Health

Trades: First responders, nurses and aides, dietician, alternative medicine, assisted-living coordinator.

- Post-construction phase

  - Workspace required: Private offices.

  - Staffing: High.

Gym

Trades: Physical fitness trainers, physical therapists, sports coaches, massage therapists.

- Post-construction phase

  - Workspace required: Gym, offices.

  - Staffing: High.

Pet Center

Trades: Pet groomer/washer, animal control.

- Post-construction phase

  - Workspace required: Kennel, treatment room, office.

  - Staffing: Low.

Learning Center

Trades: Librarian, researcher.

- Post-construction phase

  - Workspace required: Library, vocational classrooms, computer stations.

  - Staffing: Low.

Sanitation

Trades: Sanitation.

- Post-construction phase

  - Workspace required: Warehouse, small office.

  - Staffing: Low.

Electricians

- Construction phase

- Desk space required for master electrician for:

  - Planning jobs, purchasing, management

  - Maintenance of technical and training manuals and schematics

  - Maintenance of utility maps, approval of invoices

  - Inventory: Small construction trailer housing inventory.

- Post-construction phase

- Desk space required for master electrician for:

  - Planning jobs, purchasing

  - Management and training

  - Maintenance of technical and training manuals, utility maps, and schematics

  - Invoice approval.

Note: This space can be small and unmanned most of the time, as the master electrician would be on-call. Work orders could be requested on-line. Small repairs could be done at Cluster level after permission is granted, with or without on-site supervision, by master electrician. This would keep others active and trained. Work orders would be recorded, reviewed, and monitored by master electrician for trends and patterns. Work order monitoring could be done from any computer in the Village.

Inventory: Cluster garages might hold small inventory of outlets, breakers, lightbulbs, electrical tools, etc. Main trade area would maintain more sophisticated inventory and tools.

Benchwork: Can be performed from a Cluster garage.

Plumbers

- Construction phase

- Desk space required for master plumber for:

  - Planning jobs

  - Purchasing

  - Management

  - Maintenance of technical and training manuals

  - Maintenance of pipe maps

  - Invoice approval.

Inventory: Small construction trailer housing inventory.

- Post-construction phase

- Desk space required for master plumber for:

  - Planning jobs

  - Purchasing

  - Management and training

  - Maintenance of technical and training manuals, maps, and prints.

  - Invoice approval.

Note: This space can be small and unmanned most of the time, as the master plumber would be on-call. Work orders could be requested on-line. Small repairs could be done at the Cluster level after permission is granted, with or without on-site supervision, by master plumber. This would keep others active and trained. Work orders would be recorded, reviewed, and monitored by master plumber for trends and patterns. Work order monitoring could be done from any computer in the Village.

- Inventory: Cluster garages might hold small inventory of faucet repair parts, valves, pipes, tools, etc. Main trade area would maintain more-sophisticated inventory and tools.

- Benchwork: Can be performed from a Cluster garage.

Focus Management Center

- Trades: Secretaries.

- Post-construction phase

  - Workspace required: Two meeting rooms for twelve-member focus groups to meet in (along with support staff), cubicles, file storage.

Note: This would be for Main Hub and Management Forum only. This is where main groups can meet, keep their history, and maintain the continuity such a revolving group would need by utilizing permanent secretaries.

- Staffing: Medium.

Lodge

Child Care

Home School

Food Preparation

Food Raising

Chapel

TRADE AREAS

Automotive Shop

Trades: Auto mechanics, small-engine mechanics, electric cart mechanics.

- 12′ × 12′ office required.

- Three bays in 1,400-square-foot building.

- Need an initial $20,000 to equip with tools.

- Estimated cost of $200 per month for diagnostic software service.

Barber Shop/Beauty Salon

- A space of 700 square feet will allow for expansion.

- Four stations would be ideal; three are required, but a fourth would help with job sharing.

- Laundry would be done in Cluster laundry.

- Need an initial $10,000 to equip.

- Monthly supply budget of $300.

- Services would be free to residents except for cost of supplies.

- Would have to be staffed forty hours per week in order to service 500 persons. This would require minimum of six trained persons, each working twenty hours per week.

Business Office

Trades: Four accountants, two auditors, two budget analysts, three health-benefits accountants, two legal, and two small-business advisors.

Job description: small-business advisor: These persons would be knowledgeable in areas of business management, forecasting, taxes, bidding process, etc. They would be responsible for assisting residents in forming small cooperative businesses and supporting them.

Central Operations

Trades: Visitor manager, reservationists, guest lodge and campground managers, transportation coordinators (internal and external), phone receptionist, central dispatch (directs workmen to

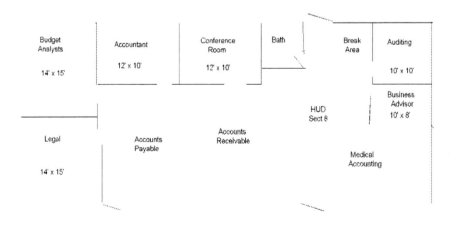

Figure 1. Business Office.

jobs), shipping and receiving (small items), post office, security, community organizer (for example, notes who is participating in which activity for the day).

• Covered parking

• Automobile unloading zone.

• Transportation personnel will assist unloading and will arrange for transportation to home.

• School bus stop

• Visitor entrance.

Child Care

Building requirements for fifty children ranging from infant to four years old:

• Requires 3,500 square feet; air conditioned building necessary.

• Four classrooms needed:

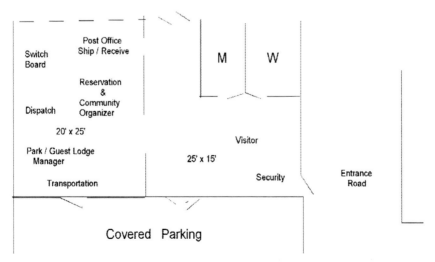

Figure 2. Central Operations.

    - Infant room with sink

    - Toddler room

    - Little kids area

    - Recreation area.

- Need 10′ × 10′ office.

- Furnished kitchen

- Lunch room

- Storage room

- Bathrooms

- Foyer area for check-in

- Arrangements for emergency lighting.

- Furnishings:

    - Kitchen: counter, stove, refrigerator, sink, freezer, table

    - Classrooms: changing tables, furniture, television, computer, toys.

- Playground area

    - Fenced-in

    - Playground equipment.

- Initial outlay of $35,000 for furnishings, kitchen equipment, and playground equipment.

Electricians/HVAC/Plumbers

Trades: Electricians, appliance repair, HVAC, electronics, computer techs, telephone/cable installers, plumbers.

- Workspace required:

- One thousand square feet required with desks and workbenches

- Air conditioned

- Bathroom

- Awning required for outside work

- Initial start-up of $3,000 to equip with shelving, workbenches, and tools.

Focus Group Support

Trades: Secretaries.

• Workspace required:

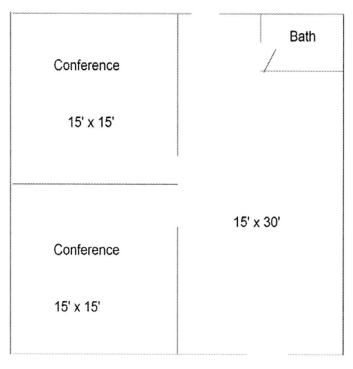

Figure 3. Focus Group Support.

- Two meeting rooms for twelve member focus groups to meet in (along with support staff); also need cubicles, file storage.

Note: This is where main groups can meet, keep their history files, and maintain the continuity such a revolving group would need by utilizing permanent secretaries.

Health Building

Trades:

- First responders

- Nurses and aides

- Dietician

- Alternative medicine

- Health benefits coordinator

- Home-birth assistants.

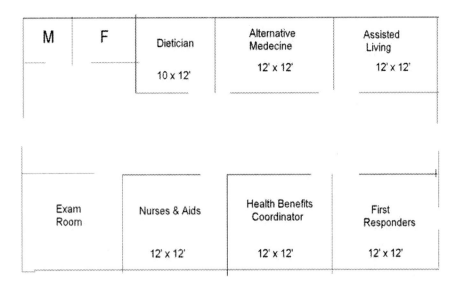

Figure 4. Health Services.

Library and Learning Center

Trades: Librarian, researcher

Uses for the library and learning center might be as follows:

• House books belonging to residents that would be available for checkout.

• House books belonging to residents in a closed stack available to other residents only upon approval of owner.

• House VCRs, CDs, and other media available for checkout.

• House reference materials such as encyclopedias, atlases, almanacs, statutes, etc.

• House job-training manuals.

• House certain magazine and newspaper subscriptions.

• Run a daily shuttle service to county library for items ordered on-line. Residents would have to be members of that library as well, enabling them to check out books there and use their computer databases to research materials on-line from their homes.

• Provide story-time programs for children.

• Provide book discussion groups.

• Provide computers for research as well as providing research assistance.

• Library might be incorporated separately in order to get grants, software, and assistance from other libraries.

• House a large classroom for training. As the library grows, this space could be used for expansion after a new classroom is built elsewhere.

• Media center—house computers, internet access, faxes, VCRs, DVD's, printers, and copiers that are used to facilitate information gathering and learning.

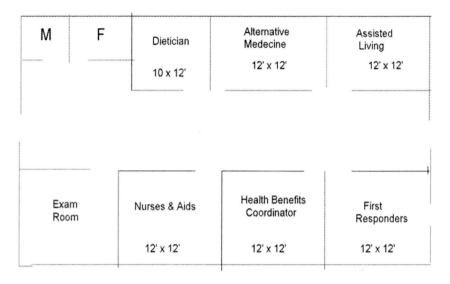

Figure 5 Library/Learning Center.

Pet Center

Trades: Pet groomer/washer, animal control

- Office should be 20′ × 10′; air conditioned

- Bathroom

- Outside kennel area.

Retreat Area

Lodge—Physical Description

- Guest rooms

    - Six large, plush rooms

    - Three rooms step out onto patio with covered, heated pool

    - All rooms handicap accessible

- Each contains two queen-size beds.

- Restaurant

  - Six tables seating four persons each.

  - Serves three meals per day

  - Excellent chefs and wait staff

  - Atmosphere might be similar to Steak & Ale.

- Lobby/lounge

  - Might contain wet bar

  - Piano

  - Couches and lounge tables

  - Dance floor

  - Seminar room

  - Has accordion walls: When folded back, dining room, foyer, and seminar areas become 2,000-square-foot ballroom.

- Other amenities

  - Swimming pool (covered and heated)

  - Two jacuzzis

  - Sauna

  - Four massage tables.

"No-Tell" Motel

- Four small stand-alone bungalows—one located near each corner of the lodge, but yet isolated.

- Each unit would contain a stocked refrigerator, microwave oven, and coffeepot.

• Must be reserved through the Visitor Center. Free to residents. Residents might have access to lodge lounge, pool, jacuzzi, and sauna only. This access would be available only if vacationers were in the Lodge. During seminars, these areas would be off limits.

• No restaurant privileges would be allowed unless invited by a vacationer.

Lodge Use

• Vacations

- Each home would have a free three-day vacation per year, reserving one room in the lodge. This could easily be done three days each week, leaving the lodge available the rest of each week for outside seminars (fee paying) or internal seminars.

- Resident vacationers could invite day guests and dinner guests until the restaurant is filled.

- Live entertainment might be provided two nights each week—perhaps a piano bar one night and a different act the next evening.

- One night might be a special-occasion dinner—perhaps a cookout by the barn, a luau around the pool or a Japanese meal on the floor of the made-over seminar room.

- Vacations might be limited to adults only.

• Seminars

- Most could be for-profit, with room and board being provided.

- The "No-Tell" rooms could be reserved those nights, making a total of ten rooms available.

Sanitation

• Fifteen-hundred-square foot shed required to house trucks

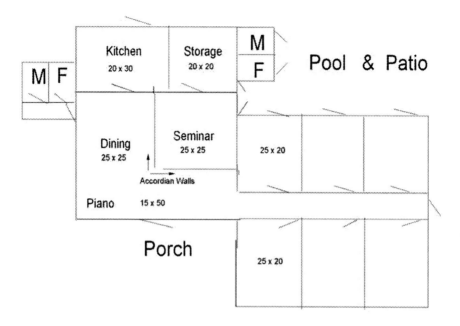

Figure 6. Lodge/Retreat

• One office/break-room (10'×10') with window air conditioner

• Bathroom with shower

• Will cost approximately $1,500 to equip with containers and tools

• Need three recycling containers.

Social Services

Trades: Recruitment, human resources, social worker, counselor, legal, entitlement manager, risk manager, safety, education advisor.

• Job Descriptions

    - Recruitment: Responsible for taking applications for residency and assisting through the admission process;

providing seminars and personal coaching to assist applicants through probation period for adjustment to village life.

- Human Resources: These persons would be knowledgeable of each resident's skills, talents, goals, and needs. They would be responsible for assisting each resident in meeting their goals and needs and at the same time matching their talents with the needs of the community.

- Entitlement Manager: These persons would be knowledgeable of benefits under Social Security, Medicare, Medicaid, federal programs, social services, and other social programs. They would be responsible for advising residents of benefits they qualify for and giving assistance in making application for them.

- Education Advisor: These persons would be knowledgeable in areas of education grants and loans, college and noncollege educational programs, vocational programs, nontraditional learning programs, and in-house training programs. They would be responsible for assisting residents in educational advancement or career training; they would help residents enroll in programs, establish housing if off-site, and secure available financing.

Warehouse

Trades: Supply, purchasing, shoppers, inventory, general store clerk.

- Three-thousand-square-foot metal building.

- Office/break room (12'×12') with window air conditioner.

- Bathroom.

- Will cost approximately $2,500 to equip with shelving.

- Located so that loading bay opens up to parking lot.

Welding Shop

- Small shed equipped with workbench.

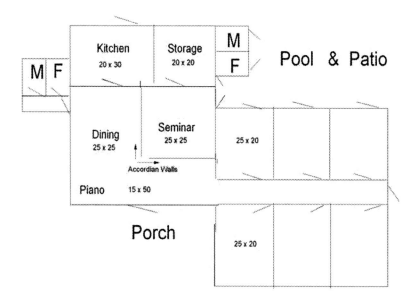

Figure 7. Social Services.

- Awning required for outside work.

- Will cost approximately $3,500 to equip with portable welding machine and tools.

- Will need approximately $1,500 in materials to construct.

- Running water required.

TRADES BUILDING CONSTRUCTION METHODS

The trades buildings might use the following construction methods:

- Framing: Framing would be with 2″ × 6″ lumber. The building codes allows for 2 × 6's to be on 24″ centers; however, we plan to use 16″ centers to give the buildings more strength and a longer life.

• Insulation: The walls will be 6" thick to allow for more insulation, increasing the R value to near R-30.

• Wall Surfaces: Internal walls would be sheetrock and external walls would be 4' × 8' hardy boards, which are cement and fiber panels with a fifty-year life expectancy. These boards are insect resistant as well as fireproof.

• Roof System: Trusses would be manufactured on site. The roof would be heavy-gauge white metal, which should reflect 20 percent of the sunlight, making the attic temperature equal to the outside temperature. The metal would be fastened to 2" × 4' purlins, negating the need for plywood decking.

• Ceiling System: The ceilings would be prepainted styrofoam-insulated panels (SIPs), 2' wide by 12' long, which would

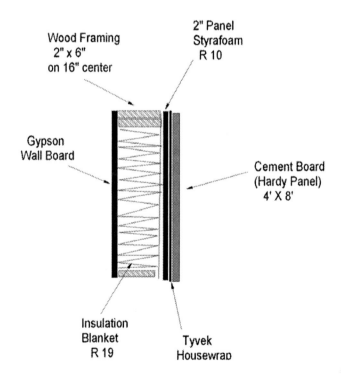

Figure 8. Wall Details.

be inserted between each roof truss. This should yield an R-30 insulation value plus a finished ceiling in two hours.

All of the above methods are such that novice builders can work with minimal supervision.

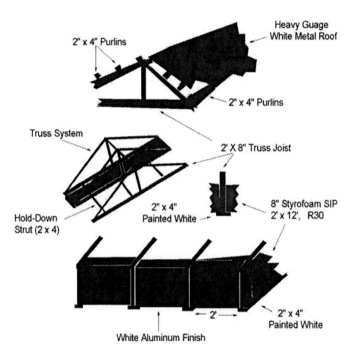

Figure 9. Roof/Ceiling Details.

Chapter 9

INFRASTRUCTURE

by Jim Costa

The Village infrastructure would consist of the following areas:

- Child Rearing
- Communications
- Education
- Fire Protection
- Food
- Health Benefits
- Library
- Power
- Recreation
- Roads and Walkways
- Sanitation
- Security
- Transportation

- Water and Sewage.

Child Rearing

1. **Choices**: Ideally, the Village will attract a diversity of people with varying values. It may be a challenge to accommodate differences in parenting ideals, which vary widely and are highly emotionally-charged. Balance between communal decisions and personal family decisions will be the key.

2. **Birthing**: Birth options include birthing at home in individual living spaces, using some part of the health building as a birth center if a midwife is available to the community, or using the nearest hospital in town. Various people will have different needs based on their level of comfort, their health, and the complications of their pregnancy. Every mother and family should feel comfortable to choose whatever kind of birth they are most comfortable with, whether at home, in a birth-center, or in a hospital. Planned, unattended births (with no licensed midwife or doctor present) can be a disaster waiting to happen, although there are many mothers, especially those who have already birthed multiple children, who advocate for it very strongly. The community would have to decide whether it would be okay to allow unattended births. The Coalition for Improving Maternity Services has a "Mother-Friendly Childbirth Initiative" with a wonderful attitude toward mother-care.

3. **Feeding**:

    a. *Breastfeeding*: Breastfeeding is best for the health of mom and baby, and mothers should be encouraged to breastfeed for at least one year and exclusively for at least six months. It would be important to have a certified lactation consultant living in the Village. Visits to a lactation consultant in town would be uncomfortable for a new family and probably more cost-prohibitive than certifying a member. Breastfeeding, of course, will save the community money—about $1,300 per infant per year. This figure is for the first year of life, after which milk/formula becomes less and less a part of the child's diet. (See http://www.kellymom.com/bf/start/prepare/bfcostbene-fits.html#table1.)

b. *Supplementing Breastfeeding*: There is a small minority of women who cannot produce enough milk, so supplementation either with other women's expressed breast milk or with formula would be an option.

c. *Solid Foods*: Solid foods could be processed in the cluster dining halls, or individually by families.

4. **Diapering**: Members/residents with infants should be strongly encouraged and enthusiastically supported to use cloth diapers. They are not the same frumpy mess with pins that they used to be. Today's cloth diapers can be put on and taken off in one piece with velcro just like a disposable (or snaps), come in a variety of colors and prints, and would be a better choice for the whole community in terms of economy, environmental concerns, and the health of the baby.

a. Washing of diapers can be done either (1) by the family in their cluster's washing facilities (this is perfectly sanitary, as long as the water outflow from the facility doesn't feed edible plants or into a gray-water system) or (2) by a "diaper service" that collects diapers every few days from each home's diaper pails and washes the diapers in a laundry facility that has the sewage-treatment capability. If diapers are to be collected together and washed, there should be a way to identify one child's diapers from another's.

b. Each family may want to use a different system, which is entirely possible given the variety of options. Therefore, there would have to be some way to keep each family's diapers separate. Another option is having everyone use the same kind of diapers, but having each family's diapers sewn with a different color or pattern. The sewing shop in one of the workshops could easily be used to sew the

Village's diapers. A diaper-sewing business could be another good source of income for the Village, especially if there is a whole team of people sewing diapers.

5. **Sewing**: Other items to be sewn by the community include slings of all styles, baby clothes, blankets, bedding, etc.

6. **Carseats**: Local carseat safety technicians can be found at http://www.nhtsa.dot.gov/people/injury/childps/contacts. Whatever person or group is maintaining the cars and checking them out to residents (once the community has pared down the number of owned cars) should also have this certification and be able to assign the correct seat for each child's age and weight. Alternatively, parents could each have their own seat stored in the auto garage, which would be installed as needed. One car should always be available and equipped with a carseat for any age infant and toddler (maybe one rear-facing and one front-facing) in case of emergency.

7. **Childcare and Schooling**

> a. *Maternity Leave*: This is an important issue, because mothers will have had obligations to the community (such as being the electrical engineer or grocery purchaser). The community would have to decide on how much maternity leave to allow for. (It should be generous.) The six weeks traditionally assigned in the market economy is a joke. A bare minimum of two weeks before the due date and three months after would provide families with a better quality of life. Some countries provide two years. The World Health Organization guidelines might be consulted on this topic.

> b. *Three months to four years*: Childcare for infants and toddlers should not be limited to simply "babysitting," but should include space for parents and families to play together and with other families rather than just dropping kids off. Also in those facilities there should be comfortable space for mothers to breastfeed their children while they are taking a break from their jobs.

c. *Four years and up*: Parents may have wildly different values about raising their children, and the Village would be prepared to support both traditional schooling (in a style such as Waldorf or Montessori) in the central classroom and home schooling. Older students may apprentice with the trades folk of the village or in town, or they may dual-enroll at the local junior college or a university.

8. **Outdoors**: Playgrounds, trees, footpaths, swings, and treehouses come to mind. Also, fences around the whole complex or just the kids' areas would be necessary. A very beautiful common building would instill a sense of community, nostalgia, and aesthetics for small people to identify with their home "town."

9. **Certifications and Endorsements**: To focus and communicate our intentions, it would be nice to be aligned with other folks who have children's needs in mind, and perhaps to link to their websites or endorse their ideals and in turn be linked from and endorsed by them. Building on the work of like-minded organizations eliminates the need for the Village to start from scratch. Two such organizations are the children's entertainer Raffi Cavoukian's "A Covenant for Honoring Children" (http://www.raffinews.com/?q=node/17) and The Child-Friendly Initiative's mission (http:// www.child-friendly.org/who/vision.html). The CFI has a program for starting a local chapter, and this could be an option for the Village, too. Also, the previously mentioned Coalition for Improving Maternity Services' "Mother-Friendly Childbirth Initiative"would offer a good option.

Communications

The communications hardware system must do the following:

1. Link 250 houses and 40 commercial buildings.

2. Provide phone service within the Village, with outside lines available.

3. Network computers at each location.

4. Allow each computer access to the Internet.

5. Monitor well systems and equipment (SCADA/PLCs).

6. Provide an In-House TV station with capability to:

   a. Provide cable service to all homes at greatly reduced rates.

   b. Broadcast live conference meetings from four intra-Village locations.

7. Include hand-held walkie-talkies with a range of two miles and costing about $35 per set. Each could be used within the Village. These sets have about twenty-six channels, so residents' last names would determine the channel they are on.

Education

1. Post–high school

The cost of education would be much less in the Village than in conventional society because in a cashless cooperative environment, state education requirements through licensing would not apply. Thus, some classes could be taught by the community, some could be taken at college, and some could be avoided completely. Each student would be free to choose because the knowledge would be more desirable than the certificate.

This would facilitate the changing of careers during a lifetime. If one tired of being a refrigerator repairman, for example, she would simply have to train another to perform those duties and then would be free to study whatever she desired for her new life, be it vocational or higher academic studies. This would certainly take the pressure off young persons to hurriedly choose a lifelong career path, costing their parents $100,000 in the process.

Training for some jobs might be provided through on-the-job training received from those already skilled. It might also require some additional classroom time, in the Village or at a local vocational school, with the costs borne by the Village. Because members might not sell their trained services outside the Village, typical certifications might not be required. With this in mind, many requirements could be ignored, such as a plumber having to take a general education class in order to obtain certification.

Within the Village: Education following high school should offer a lifetime of learning to all residents. It would afford each individual the opportunity to re-create themselves as life progresses, allowing each to expand their horizons as he or she chooses. The majority of the learning would be a direct benefit to the Village as a whole. Some of it would be of benefit to the particular resident only. But always the learning would expand the Village as each person grows and is happiest discovering himself. People are constantly growing and evolving, learning about the world and themselves, and the Village provides the unique opportunity to get off the market-economy treadmill and pursue the many twists and turns of a lifelong education. For example, someone working in the community as a plumber for seven years may find him- or herself gravitating toward a role as a personal counselor, and should be encouraged.

Outside the Village: Education following high school, but outside the Village, should allow for formal higher education so that young people will have the opportunity to go out into the market economy in order to pursue any life they choose, and to share what they have learned about sustainable cooperative living.

2. High school

- Traditional schooling

- GED

3. Middle and elementary school

4. Preschool

5. Degreed teachers (possibly state certified) could be available to:

- Assist with lesson plans

- Assist with presentation methods

- Diagnose and work with learning-disabled

- Motivate

- File forms to the state

- Monitor class activity

- Utilize testing methods

- Train and supervise instructors.

6. Course instructors could:

- Teach areas they are knowledgeable in

- Mentor students expressing interest in a particular subject

- Teach subjects such as automotive, math, plumbing, science, family planning, etc.

A teacher or other adult would remain in the classroom with instructors until a certain grade. This would provide a place for parents to be involved and would ease the transition for younger students to a new environment. This could tie into the apprenticeship program for those students wanting to go into the trades of the Village.

7. Subjects covered could include:

- Usual subjects as well as the traditional English, science, math, social studies, etc.

- Foreign language, as knowledgeable instructors are available

- Life skills such as nonviolent communication

- Health education, including sex, birth, and family planning with small groups of students of the same age and gender.

8. Structure

- School could be in session all year or with summers off. One subject at a time could be taught for six weeks each, or individual classes could be taught throughout the day. The education advisor and committee will have to decide and remain flexible to parent, student, and teacher needs.

- The school might choose to affiliate with or follow some kind of established program such as Waldorf or Montessori.

9. Scouts, clubs, etc.: The Village may opt to have its own chapter. A decision would have to made regarding how much the residents want to go out of their way to foster group activities with people out in town.

10. Alternative classes

- A school for resident children—preferably a Waldorf school, possibly Montessori-style—is an option. Waldorf schools produce creative, intelligent children with broad interests and skills. They have a balance between creative and academic work, and focus on arts, spirituality, and social skills, in addition to the usual academic subjects. They learn several musical instruments and foreign languages from age seven and are much sought after by universities as amazing, broadly developed individuals. Montessori schools focus on letting the student learn on his or her own initiative.

- A school for adolescents, preferably s Waldorf high school.

- A technical school for adults, which could share classes and facilities with the high school.

- A "mystery school," for exploring the secrets of all of the various religions and traditions throughout history. Included would be:

11. Comparative religions

- Meditation

- Yoga

- Eastern mysticism (Hindu, Buddhist, Taoist)

- Western mythology (Roman, Greek, Norse, Jewish, Moslem, Christian, Druid, Pagan)

- Western mysticism (Theosophy, Rosicrucian, Cathars, Bogomils, Grail myth, Gnosticism, Sufis and Assassins, Christian Mystics [St. Francis, St. Theresa, St. Hildegard, etc.], Meister Eckhart, Emerson, Swedenborg, New Thought movement)

- Native American and South American spirituality, including shamanism

- Entheogens

- Alchemy

- Sacred geometry, including Feng Shui

- Practical magic, including the science of prayer; Findhorn gardening; biodynamic gardening; manifesting

- Energy healing, including Reiki, reconnective healing, Qi Gong, dream healing.

Fire Protection

Fire protection could be achieved by the following:

- Home and building level

- All wiring could be one size heavier than required by code (for example, #10 wire, which is thicker, could be used in place of #12 wire). Nothing smaller than #12 wire would be used. All of this would give more protection from circuit overload.

- All wiring would be placed in electrical PVC conduit, giving more protection from fires caused by lightning.

- Range hoods would contain automatic chemical fire extinguishers.

- Washers and dryers would be housed in separate laundry buildings.

- Most interiors would be sheetrock, yielding more fireproofing.

- Fire alarms could be monitored by computer system as well as with an outside horn to notify the Cluster.

- All buildings would have large portable fire extinguishers.

- Metal roofs would greatly reduce wildfire damage.

- A minimum of fifty feet from the heavily wooded areas would be maintained as a fire break.

Fire Department

- First responders would be trained as firefighters until arrival of county fire department.

- Security would monitor and respond to all fire alarms.

- Well adapters would be on hand so that a volunteer fire department could refill its tanker trucks from wells and cisterns on site.

- Fire hydrants could be installed using a 500 psi diesel fire pump located at ponds; manifold plumbed to three hydrants at each cluster. Each hydrant might have 250 feet of 1½-inch hose with a select flow nozzle.

- Each Cluster might have two short-term breathing apparatuses.

- A small first responder fire truck could be equipped and kept on site.

Food

Food for the village might be provided in the following manner:

- Food raising

   - Up to 600 acres might be made available for food growing.

   - Homes would be landscaped with edible plants and small gardens drip-irrigated from household gray water.

   - The Village might choose to contract with a local farmer to purchase (organic?) food not raised by the Village.

   - The Village might lease a field and provide the labor to work it.

   - Residents could visit U-Pick farms during the growing season.

   - Clusters would use food scraps to make compost.

- Food storage

   - Most residents could be available at harvest time for picking.

   - Harvested food could be canned in jars or frozen. This would eliminate most preservatives in foods currently purchased.

   - A walk-in freezer would have a moveable wall for efficiency. Frozen foods would be consumed first, then jarred foods.

- Food costs

   - All of the above might bring the cost of food down to about 25 percent of what it currently is.

Health Benefits

It must be understood that there will be a drastic difference in health benefits between the first year and twenty years after startup. This is because of the anticipated increased health of the population, the size of the population, the changing age of the population, and the number of residents drawing outside health benefits, as well as the federal government's involvement in Medicare, Medicaid, and health coverage.

- Health benefits during the third year of operation, for example, might be as follows:

- Pre-existing coverage: Those persons currently covered by health benefits under entitlements such as retirement benefits, Medicare, etc., would keep their coverage. This group might be as high as 25 percent of the overall population.

- Village coverage

  - A group catastrophic health policy would be purchased to cover those who do not have entitlement health coverage.

  - The Village might contract with a local medical group for primary healthcare for self-insurance, with X percent of the fees paid for by the Village and the balance paid by the resident. Over a period of time, the full amount might be paid by the Village.

  - A pre-existing medical condition clause may be required to protect the Village from being overburdened by current catastrophic conditions. This clause probably would be required by the insurance provider but might apply to the Village self- insurance as well.

  - In the event of a preexisting condition, that person could still obtain medical assistance but at the expense of the medical industry as an indigent. The Village would still be in a position to give other support.

  - Self-insurance benefits would change from year to year based upon budget constraints.

- The Village would maintain insurance clerks, advisors, actuaries, budget analysts, medical advisors, and others necessary to provide a viable health-maintenance plan.

- Medical policy would be managed by the "How Do We Vitalize Ourselves" focus group.

• All residents:

Preventative maintenance systems would be maintained by the Village and would be available to all its residents, keeping in mind that 80 percent of medical problems are stress-related. These systems might include:

- Dieticians

- Exercise equipment and trainers

- Active sports

- Nurses to assist with research and advise when a doctor is needed

- Massage therapists

- Yoga and meditation

- Medical aides

- Advice and help with alternative healing

- Entitlement advisor (knows what outside systems can assist residents).

- Hypnotherapy

- Homeopathy

- Free vitamins and supplements

- Family planning and contraceptives

- Maternity Assistants, including Midwife, Labor Doula, Lactation Consultant, Fertility & Maternity Counselor.

Library

The library and learning center might be used as follows:

- House books belonging to residents that would be available for checkout.

- House books belonging to residents in a closed stack available to other residents only upon approval of owner.

- House VCR, CDs, and other media available for checkout.

- House reference materials such as encyclopedias, atlases, almanacs, statutes, etc.

- House job-training manuals.

- House certain magazine and newspaper subscriptions.

- Run a daily shuttle service to county library for items ordered on-line. Residents would have to be members of that library as well, enabling them to check out books there and use their computer databases to research materials on-line from their homes.

- Provide story-time programs for children.

- Provide book discussion groups.

- Provide computers for research as well as providing research assistance.

- The library might be incorporated separately in order to get grants, software, and assistance from other libraries.

- House a large classroom for training. As the library grows, this space could be used for expansion after a new classroom is built elsewhere.

- A media center could be used to house computers, internet, faxes, VCRs, DVDs, printers, and copiers that are used to facilitate information gathering and learning.

Power

The power system might be as follows:

- Currently, solar electric systems are cost-effective only if unused power is stored on the utility company's electric grid system. This is known as nega-watts, where the utility buys your unused power and sells it back to you when needed. Otherwise, expensive batteries, relays, and converters are required to store energy for night usage. Only 50 percent of the states have legislation requiring utilities to have a nega-watt system. It appears that this section of Florida does not have such a system. Therefore, it is recommended that homes and trade buildings be constructed as energy-efficient as possible, reducing the demand for energy by:

  - Use of energy-efficient appliances and fluorescent lighting

  - Super-insulation

  - Use of skylights

  - Ample use of awnings and white roofs

  - Placing all buildings running east to west to passively manage the sunlight impact

  - Wiring the buildings in anticipation of installing solar systems later as prices drop

  - Installing solar water heating, which is cost-effective

  - Installing solar floor radiant heating

  - Lighting sidewalks using solar energy as much as possible.

Sanitation

Sanitation for the village might be accomplished by:

- Collection cans in each Cluster, marked as follows:

- Green: Compost scraps.

- Purple: Recyclables such as trash, paper, plastic, metal, glass, etc. Some sorting could be done in the Cluster.

- Red: Garbage such as chemicals, tampons, diapers, noncomposting food, scraps and containers, bandages, biologically dangerous articles, etc.

- Collection method:

  - Green: Emptied by Cluster residents into their own compost piles.

  - Purple: Collected and later sorted and reused by the sanitation focus group.

  - Red: Collected and emptied into large commercial dumpster at outskirt of Village to be removed by commercial carrier.

Security

The security system might be as follows:

- Only identified autos would be allowed past the parking lot.

- Visitors must enter and leave through the Visitor Center and must sign in. Security would then notify the sponsoring party of their arrival.

- Eighty percent of the parking lot would be locked from 10:00 p.m. until 5:30 a.m. daily. Access to this area during lockdown would be gained through the Visitor Center only.

- Twenty percent of the parking lot would be unlocked for late arrivals. After 10:00 p.m., all persons must enter and leave through the Visitor Center.

- Security cameras could be placed in the unlocked parking lot area, with entrance alarms to notify security of lot activity at night.

Transportation

The transportation systems might be as follows:

- **Internal**:

  - A fleet of electric carts, bicycles, and wagons would be provided.

  - A shuttle bus might make rounds every half-hour, especially during bad weather. More rounds could be made for school children to get them to the county school bus stop.

  - The transportation department could be contacted for village taxis for those in need.

  - Mail service and other deliveries would be made to the Visitor Center and distributed from there, keeping delivery vehicles out of the Village as much as possible.

  - The goal is to free up the roads as much as possible for pedestrian traffic and for children to play in.

- **External:**

  - All autos would have access to homes to unload large items.

  - Some autos would be parked in a cluster on an as-needed basis, such as someone who works out of the Village, physically impaired persons who continually must visit the doctor, etc.

  - All other autos, boats, and RVs not being used would be stored in the main parking lot and be locked up at night.

  - A fleet of autos and trucks would be owned and maintained by the Village and would be available to residents when needed. Reservations could be made online. A taxi might be called to deliver the resident to the parking lot.

- Professional shoppers would make daily runs to the city and could be used to run some personal errands.

Water and Sewage

- **Drinking water:**

  - Recognizing that Florida expects to double in population over the next five years and that drinking water is becoming more expensive to supply, the following is recommended:

  - Homes: Cisterns would be used to collect rainwater, which would be filtered and treated. Clusters would have wells as back-up and to supply water under pressure needs. These faucets would be painted blue.

  - Larger buildings: Wells might be monitored by computer (using a SCADA system) and by a safety person.

- **Grey water**: Water from all sources except toilets would be collected and used for irrigation of edible plants. These faucets would be painted with red stripes.

- **Septic**

  - Homes: Composting toilets would be maintained by the sanitation department.

  - Larger buildings: Septic tanks would be used.

  - Campground: Septic tanks would be used.

Chapter 10

SIMPLIFIED BUSINESS PLAN

by Jim Costa

A. COMPANY DESCRIPTION

B. MAIN PRODUCT

C. SECONDARY PRODUCT

D. FINANCING SOURCES

E. MARKETING PLAN—MAIN PRODUCT

F. MANAGEMENT

G. "AT-WORST" FALLBACK POSITION

A. COMPANY DESCRIPTION

Name: Co-op Village Foundation, Inc.

Date of incorporation: 5/23/2005

Type: Not for profit

IRS status: 501(c)(3)

Purpose: Community land trust

This corporation will own land, buildings, and certain fixed assets only.

Other legal issues: Other, nonrelated corporations will be owned by the residents for the purposes of daily operations and income production. This will give legal and financial protection to the land trust.

CLT: A community land trust is a corporation whose purpose is to hold, protect, and conserve property forever to be used only for the purpose spelled out by its charter.

Mission: To give mankind an optional way of living by promoting the building of villages of 500 persons based on cooperation, and having its own internal economy, being self-sustaining, forever. This would promote a way of life that would be healthy for both the individual and the planet. Based on the ideals of moral and political egalitarianism, we recognize that every individual brings their own gifts and needs, but in the decision-making process each person is considered equal to the others. This would be a place where all decisions would be based on what is in the best interest of all concerned.

Our means would be twofold.

1. Design such a village and share our ideas and experience with others for free.

2. Build such a village in northwestern Florida.

B. MAIN PRODUCT

Construct and operate a village in Escambia or Santa Rosa County, Florida, having the following features:

1. Provide affordable housing for 500 persons on 500 to 1,000 acres.

2. Cooperatively, provide for life:

   a. Food

   b. Utilities

   c. Maintenance

   d. Transportation

   e. Child care

   f. Assisted living, if necessary.

3. Provide jobs and job training to residents that need them.

4. Provide health benefits to residents that need it.

5. Provide advanced education and homes for resident children that mature and choose to remain.

6. Provide commercial buildings to work out of.

7. Area would be extremely earth-friendly.

8. The Village would be self-sustaining as much as possible.

9. Governance would be by consensus of all residents.

10. The Village would be operated by cooperative corporations owned only by residents.

11. Internal economy would be cashless.

12. The Village would provide financing for those who cannot make initial full payment.

13. Full financing payments may be as low as $100 per month.

14. Construction to be done by residents.

15. Diverse population (age, race, faith, sex, income, education, health, etc.) would be expected.

16. Unit cost would be $40,000 per person. Cost to children may be deferred until adulthood.

C. SECONDARY PRODUCTS

Subsequent corporations would be formed for the purpose of generating outside cash for residents and the Village. Features are as follows:

Products: Construction, plumbing, electrical, solar energy systems, health insurance, etc.

Residents would partner with the Village in starting businesses that are deemed low-risk by the Village business department.

Training: Most employees would be residents who have been trained by the Village.

Support systems: The Village would maintain a well-developed and well-staffed business office, fleet transportation system, supply department, training program, business financing, etc., to manage and support such ventures.

Competitive Edges:

• Workforce can be laid off for months at a time without harming them in lieu of taking low-profit work just to maintain the workforce.

• Resident employees have room and board covered for life and therefore are not in need of cash.

• Ample supply of workers available.

- Storefronts need not be maintained.

- All profits, most wages, and most overhead stay within Village.

- Most other trades are available in the Village to back up project (welders, legal, a/c, etc.).

- Mass transportation for workers.

- Most of the labor would be free.

- Ability to avoid payroll taxes and worker compensation insurance.

- Due to extremely low overhead and all profits remaining in the Village, competitors' prices can always be undercut, allowing the ability to "cherry-pick" contracts.

D. FINANCING SOURCES

Financing will be utilized from the following areas:

- Resident investment

- Private investment

- Department of Housing and Urban Development (HUD) and Department of Agriculture:

  - Plan development seed money

  - Land acquisition

  - Construction

  - Energy system

  - Water/wastewater system

  - Library

  - Infrastructure

  - Farm loan

- Fire department.

• HUD

This is a Section 8 program to subsidize rent payments. Note: Once a tenant has paid $40,000 in rent, he will then have a life estate interest.

- Grants

- Green building/Safe buildings

- Intentional community buildings

- Department of Energy—alternative energy systems

- EPA—alternative water/wastewater systems

- Interim construction loan

- Land seller financing

- One parcel will be purchased for each phase, with options to purchase the remaining parcels as needed.

- Small Business Administration

- Business development/job creation

Note: All mortgages are planned to be paid off within ten years in order to leave the Community Land Trust free and clear.

E. MARKETING PLAN—MAIN PRODUCT

For the Village to be successful, its demographics need to match the local overall demographics. This is especially true with regard to age. Therefore, the Village must appeal to all age groups; and within those groups, it must appeal to those with high income and middle income, to the working poor as well as the poor.

- Benefit messages to be delivered to age subgroups:

  - Young persons. The community can help these persons by providing a means of home ownership in three to six years, help with child care, experienced advice and training, a lower cost of living, security in the event of unemployment, dinners prepared during busy evenings, possible financial assistance, access to unaffordable assets, and dignity while starting a family and career.

- Middle-aged persons. The community can help these persons by providing a network of caring relationships, the opportunity to reduce working hours, lower cost of living, daily adventure, and an opportunity to serve others.

- Retired persons. The community can help these persons by providing caring relationships, an opportunity to serve others and use their skills, home security while traveling, a lower cost of living, daily adventure, and caring assisted living when they need it.

- Children. The community can help these persons by providing help with child care and child rearing, caring relationships, stability, transportation, advice, experience in maintaining unselfish relationships, community involvement, and learning cooperation instead of competition.

- Elderly and physically handicapped persons. The community can help these persons by providing caring relationships, involvement, dignity, concern and attention, transportation, physical work and assistance, repairs, a lower cost of independent living, protection, and a need for their advice and knowledge.

- Homeless persons. The community can help these persons by assisting in the financing of home ownership, job training if necessary, providing jobs, a low cost of living, transportation, dignity, caring relationships, and access to unaffordable assets.

Home ownership message to most age groups:

• Outside the Village:

- Access to a new home in our current economic system costs approximately $200,000.

- Village offering:

  - Access to a new home in the Village will cost each adult only $40,000.

  - Credit history/rating is not an issue.

  - Housing can be financed by the Village for up to forty years.

  - Jobs and job training will be provided for those that need it.

  - Food and utilities.

  - Child care.

  - Transportation.

  - Healthcare.

Security message to all age groups:

The Village economy would provide a lifetime shield from the financial impact of the dreaded "D's" (being: downsized, divorced, death of a partner, disease, disability, dementia, delinquent utility bills).

F. MANAGEMENT

The Village intends to build a business office and staff it with the following professional persons to manage the business affairs:

- Accounting (four people)

- Auditors (two)

- Budget analysts (two)

- Health benefits accounting (three)

- Legal (two)

- Small business advisors (two)

- Human resources (two)

- Entitlement advisors (two).

G. "AT-WORST" FALLBACK POSITION

Some options to the Village in the event of financial difficulty are:

- Increase the residents' workweek above the twenty-hour standard week.

- Postpone the plan to pay off mortgages within ten years by utilizing the government's payback term of forty years.

- Construct an additional nine clusters with resident fees at $60,000. This would yield net cash inflow of $3 million, after construction costs.

- Convert one cluster (out of fifteen) to an assisted-living facility or nursing home capable of housing fifty persons. This would generate revenue of as much as $150,000 per month with extremely low overhead and no wages. This should yield about $1 million per year in profit to repay the $5 million loan.

- Revenue would come from Medicaid, Medicare, SSI, HUD Section 8, etc.

- This could be done for more than just one cluster.

- Convert one cluster for seminars to teach the new technologies and systems utilized by the Village.

Chapter 11

COMPARISON TO OTHER COMMUNITY MODELS

by Jennifer Chendea

I have long been interested in the idea of intentional community. I visited the Lama Foundation in New Mexico when I went on a road trip in college, and I loved the way of life there… slower, less insular, more interconnected than the way I grew up in the suburbs. There's something in there too about the sound of birds and the light filtered through the trees that you just can't find when you live in a development wherein the whole land was stripped and some token maples were planted amongst the sod. After college, I went to midwifery school, with the vague intention that I was on my way to some community out there ready to welcome me.

Then I met my husband. Everything after that is sort of a blur, but now here I am years later in Virginia waiting to see if the Navy will let us go to Pensacola, which I call home. But as much as my husband derailed my life plans, our son helped me remember them again (that is except for the midwifery—giving birth to him was enough birthing for one lifetime). Watching him play in our small backyard with sticks and mud puddles, teaching him about composting, and tending our kitchen garden while he asks in his toddler voice to play with the neighbor kids, I am more determined than ever to invest in a better future.

However, I am a fierce skeptic and an even fiercer protector of my son—how can I be sure that the alternative future I find for my son is a safe one? Living with my parents in Pensacola during my son's first winter, while Andrei was out to sea, I was leading a cloth diaper workshop at the health food store when I saw a flyer for the Co-op Village. I thought these things only started up out west! Because I was raised in Pensacola and want to settle there, this was exactly what I was looking for. But I was reticent. I half expected to walk into this meeting and find a bunch of rebellious students and druggies with no real direction… or worse, some religious extremists trying to leave our society behind. What I found was a core group of very committed people–accountants, electrical engineers, therapists–people who want just what I want: a sane way of living on this complicated planet.

So I aim to explain, after working with the Co-op Village Foundation for more than a year, how it is not a group of religious fanatics and how it very definitely has direction. It is not a cult, not a religious group, not exempt from the laws of our country, not the sole property of any one person, and most of all not a utopian ideal. The Co-op Village concept is a tool to rescue us from our own spiraling mismanagement of resources (money, environment, body, time, psychology, families…). It is an experiment in answering the warning signs that we have thus far been trying mightily to ignore.

Any venture like the Co-op Village primarily brings to mind the idea of utopia, a naïve idea that one can create a perfect society. From Plato's Republic to Orwell's 1984, the idea of utopia has figured large in the consciousness of the western world, but history has shown us that investment in the idea of utopia is often a fatal hubris. While we share a common yearning for a peaceable, plentiful, just world, we also share a gut-level suspicion that if you can't be happy right where you are, then where do you expect to be happy? Utopia itself is a play on words, a Latin pun we inherit from Thomas More's book of the same name, meaning either (or both) "eutopia," a good place or "outopia," no place. To this day, we have inherited More's ambiguity, and we commonly feel that a utopia is a perfect place that does not—cannot—exist.

COMMUNITIES

The object of this chapter is to address some apprehensions or preconceptions regarding intentional community by offering a review and comparison of some of the many community-living experiments that have occurred in recent memory. Some of these were the product of the hippie movement, such as The Farm in Tennessee. Other ventures involved mass migration to a new country, such as when Jews, displaced from Eastern Europe by escalating violence and alienation, settled in then-Palestine in communities called kibbutzim (singular, kibbutz). The Amish migrated to America during the 18th and 19th centuries, also escaping persecution, and their Anabaptist values led them to insulate themselves into communities. In contrast to these successes, in the 1970s Jim Jones used a utopian rhetoric and cult methodologies to lure a thousand people to their deaths in "Jonestown," British Guyana. An overview of these communities may serve not only to define the Co-op Village by comparison, but to serve as lessons for its growth.

As if offering substance to our fears of utopian movements, the "community" at Jonestown became a national tragedy in 1978. It was a horror that was rooted decades before with the formation of the Peoples Temple by Jim Jones, the charismatic but psychopathic leader who used communist rhetoric to lure a thousand disenchanted, poor, or otherwise vulnerable victims to an isolated compound in British Guyana. Nearly all of them died there, in a mass murder perpetrated by a few of Jones' loyal and brainwashed devotees. Thus ended a journey that had begun with simple attendance at Jones' church and slowly they were drawn in to his web of lies, calculated manipulation, kidnapping, and coercion. The calculated mind-control techniques that Jones had developed for decades facilitated his manipulation of these people for his own financial gain, twisted psychological satisfaction, and as an ultimate route to lasting, if posthumous, fame.

Amish communities could hardly be more different than the compound at Jonestown. There are nearly 200,000 Amish in the U.S., mostly in Pennsylvania, Ohio, and Indiana. Centuries before coming to America from Europe, the Amish were originally Swiss Anabaptists, breaking away from the Catholic Church in the 17th century. By the end of that century, they had experienced a split with the Anabaptists and in the 18th and 19th centuries migrated to America to escape persecution. Now, they are commonly known as a reclusive, nonviolent religious group wearing uniform clothing and avoiding modern technology such as Velcro and motor vehicles. Each Amish community itself is small, with less than 200 people–the location must be small enough to be navigated by horse and buggy and the population must fit in a barn for meetings. While they remain secluded in order to avoid the sins of worldliness, their art and culture permeates the mainstream, particularly in Pennsylvania Dutch country.

The kibbutzim have similarly left their mark on Israel, and are also in other ways similar to the Amish communities, originating from a large migration to escape persecution, and sharing religious doctrine. They are communities in Israel of about 500 people that have been thriving throughout most of the twentieth century. The first kibbutz was founded in what was then Palestine in 1909 as part of a reaction to anti-Semitic persecution in Eastern Europe. The kibbutz movement upheld ideals of community, hard work, and living off the land in the agriculturally barren areas of Palestine. The movement remained strong as it played a vital role in the establishment of the state of Israel, and is at the present time still a vital component of its economy. Each of the more than 85 kibbutzim is unique in the way it deals with such issues as individual ownership and methods of earning a living, but they share a similar heritage. Though the focus of the movement has changed from an anti-materialistic back-to-the-land communal ethos into manufacture, industry, and individual independence, the kibbutz represents a very successful community movement.

50 years after the first kibbutz was founded along the Mediterranean, a similar movement grew among the hippie culture in America. The Farm in Tennessee was founded in 1970 by 250 people of all ages who followed Stephen Gaskin from San Fransisco and set up a remarkably self-sufficient community. Today, the Farm is well-known for its midwifery practice and sustainable building workshops, and as an example of community living based on compassion and environmental responsibility. Like the kibbutzim, the Farm has undergone radical changes, especially in the late 70s and early 80s, when the population grew to an obese 1,400 members and the original ideals became diluted. This led to a 1983 restructuring from a collective into a cooperative,

abandoning the communal wealth model for a situation in which members are responsible for supporting themselves and paying dues. The Farm today is a hopeful, small, 200-member example of communal living.

How is the co-op village concept similar to these experiments in history? How does it differ? Most importantly, what must we learn from them in order to make this experiment work? The Village concept must incorporate fail-safes to prevent an unthinkable Jim-Jones event–these preventive measures include the adherence to consensus and the governmental structure explained elsewhere in this book. We must watch carefully the balance of isolation, not becoming reclusive like the Amish, but avoiding the dilution of ideals experienced by Farm. We must, however, remain with at least one foot in the great tradition of idealism embodied by those Anabaptists defying the powerful Church, by the Jews in anti-Semitic Russia who dared to hope for freedom, and by the hippies seeking to leave behind materialism and violence. Our imperative is no less sacred for being secular: our ecological fears are amplified concurrently with the destructive powers we are just beginning to understand. We share with the Farm, the kibbutzim, the Amish, and even the poor souls who joined Peoples Temple, an aversion to violence, a criticism of materialism, and a yearning for a better life.

COMPARISONS

Children working in California for the Peoples Temple before they moved to Jonestown was sent out to beg. The begging done by his members was a lucrative source of income for Jones. He warned the little ones that if they stole the money they received, Jones would know and the offender would be struck down by God. One little boy pocketed $10 and, when nothing happened to him, he quit the church because he saw that Jones was a liar. His skepticism saved his life. In addition to begging, the congregation of Jim Jones was allowed to have outside jobs before the move to British Guyana, but all money earned was to be given to Jones. Children were made to beg and threatened not to steal because Jones, being God, would know. When living in California, the congregation made weekly trips to San Francisco and L.A. for choir performances and miracle healings, from which Jones made a lot of money.

While members of The Co-op Village, of the kibbutz, and of the Farm have the freedom to pursue right livelihood outside the community if they choose, those living in Jonestown as well as the reclusive Amish limited outside contact. In Jonestown, Jim Jones was the only conduit to the outside world. He alone had access to the single method of outside communication—a guarded radio— and he used his position to convince those living in the community that the rest of the world was falling apart and they had to remain as the last place of true morality. This isolation was a continuation of the mind-control tactics he used in recruitment and part of the road to the ultimate mass murder he committed.

For Jim Jones' followers, there was no adherence to the laws of the surrounding area. Jones fled to Guyana with his congregation to avoid paying taxes and to avoid being discovered in his many illegal activities, including fraud, child abuse and neglect, sexual abuse, and drug abuse, among other things. The capitalist world was painted as evil, and that those in the evil outside world would see any achievements by the Peoples Temple as a threat. With teachings such as these, Jones fabricated a world in which he was the only refuge of safety and comfort. It would be easy to resolve that the isolation of the residents of Jonestown was their downfall, and that the village concept should avoid such isolation.

However, the Amish are isolated as well, believing that the world is full of corruption, materialism, and selfishness. They particularly avoid seeking modern comforts, love of material things, and self-enhancing activity, which they believe keeps them pure and eligible as a community to enter heaven. These motivations prompt them to ask, "what fellowship has light with darkness?" (where presumably, mainstream culture is 'darkness'). This pious isolation seems overall to have served them well, except where it inhibits medical care and help from social programs.

The Amish communities throughout the northeast US, as well as the various kibbutzim throughout Israel, each have found their own balance of interaction with the outside state. It then follows that each co-op village that is built will reach an equilibrium of interaction with the outside world that will be comfortable to those members. If a group of Mormons takes on the village model and chooses to keep their village secluded, that will be acceptable because the model is basically a tool for use that we hope will help bring the world into balance ecologically, economically, and socially.

The members of the Farm still advocate for this balance, as they always have, minimizing reliance on the fossil-fuel power grid and adhering to what the Farm calls "right livelihood." Right livelihood is a Buddhist principle requiring integrity between one's work and one's values. For example, if the collective intention of the members of the Farm is to live sustainably, then a member working outside the community, say in Nashville, should evaluate the ecological impact of that job. Is the 45-mile drive each day, relying on fossil fuels, worthwhile? How does this affect the environment, and how could that money be better spent? Is the work very important and worth the sacrifice? This involves thinking not so much about the good for oneself, but about the common good.

The Co-op Village members will face similar choices, and should be encouraged to discuss such issues. Right Livelihood is an element of any successful community. The Amish hold strictly to their ethics by avoiding contact with the outside world–this, as well as their avoidance of higher education, limits their pool of available occupations. Some Amish are branching out while maintaining their integrity, for example building homes that are competitive because of their refusal to make much profit off the sales.

The Kibbutzim set out in the beginning of the century to live off the land and restore the vitality of the human being through hard work, very similar to the Amish. Although much has changed for kibbutzniks, including manufacture and even tourism as methods of livelihood, much consideration and debate centers around adherence to values. Where there is no discussion on right livelihood, as in the monologuous power held by Jim Jones, there is a sick or dying community.

The Amish community relies not only on its integrity, but the physical integrity of its ecosphere. Lancaster County, Pennsylvania, home to the largest settlement of Amish people, has the most productive soils in the country. Amish farming practices probably account for this fertility—they grow a diversity of crops incorporating woodlands and pastures, employ crop rotation and fertilize with manure. Moreover, the Amish rely very little on fossil fuels, and have been shown to use less energy than other farmers while producing the same yields. The "old-fashioned" mindset of the Amish, who are distrustful of modernization, has led them to more slowly adopt or completely avoid farming practices such as the use of tractors and manipulation of animals to produce more. It appears that what seems unethical to the Amish are often the very same practices avoided by modern organic agriculture, and the result has been a successful stewardship of the land.

Land stewardship and ecological living, although not entirely embraced by the Amish, are basic tenets at the Farm. Because they are a much smaller community and not reclusive, their impact on the environment has not been limited to the land on which they farm. The Farm is active in educating others in environmentally sustainable living, on every topic from vegetarianism to building techniques to solar power.

Similarly, the kibbutzim began their life with ideals of hard labor and living close to the land, based on Biblical passages and religious yearning. Today, many kibbutzim use organic and biodynamic methods to grow food that feeds the community. Some kibbutzim, such as Sde Eliyahu, become centers for agricultural education, spreading the organic ideals by educating other farmers and sharing knowledge. Like the Farm, this is their contribution, in addition to their stewardship of the land.

The Co-op Village hopes to incorporate these ideals, stewardship, and sharing knowledge. While the impulse is to invite a vigorous dialogue and share the knowledge and experience we will surely build up, one must recognize the intention of the Amish and their results. Because they wished to remain separate from "the world" in order to remain purely themselves and avoid corruption, they have greatly slowed their adoption of new techniques. This delay resulted in them being allowed to see the consequences before they adopt a new technology, such as tractors compacting the soil when it should be aerated to be healthy. The Village must remember to keep its center.

Individual ownership of items and money is an issue all communities must address, and often one that figures into the very reasons for founding a community at all. Of the bubble economies of the communities studied here, the kibbutzim and the Farm began as experiments in holding money and possessions communally, and both have abandoned the practice.

The kibbutzim originally maintained strict rules against propriety, believing that communal wealth would reinforce community togetherness and reduce materialism Community was forced, or strongly encouraged, by such practices as disallowing married couples to sit together and disallowing teakettles in homes to encourage people to come to the dining halls. Also, gifts of money and goods were put into a common pot for everyone's use. One important problem developed—when members were not paying utility bills themselves, they had no incentive to conserve. The return of private accounts led to more moderate usage of resources. Gradually, this practice evaporated and the practice of maintaining equality by providing items which become popular so that no one is deprived of, say, a TV or radio. Today, the issue varies between individual kibbutz. Kibbutz Tammuz requires that one have a full-time job and that one's paycheck be turned over to the community in turn for receiving a household stipend. Now that kibbutzniks have begun to lead more private lives, with dvds and internet like other families, group activities are much less attended.

The individuals involved with Jim Jones' Peoples Temple could not keep their own wealth, and there was absolutely no financial independence. Collection of social security and government checks was a substantial source of income for Jones-all members were required to turn them over. Jones convinced every person who joined to turn over all individual property, including homes, cars, jewelry, and millions of dollars of real estate. The Had followers, especially a lawyer named Tim Stoen, manipulate the federal and state governments so that he could remain off their radar while collecting social security and foster-care checks for the people he had brainwashed and was housing in substandard housing. The manipulation of governmental agencies by Jones and their failure to catch this cult before it became a mass murder continues to baffle and enrage survivors and family members of the deceased.

The Amish and the Farm have no restrictions on personal ownership or income, although both share a distaste for consumerism and greed. The Amish believe that striving for material things is one of the evils of worldliness, and that it can lead to an exaltation of the self. However, in Jonestown, while no one was allowed to own anything, the prevailing reason for that was Jones' own greed. He owned everything of value, including real estate, furs, jewelry, and other valuable that he insisted members must hand over to him if they were truly committed to "the cause." The Co-op Village, of course, will have no identified leader to coerce members' belongings away, and neither will it require members to give up their tea kettles. The Co-op Villages' approach to ownership will be more like that of the Farm, with communal spaces and property, but with respect for individuals' own property.

Since 1983 on the Farm, members must support themselves financially, but originally resources were pooled. The communal wealth system of the founders, who traveled out to Tennessee from San Francisco, made it possible to by the original land at $70 per acre, and build a successful community. Eventually the complications of the system as well as the enormous population size were overwhelming and a change was made to the current system wherein there is officially no shared wealth. However, there are many common spaces and some community-owned property, such as farm equipment. All of the members of one urban kibbutz, Kibbutz Tammuz, work outside the community and it has no enterprises of its own. still

In the Co-op Village, no one's forced to give over their 401(k), but wealth will generally be shared as one family. There will probably be a period of about 20-30 years during which we transition to this communal wealth as people become more comfortable with the community atmosphere of sharing. Upon joining, there will be a fee, just as there is for new members of the Farm. The Amish are almost always born into the community, and kibbutz members sometimes do not pay a joining fee at all.

Joining a community, such as the ones we're studying, often involves a typical process of visiting, expressing interest, visiting more, finding a mentor, attending some classes or orientation, and often a fee as mentioned above. While the Amish are very suspicious of outsiders and the compound at Jonestown has been abandoned for nearly 30 years since the massacre, the Farm and the kibbutz are open to new members. The Co-op Village also has an open-door policy. Anyone interested in the community will be allowed to apply, just like the Farm and the kibbutzim, and the application process is very similar. Jones recruited his members specifically for traits that made them easy to manipulate, and he used mind control techniques on them that were later found highlighted in his library. For example, the initiations into the community increased incrementally in their commitment and their demands in order to make it difficult to leave, the idea being that once a person has gone so far they are unwilling to admit they'd been wrong all along. Researchers are still baffled at how well his strategies worked.

Anyone is free to leave and then return at the Farm, the kibbutzim, and the Co-op Villages, but the Amish face shunning if they leave and will never then be allowed to communicate with their families thereafter. Jim Jones was famously enraged by those members who managed to escape and especially by those who formed a group to try to stop him. The Co-op Village will, of course, allow members to come and go as they please, and help members who leave to regain their footing in the outside economy.

The kibbutzim are currently the largest of the communities studied, at about 600 people per kibbutz. The Amish district, which is the smallest unit of government, oversees about 100-200 people. There are 200 people on the Farm, and the Co-op Village will support about 500. Although Jonestown is extinct as a community, it is worth mentioning that at the time of the massacre there were more than 900 people there. None of these communities restricted membership based on age or gender, although gender dynamics vary.

The Amish woman is a domestic, caring for the children, sewing, cooking, tending the garden, doing the washing and cleaning, but not working in factories or an outside job. Her occupations are not subordinate, however, they are a boon to her family and rewarded by her community. The men tend to the farms, work in paid professions, and occasionally help with more rigorous household chores as directed by their wives. The men make official decisions and speak up in church, whereas the women follow the literal interpretation of the bible indicating their voices should not be heard in the church.

The gender dynamics and sexual perversion at Jonestown are hardly worth mentioning in this context, except to say that they were a direct outgrowth of Jones' psychological perversions, and no one was safe from his discrimination and abuse. The Farm's seminal period, however, was during the sexual revolution and the birth of second-wave feminism, when both genders were encouraged to break free from traditional gender roles. With young families, the trend is and has been to a somewhat traditional setting, with a father as breadwinner (as well as diaper-changer) and a mother as nurturing childcare provider. The collective interest in home birth, breastfeeding, and attachment parenting could be related to this trend, because of the tendency of a mother to remain in close contact with a breastfed baby for a long period of time. As children get older, mothers tend to become free to engage in professions full-time and become more independent.

Women wanted to and were encouraged to work in the fields just as rigorously as men and the kibbutz communities originally freed women from what they saw as the obligation of constant childcare by setting up communal childcare. This had the dual purpose of demoting the family as a central unit of consideration and promoting the community as the primary unit. Much has been written on the experiences, sometimes negative effects, leaving them to cry and suckle only every 4 hours, of children cared for communally in these settings, and the practice was eventually abandoned completely in favor of what we would see as a more typical day-care environment.

On the Farm, children grow up in a safe, gated community surrounded by caring and supportive adults. Children will be similarly cared for in the Co-op Village. Young families will be encouraged to have time together and enter into preschool or elementary school at their own pace. Children will be allowed to enter public school nearby or the school on site at the Co-op Village.

Amish families average 7 children, and they are never educated past the 8th grade when they enter "rumspringa" or the period when they experiment with modern ways and ultimately decide whether or not to commit to Amish life. Families in the kibbutz are honored whereas, early in the life of the movement the community was often revered above the family. The early kibbutzim put children into communal housing where they were allowed family time only 4 hours or so a day. Many studies have been done since then on the psychological effects of this practice and it has since been abandoned in favor of traditional day care. In stark contrast, children at Jonestown were abused, neglected, and certainly not allowed schooling of any kind.

Education in the Co-op Village is seen as a lifelong endeavor. Career-switching, sharing of information, and simple soul-searching will be abundant. Advanced education such as college, whether used to return to the community or to venture forth on one's own, will be encouraged and provided for if financially possible. Of the other communities in this study, only the kibbutz provides for advanced education. The cost of higher education is on a much larger scale than the simpler life of intentional communities, and even when it is seen as a priority, tension remains over its outcomes. Are the students in question going to come back and return their knowledge to the community or simply leave? Will they study a vocation that is needed within the community, such as plumbing, or something they may dearly love but for which the community has no outright need? These questions require compassionate answers and considerable attention.

One hopes that some of those students will pursue education in the health sciences and then return to care for the community. This is the ideal for the Co-op Village, whose rainbow of alternative and allopathic healers would ideally provide for the medical, dental, and psychological care of the whole person, of each person. However, with a self-selected community of 500 people, it will be necessary to seek outside care in the area of, say, dentistry, if there are no dentists or hygienists living in the community. Open-heart surgery will undoubtedly be the job of local hospitals.

The balance between outside help and self-reliance is maintained by all the communities studied, except of course for Jonestown, whose members were infamously neglected and undernourished. Of particular interest are the Amish, who have a delicate relationship with healthcare providers. Although they eschew contact with outsiders, they also have no members educated above the 8th grade. Thus, they must find English doctors who they trust. The complications only begin there, however. They do not take out health insurance or rely on aid, so paying medical bills can be a bit of a problem. Because of their distrust of and isolation from the outside world, they have no knowledge of pharmaceuticals and distrust strong medicine or pills. Because they favor personal integrity and bedside manner over advanced education (which they tend to distrust) they tend to visit more often chiropractors or alternative healers.

For the Co-op Village and the other (sane) communities, healing begins preventatively, with lifestyle. The healthfulness of a pedestrian lifestyle is interrelated with the other elements of community living. It encourages fitness, enjoyment, community intimacy, and communication among members, among other benefits. A pedestrian atmosphere and often a natural setting are shared by all the communities in this study. We cannot look favorably upon Jonestown given the circumstances, but members of the Farm, the Kibbutzim, and the Amish have all reflected on the joy inherent in this type of living. We hope that the Co-op Village's small atmosphere and reliance on biking and walking will not only improve the health of its members but also build intimacy and fun into everyday life.

The nutrition of the community is similarly vital to its health. Sharing community meals–a practice embraced by all the other communities, generally helps contribute to a joyous, intimate lifestyle. All communities addressed in this chapter grew at least some of their own food, even Jonestown. In fact, eating nothing that one has grown oneself is an aberration of modern life wherein our food travels many miles to reach us, causes the consumption of a great proportion of our fossil fuel consumption, and relies on cheap labor.

Jim Jones, however, relied on slave labor. Once he and his most loyal members had duped others into joining his Peoples Temple, he coerced, kidnapped, and brainwashed them into moving to his compound at British Guyana, where his elite and very loyal armed guards oversaw people working in the fields, punishing them if they stopped for even a moment. The only thing that could be grown in the weak soil was a local root vegetable called, "eddoes."

This and rice constituted the diet for everyone at Jonestown except Jim Jones, his loyal members, and his guards.

The specific diet eaten by these communities is directly linked to their ideologies. The Farm was originally strictly vegan and may have relaxed its standards slightly, whereas kibbutzniks eat Kosher meals. Both enjoy foods grown at home. The Amish diet of homegrown foods includes meats, eggs, and dairy, and they have a tendency to over-sweeten and overcook their foods, which are already heavy in carbohydrates and fats. This nutritional danger may be counteracted by the Amish lifestyle of daily hard work.

Life in the early kibbutzim was laborious as well, although the hard labor was not forced as at Jonestown. It was instead an integral part of the back-to-the-land ideals of that communal movement. For decades, the kibbutzim subsisted mostly on their own agriculture. In more recent years, they have branched out into other livelihoods such as manufacturing and tourism. The extent to which each kibbutz grows its own food depends on that community's industries and abilities.

The Farm also grows much of its own food, and an intention of the community is to have as small an ecological footprint as possible–a goal that the Co-op Village concept shares and that is necessary for the continuation of life on earth. Living sustainably in this way necessitates not only living off of what can be grown on the land locally, but also being mindful of what one actually eats. The awareness of this "footprint" of consumption is why the Farm was originally vegan, and why it remains largely vegetarian to this day.

Although part of the Farm's seminal culture was drug use for spiritual exploration, Gaskin has since abandoned the practice. Drug use is not allowed, while alcohol and tobacco use is discouraged. The Amish similarly disapprove of them as unhealthful, but pipe tobacco and cigars are tolerated in some districts. Drug use was a vital part of Jones' systematic mind control—anyone who tried to escape was subsequently drugged and constantly watched by the guards. Alcohol was available as a reward for loyalty, especially to his guards. Toleration of these substances will be determined at the Co-op Villages by consensus. Illegal drug use will not be allowed because of adherence to all state and federal laws.

The consensus process itself is a unique feature of the Co-op Village concept. The Amish govern themselves within their districts democratically, but decision-making power is in the hands of ministers and deacons who are ordained and never retire. Though there have historically been legal issues over school attendance and other matters where the mores of the Amish conflict with the laws of the state, the Amish have a deep respect for government. They pay all taxes except social security because they do not accept it themselves. They do not accept welfare and they refuse to rely on help, believing staunchly in self-sufficiency. Members who violate the rules of the community are shunned or split off into splinter communities.

The Farm, however, manages itself with an elected board, town meetings, and community voting–a method they refer to as close to consensus but not quite. Although Stephen Gaskin was the driving force in the creation and progress of the community, he maintains that he is a teacher not a leader. The non-hierarchical nature of the community reinforces his assertion. Each member has a vital role to play, and there are no social positions.

The kibbutzim are similarly democratic, run by a system of coordinators and secretaries who lead committees overseeing particular areas such as farming or education. These positions are held temporarily and service is seen as a duty for all. The kibbutzim comply with all of Israel's laws. Crime rates are very low, and serious crimes are reported to the authorities.

Jim Jones was the single decision-maker at Jonestown, teaching his followers that he was actually God. He used every method he could–violence, mind control, careful selection of members, propaganda, forced drugging, and more—in order to have his way. He was a manipulative, drug-addicted sadist whose destiny as a cult leader was evident even in his childhood. He acted out the very same scenario that happened at Jonestown, taking in animals, making them trust him, and then killing them and holding elaborate funerals. When local press finally began to catch on to his perversion, he fled the country for British Guyana with his followers, taking some children while their unwitting parents were at work. This was just one more way that he lured some parents. It is important not to understate his genius and his perversion in order to avoid confusing Jonestown with a genuine intentional community.

There was no system of governing at Jonestown, only Jones himself. No other community studied here has a single identified leader. The communities of the Farm and the kibbutzim provide excellent models for the Co-op Villages. Consensus and rotation of leadership are major ways that the Co-op Village will avoid such a tragedy. Also, careful admission processes and adherence to the laws of the state will assure that each member is treated fairly and compassionately by the other members.

Generally, the communities so far have shared a spiritual path–the Amish share theirs Anabaptist roots, the hippies on the Farm shared Gaskin's spiritual leadership, the kibbutzniks are Jews; although many communities are or were founded as atheist endeavors.

CONCLUSION

When describing communities, I have not been entirely ignorant of the ideological problems of what exactly qualifies a community as "successful." Because avoiding all reference to whether or not a community is now a success or failure would be difficult, I have considered only the crudest elements of success in my estimation. Evaluating the success of communities is essential if we are too look to them for our own learning and for the benefit of our future communities. For the purposes of this chapter, a successful community is one that has maintained relative longevity, generally benefits economically and environmentally to the surrounding area as well as its members, holds onto a measure of self-sufficiency, manages to adhere to at least some of its founding principles, and does not overtly cause harm or death to its members.

Located across the globe, intentional communities are not merely small bubble societies with their heads in the sand. Their vitality and compassion are models for living and hope. The time has come for the community model of living to insinuate itself into the fabric of modern life. The transition from the alienation and environmental disaster of modern life can be seamless for those who prefer only small changes to their lives or it can be revolutionary for those who are longing for a new evolution. However, what it must be is available.

A popular internet site, "Intentional Communities," or www.ic.org, is a definitive resource in finding and building community. However, most of the communities are simply a few folks sharing housing and trying to be mindful ecologically, or very expensive gated communities. Few communities provide the kind of large-scale and replicable solutions that the Co-op Village project has been designed to address. The first Co-op Village will be an experiment in practicality, a living blueprint which could then be offered up as a model for the next Co-op Villages, wherever they may be.

How do we share our abundance? In other words: how is wealth understood and shared by members/residents?

	Co-op village	The Farm	Kibbutz	Amish	Jim Jones
Can you keep your wealth? (financial independence)	Your wealth will be yours. But everyone will work 20 hours a week serving others or contributing to the general wealth.	Since 1983 members must be financially independent, but originally members pooled their resources.	Individuals are allowed a personal budget, generally equal to others', allowing for things such as travel, clothing, spending. originally gifts and income from outside turned over to communal treasury, trended to individual ownership in the latter half of the 20th century.	Yes, but Amish life requires living simply and without greed.	Absolutely no financial independence. One child, sent out to beg, had been told if he kept any of the money he received, Jones would know and he would be struck down by God. He pocketed $10 and nothing happened to him, so he quit the church because he saw it was a lie.
Shared Income	Yes and no. Income from village industries, for example construction, goes into the communal wealth, but those working outside do not have to turn over all their wealth. If you wish to work more than 20 hours a week then that income is yours.	Not at the present time.	Yes.	No.	No one shared the wealth that Jones enjoyed. He collected any passive income of his congregants.

Personal Expenses	Those working for the village will be provided for with their monthly stipend, while those earning enough by working outside will not receive one.	Members must support themselves.	Members given a stipend to cover personal expenses.	Amish are encouraged to be frugal, and wives are given a household purse to use for their needs, while the husband manages the money.	N/A
Ownership of Items	Residents will own personal possessions.	Many items and common spaces are community property, but there is no official restriction on individual ownership.	Originally ownership of anything was not allowed, gifts of money and goods from outside are no longer disallowed but quietly frowned upon.	Yes	Jones convinced "members" to turn over all individual property, including homes, cars, jewelry, and millions of dollars of real estate.
Join Fee?	Non-refundable, large enough to show commitment but not too large as to exclude people. Somewhere between $100 and $1,000.	One-time membership fee paid in installments.	Varies.	No	As much as Jones could get, including real estate and any property of value.

| Regular Fees? | No regular fees. However, those with outside full time jobs will simply give the cost of living plus 10% of their income to the community general fund. $ | 75-125 per adult per month. No. | No | All earned income and money from begging was taken under threat of punishment, and members were encouraged to try to solicit money from relatives, only reason to keep in touch. |

How do we reach consensus? In other words: how are the communities governed?

	Co-op village	The Farm	Kibbutz	Amish	Jim Jones
Is it a Cult?	No.	No.	No.	No.	Yes.
Decision Making	Consensus.	Elected board, town meetings, and community voting.	Self-governing democratic, seen as a municipality by Israeli government.	Religious leaders ordained and never retire.	Brainwashing, propaganda, and drugging of residents who disobey or consider leaving.
Identified Leader	No. Leadership on rotation basis so all may serve.	Stephen Gaskin was a driving force in the creation and sustaining of the community, but claimed to be a teacher not a leader.	None.	None.	Jim Jones, a manipulative sadist addicted to thorazine, amphetamines, and other drugs who taught that he was actually God.
Hierarchy	None. No social classes helps eliminate discrimination.	No social positions, each has a vital role to play.	Run by a system of impermanent coordinators and committees governing specifics like farming, education, etc.	Deacons and ministers hold power over rule-breakers, and within the family the father is head and the older boys assert dominance over the girls	Jones above everyone. His armed guard had perks like alcohol and some food, but ultimately everyone was his victim.

Adherence to Laws of Surrounding Country	Yes.	Yes.	Yes.	Generally. There have been legal issues over school attendance because the Amish do not allow schooling over the age of 15. They do have a deep respect for government and pay all taxes except social security because they care for their aged. Do not accept welfare.	No. Jones fled to Guyana with his congregation to avoid paying taxes and to avoid being discovered in his many illegal activities, including fraud, child abuse and neglect, sexual abuse, drug abuse, and more.
Incidence of Crime, how dealt with	Transparency with law enforcement and a committee to remove members who are grossly malicious.	Standards for conduct include nonviolence and vegetarianism, however the enforcement has varied over the life of the community.	Very low, serious crimes reported to local authorities.	Members who violate the rules of the community are shunned or split off into splinter communities. Amish submit to the authority of the state when it does not violate their principles.	Followers were cruelly and sadistically punished for committing any transgression such as favoring one's own children over others or speaking against Jones.

How do we interact with our enviromnent? In other words, environmental responsibility.

	Co-op village	The Farm	Kibbutz	Amish	Jim Jones
Conservation Measures	Ecologically mindful in its design, construction, and usage. Organic farming.	Ecologically mindful in its design, construction, and usage. Organic farming.	Some kibbutzim, such as Kibbutz Tammuz, are highly mindful of the state of the environment. Organic farming.	Schools built to use natural light so no electricity is needed, kids walk to school, almost no use of fossil fuels	None.
Outreach	Creation of new communities, educating visitors, and more to be determined by the interests of the members.	Holds workshops on sustainable building, publishes books, and educates visitors. Advocates vegetarianism.	Visitor programs to some organic farms, education.	None.	None.

How do we beautify our environment? In other words, how communities designed and constructed?

	Co-op village	The Farm	Kibbutz	Amish	Jim Jones
Basic Infrastructure	See chapter on Infrastructure.	27 original multi-family residential buildings as well as a number of communal and many newer buildings.	Neighborhoods located around common areas such as dining halls, workplaces, and child-care centers, usually run on typical electricity with in-home toilets, etc.	Traditionally-built homes and common buildings, horse-and-buggy travel, small locale to keep 30-40 households close, no electricity.	150 buildings planned, only 50 built, severe overcrowding, only two toilets.
Cars Allowed Inside Community?	Generally no. Only a few permits will be given to those that absolutely need them.	Yes.	Restricted to necessity.	No, not allowed at all.	Unknown.
Creation of New Communities	Inherent in design, necessary to reach goals.	No, but connections with scattered other communities.	Ongoing.	Growing with the Amish population.	No.
One Community or Part of a Network?	Ideally, the village will connect, sponsor and support the many other villages.	Single community.	Network of at least 85 communities.	Around 900 districts (individual communities).	Single Community.

Location	N.W. Florida, USA	Southern Tennessee near Summertown.	Israel.	Throughout US and Canada, mostly PA, OH, and IN	Redwood Hills, California and later British Guyana.
Urban/Rural	Rural	Rural	Originally rural, urban kibbutz such as Kibbutz Tammuz are newer.	Rural.	Located amid a thick jungle chosen to make communication impossible.
Method of Construction	Varies by community. Buildings designed to be fireproof and last 100 years.	Various cost-effective and energy-saving designs using recycled materials.	Varies by community.	Labor of the members. The barn-raising is a common community event.	Slave labor by brain-washed participants.
Time Period of Construction	All buildings completed within 12 months.	Built over time as part of workshops and income.	1909 to present.	Waves of emigration from 1720-1770 and 1816-1880. Construction continues today.	Unknown. Was partly constructed before Jones' arrival in summer of 77 but thereafter left incomplete.
Period of Existence	Forming in 2007.	1970 till present day	Varies, some kibbutzim are as old as the movement itself, and others were built as recently as the 80s.	1700s to present day.	Moved to Guyana in summer 1977, mass murder in November 1978.

How do we enrich ourselves?

	Co-op village	The Farm	Kibbutz	Amish	Jim Jones
Income from External Economy?	Yes.	Workshops, services, manufacturing, midwifery, construction, book publishing, free and low-cost visits, and more.	Yes.	Yes. Selling surplus crops and dairy help support the rising cost of farmland. Obstacles to this include practices such as avoiding tractors and not conducting business on Sunday.	Jones collected social security, foster-care, and other checks for his followers, had children beg in the streets, and ran an exhaustive choir in SF and LA for large amounts of money.
Interaction with Outside World?	Yes. Some residents will live in town or commute daily. Young adults will be given a few years to live outside to see if that is where they belong.	Yes. Some members work in nearby towns, relations with neighbors and local businesses are generally good, aside from some local kids.	Yes, selling farmed and manufactured goods, intermarrying. Kibbutz played an important role in creation of Isreal.	Believe that they must live separate from the world, not required to pay ssi because they do not accept social security payments, avoid courts if possible.	Prohibited, only one road leading to compound through jungle, no telephone, one guarded shortwave radio, manipulated governments to remain uninvestigated.

How do we find enjoyment?

	Co-op village	The Farm	Kibbutz	Amish	Jim Jones
Group Recreation	Yes	Yes, also meditation.	Yes.	Yes, also church.	No.
Pedestrian Community?	Yes	Yes.	Yes.	Yes.	Yes.

How do we coordinate what we love to do? In other words, how do communities decide what members jobs will be?

	Co-op village	The Farm	Kibbutz	Amish	Jim Jones
Allowed to work Outside?	Yes, but required to pay living expenses if 20 hours per week not worked within village.	About one-third of the adults in the community work in the surrounding area. The principle of Right Livelihood guides members.	Generally allowed.	No, that would bring shunning on the Amish who spends time with outsiders.	Yes, before the move to British Guyana, but all money earned was to be given to Jones. Children were made to beg and threatened not to steal because Jones, being God, would know.

Typical jobs available inside the community	Infrastructure upkeep, energy maintenance, farming, cooking, counseling, childcare, healthcare, (any of the needs for the community) or starting one's own business according to one's passion.	Working in any of the industries on the farm: mail order catalog, book publishing, electronics manufacture, farming, childcare, and much more.	Farming is the most common livelihood, while some Amish do keep shops, shoe horses, serve as butchers, or even publish newspapers.	There was a small medical clinic staffed by those who gave out the poison, and some people served as armed guards, otherwise they were forced to work in the fields.
Labor Contribution Required	Residents who do not work outside the community work at jobs within the community 20 hours a week, according to their skills and inclination, and the need of the community.	All members contribute some of their time to the community.	Typical full-time workday unless the member works in the community, then they pay a fee to cover their living expenses.	Every person works in the Amish family, even children after school, and physically rigorous labor is thought to maintain health.	Compulsory.

How do we nourish ourselves? In other words, food and agriculture.

	Co-op village	The Farm	Kibbutz	Amish	Jim Jones
Alcohol Use	To be determined by consensus of all.	Discouraged	Varies by community.	Usually only by the young during rumspringa, generally disapproved of but allowed.	Only by guards and most loyal members.
Tobacco Use	To be determined by consensus of all.	Discouraged	Varies by community.	Varies. cigarettes are disapproved of as worldy, but pipes and cigars are allowed in some districts while many others officially discourage its use.	Unknown.
Drug Use	Illegal use of drugs not allowed.	Originally use of LSD and other "spiritual" drugs was condoned, but today is discouraged.	Varies by community.	Not tolerated, suspicious of modern pharmaceuticals.	Mushrooms, lsd, thorazine, amphetamines, and finally cyanide used to kill everyone except escapees, who were shot.

% of food grown	90%	Varies widely from none in some urban kibbutzim to a large amount in rural ones.	Stewards of the earth, not exploiters.	Almost none, only a local root vegetable called eddoes.
Share Community Meals	Yes	Often.	On Sunday and at weddings, but daily meals are a family affair.	Probably.
Dietary Practice	To be determined by consensus of all.	Kosher.	Mostly local or homegrown foods, including produce, dairy, eggs, and meats.	Almost everyone, except the guards, the most loyal, and Jones himself ate only rice, sometimes maggoty rice.

How do we vitalize ourselves? In other word, how do communities encourage health and wellness?

	Co-op village	The Farm	Kibbutz	Amish	Jim Jones
Health Care	To be provided to residents.	Members must support themselves.	The community cares for itself as well as it can, and calls on outside help when it must.	Have no doctors because higher education is prohibited, rely on trusted outsiders, distrust pills and strong medicine, very low immunization rates, most avoid health insurance, home birth is common.	"Even when people were vomiting, they had to continue to work in the fields." Wooden, 177. Elderly were given no medical care at all. Medical unit was mainly used for punishment and to drug those who tried to escape.
Pension / Retirement/ Disability	All residents will be supported.	Members must support themselves.	The community cares for itself as well as it can, and calls on outside help when it must.	Parents retire and leave home/farm to kids and move into attached home, system of care and social participation very humane.	Collection of social security and gov't checks was a substantial source of income for Jones - all members were required to turn them over.

How do we communicate? In other words, how did communities foster communication skills in individuals and the practical technology of communications?

	Co-op village	The Farm	Kibbutz	Amish	Jim Jones
Reasons for Creation	Answer to the problems of our time.	Shirking the increasing violence and materialism of the time, "back to the land" living, escaping persecution as "hippies".	Immigration to a Israel from Russia because of discrimination and pogroms.	Immigration to the US to escape religious persecution and compulsory military service in Europe.	Move to Guyana was for tax evasion as investigations by the IRS heated up, Jones' desire to control this group of people totally, and have them all commit a mass suicide
Shared Spiritual Path?	No.	Yes. Stephen Gaskin's ideas guided the community and still do, although emphasis is placed on finding your own way	Yes, Judaism	Same religion.	Same religion, Christian at first, then became brainwashed that Jones was God himself

Ambitions, Shared Goals	Live sustainably, stress free, with control over our own lives.	Living with compassion and community with fellow beings on the planet, helping the world become a better place, reducing the negative environmental impact of humanity.	Kibbutzim had a hand in the creation of Israel..	Mainly, to enter heaven as a community by avoiding the sins of worldliness, particularly self-aggradizement, seeking comforts, and materialism.	"Jonestown was the final communal-living design, conceived by Jones not as a human experiment in living and growing, but as a devious plan to lure and trap people, and to direct their modest streams of dollars into a river of millions to be stored in foreign bank reservoirs."
Viewes Itself as Utopian	No.	Yes, originally. What began as a social experiment became a simple way to live compassionately and in service to others.	No.	They don't share the cultural context of the idea of utopianism, but do believe that theirs is the only right way of living.	Yes. Jones was the only source of outside "news," he convinced them that the rest of the world was falling apart and they had to remain as the last place of true morality, according to him.

How do we bring forth inner wisdom? In other words, education, community beliefs.

	Co-op village	The Farm	Kibbutz	Amish	Jim Jones
Provide Advanced Education	Yes.	No. Families are responsible for taking care of themselves.	Yes, tension exists over whether the purpose is to come back and serve the community or leave and work outside, thus whether one should be allowed to study one's own passions or encouraged to study what is needed.	No.	No - some classes on obscure subjects were offered late at night to cause sleep deprivation.
Raising Children	Families are given support and allowed to unfold in their own manner	Children are surrounded by supportive adults but parents are ultimately responsible.	Originally very strict separation of the family, but now a conventional atmosphere.	Avg # of kids = 7, not educated past 8th grade, rumspringa.	In CA, allowed to attend public school, parents were forced to sign releases allowing their children to be terrorized, physically and sexually abused.

How do we expand our community?

	Co-op village	The Farm	Kibbutz	Amish	Jim Jones
Population	500	About 200. Peaked at 1200 in 1982.	About 90,000, each kibbutz with about 600 members.	189,000 (144,700 in 1990, and doubling every 23 years).	950
Adult Members	Mimicks outside demographics	Exact number unknown.	Varies	Slightly fewer than typical rural Americans.	About 600.
Child Members	Mimicks outside demographics	Exact number unknown.	Varies	Much more children and adolescents than typical rural Americans.	276, of which 240 were under age 16, not including those who escaped.
Gender Balance	Mimicks outside demographics	About equal.	Men, women, and families as residents	Nearly equal population.	Unkown. Most bodies were not identified.
Age restrictions	Mimicks outside demographics	None. Caring for elders and children is a "sacred duty."	None	None.	None, Jones particularly preyed upon children and the elderly.

Non-Member Residents/ Transients	Members must be residents.	Unknown	Yes, including temporary volunteers (often students), immigrants, and ulpanim, people involved in an intense hebrew language study, transient workers in early years to sustain community financially.	Joining Amish is converting to religion, very rare, and the Amish avoid interaction with outside influences, asking: "what fellowship has light with darkness?"	No, followers of Jones were handpicked and subject to mind control, and not allowed to leave.
Open to New Members / Admission Process	Yes. Process includes filing an application, attending orientations, being voted in, and paying the entrance fee.	yes. Process includes visiting, finding a sponsor, being voted in, and paying application fee.	Yes, only Jews, the process varies.	Not unheard of but rare.	People were systematically manipulated and coerced, sometimes by the kidnapping of their children, to move to Jonestown.

Romantic Relationships	Unrestricted	Gaskin is quoted as saying, "If you're having sex, you're engaged. If you're having babies, you're married." Now, members are more free to do as the please.	Heterosexual marriage strongly favored, Westermarck effect leads to not finding a mate within community and thus abandonment of communal life as an adult.	Encouraged as the foundation of the family. Young people begin dating during "rumspringa" at about 16 and marry around 23. Dating occurs at community events and in the girl's home.	Sexual acts w/ Jones in front of everyone.
Allowed to Marry an Outsider?	Yes.	Yes	Yes	Not unless they leave the community and accept shunning.	No. Followers often faced splitting up their families by joining, and Jones dictated the pairings that were allowed within the community.

	Free to Leave Then Return?			
	Yes.	yes	Yes	Teenagers are given the option to leave the community during their "rumspringa," around age 16. If they leave, or if anyone "sins" severely, they are shunned and lose all contact with the community.	According to survivors, more than 90% wanted desperately to leave, but were prevented by the breakdown of family alliances and the constantly vigilant armed guards who were brainwashed, loyal, and armed with shotguns, semiautomatic rifles, and crossbows.

Chapter 12

COMMUNITY CLUSTERS

by Jack Reed

So, once we get the model demonstration Community going, what's the next step? Given its success, one of the things that will happen rather quickly is that this "Highest Good For All" model for living will be replicated at various places around the planet by people who see that this holistic systems-approach to the planet's challenges is not only what is needed but needed immediately. Therefore, the next major step would be to create a cluster of cooperative Communities all physically connected to each other. A cluster of Communities would be able to provide the social, intellectual, cultural, recreational, and economic diversity to not only help stabilize the Communities, but also provide ample opportunities for enrichment on all levels of living.

Let's take an area of, say, ten thousand acres where we're planning on creating a cluster of Communities. We would create the first Community on only a small portion of the land, and then later create Community #2, then #3, etc., until we had five or six Communities of four to five hundred people each. Naturally, the area of land needed for each Community would depend on the particular area and what the land could naturally support in keeping in harmony with *all life*. These Communities would be planned in harmony and cooperation with each other so that they could share many of the same resources, thereby also limiting the number of unnecessary buildings. In addition, through sharing resources, the Communities would be able to reduce the total amount of equipment per person that they need and also eliminate several job duties. However, the Communities are close enough together so that it is easily possible to walk, ride a bike or electric cart from one Community to another on natural paths and a minimal road system. But again, the key is that all the residents are committed to acting for The Highest Good Of All and to enjoying the abundance of that approach rather than the limitations of the everyone-for-themselves, win/lose, let-me-fence-off-my-area system.

A most important benefit of the clusters will be that they will generate many times the attention of the initial single model Community. When people hear that a couple of thousand people in one area are living what can only be considered a very successful and happy yet radically different lifestyle, then that will really grab their attention. This will become of progressively greater importance as people search for solutions against the backdrop of the planet's progressively greater problems. The mindsets of people, which have been based on thousands of years of programming, will be challenged and changed as they see a different and better way of living for all life. There will be media coverage dwarfing the amount of coverage that, for example, the Biosphere project near Tucson, Arizona received. There will be scientific studies in all the various disciplines as the very fabric of the world's system of interrelating economically, socially, politically, and interpersonally is challenged.

COMMUNITIES COOPERATING

Now let's take a town of about 10 thousand people made up of 20 to 25 Communities of four to five hundred people each, all operating on the principle of the Highest Good For All. First of all, through the commitment to make this larger Community work for all of the residents, we no longer need to consider the question of unemployment, even though we can eliminate many traditional jobs which, as we discussed earlier, are based on the lack of cooperation between people. We also have no need for welfare or disability benefits because, in a cooperative Community, there is always something that every resident can do to contribute to the

Community, the larger Community, and/or to the planet. Given the number of traditional jobs that are no longer needed, other jobs will be created as we restore the environment locally, produce more of our own food locally, and begin to build fun and nurturing back into our lives. Although we obviously can't replace all the jobs, there's nothing wrong with reducing the number of hours that people spend working. It's interesting that this seemingly liberal approach to changing the way we live together is actually more in line with the conservative agenda of eliminating public assistance, returning decision-making to the local level, and downsizing the need for government.

This larger Community would also have the ability to share many additional resources not practical in the four to five hundred person Communities. For instance, they might have a hospital, a large recycling facility, etc. But, again the principle is that the number of buildings are kept to a minimum, they are multi-use, and they are available for the use of all the people in all the connected Communities at no cost, because this entire cluster of Communities is based on the philosophy of cooperating for The Highest Good For All. Thus, we have little or no use for lawyers, accountants, and paper shufflers of all types except for those who are necessary in the Highest Good model for tasks such as inventorying and ordering.

The elimination of those jobs which are based on lack of cooperation frees up a tremendous amount of space as well as jobs. Just look at any business street and see how much space is used for stores with huge inventories of products, products which may sit there for long periods of time before being sold to individual homes where many of them may sit around in disuse for years before entering landfills. Then check out the number of stores that are selling the same things but are in competition with each other. These jobs, born out of the everyone-for-themselves' need to create jobs and amass money, along with the space they occupy and the resources they use, are not necessary in a cooperative model. In fact, they diminish the quality of life we could have. This Community of ten thousand would truly demonstrate that people can live cooperatively on a large scale with all residents able to afford the richness of what the Community has to offer. If one Community has a need, the representatives of all the Communities get together to figure out how to deal with the issue. Without the influence and restrictions of government, very creative systems-approach solutions can also now be found— solutions which heretofore were not possible in traditional living models. Using money as an excuse for not being able to do something becomes a virtual non-issue as compared to the way our lives are currently set up.

The larger Community could also grow just about all of its own pesticide-free and chemical-free food as well as start to renew the topsoil. Some of the Communities would choose to grow certain more specialized foods (sometimes in specially created environments), and it would now make more sense to grow the larger grain and legume field crops. The key, though, is that the food is still being grown locally as opposed to our present day practice of shipping it over 1500 miles to market.

However, as contrasted to a current typical town of ten thousand, we have many times more open area and nature with natural habitat. While our lifestyles are far more abundant, we have far fewer structures, far less space under roofs, and more than 95 percent less land under concrete. This larger Community is also mainly a pedestrian Community with no traditional street system leading up to individual houses, no driveways and garages (remember that the few number of cars necessary for the smaller Communities are kept on the outskirts of those Communities). Instead, there are walking and biking paths and a minimal road system interconnecting the Communities, and these roads are used mostly by solar electric powered carts, transports and shuttles. In fact, the larger Community would plan all the Communities in such a way as to create a beautiful, balanced inter-relationship with nature.

Of course, my personal favorite aspect of the larger Community is that the capacity to have fun in our lives increases exponentially. Through the benefits of sharing, the larger Community will enable us to have the option of spending even less time working. Also, the kinds of resources that the larger Community can provide the opportunity for almost any kind of recreational, artistic, and creative interests that one may have—

from hang gliding to playing in an orchestra. All these pursuits then suddenly become affordable and available to all residents as opposed to what we now do, which is dream about doing these things if we had the equipment and/or the money, the time, the proximity, and the friends with whom to do these things—which translates to "we just don't get around to doing many things on a regular basis that would add more enjoyment and excitement to our lives."

SO THE WORLD CAN SEE

Imagine the impact that a Community of this size would have on the world. We would be addressing the environmental concerns by being basically non-polluting, by being energy self-sufficient, by eliminating the need for almost all packaging and other landfill materials, by making it easy to recycle almost everything, etc. We would also reintegrate our lives with nature while at the same time bringing fun, creativity, nurturing, and really connecting with others back into our lives. With a Community on this scale which boldly redefines how we as people can live together, the media coverage will bring this model to the attention of the world.

Just as the current model of the way we live together continues to disintegrate, people all over the planet will be quick to respond to a better way of living both for themselves and for the planet. It is then just a question of how long it will take before most of the world starts forming Communities based on the concept of *The Highest Good For All Life.*

As Communities spring up around the planet, they will have different looks depending on the area and climate. One of the exciting things design-wise is that, in planning Communities for The Highest Good Of All, it opens up some interesting opportunities for improving the quality of life in relationship to the whims of our weather. For example, as I described earlier, it's possible to put domes over Communities to lessen the inconveniences of winter snowstorms. These domes can be of any size from the 350 person Community I saw the blueprints for to a whole town. Imagine still being able to enjoy the snow while also having the

CONCEPTUAL DOMED COMMUNITY DRAWING BY THOMAS SLAGLE

option of being able to live and go to work in the Community without having to negotiate the trials of the season.

Is it possible that we can successfully live together in Community? Well, it's actually happening and has been happening for hundreds of years. There are many books in print about the multitudes of today's intentional communities. The authors of one of the most informative intentional community books, *Builders Of The Dawn*, state that "Information of today's communities is lacking" and "The majority of communities shun publicity." It's like what has been happening in the very successful Basque cooperatives—the news hasn't been getting out that cooperative living and working has been very successful.

The early American colonists shared resources and were like the intentional communities of today, so what we are proposing is not un-American. However, unlike anything else that has been done, what we are proposing is a much larger model which integrates technology and the kinds of amenities, opportunities, and nurturing that would make Community life appealing to almost everyone in terms of lifestyle. The other big difference is that this model would not shun publicity but instead would make sure that the world takes notice that we can make life work abundantly for everyone.

But again, let's keep in mind that this Revolution in the way we live together involves both the change in the form to the Highest Good model and *the commitment in consciousness* to go for The Highest Good Of All. As this Revolution then spreads around the world, improving life all across the planet and bringing prosperity—while also restoring the environment in even Third World countries—the quality of life evens out to a very high level worldwide. As people gain years of experience in being committed to The Highest Good and as the Community model for living that principle spreads across the planet, we not only will be sharing resources in the larger cluster Communities and seeing ourselves as part of the local areas, but we will also be seeing ourselves as part of the worldwide network of Communities. With that global consciousness, we will be committed to life working abundantly for all Community members (and for everyone) everywhere.

Chapter 13

COMMUNITIES AROUND THE WORLD

by Jack Reed

So, let's take a look at what would happen with this future global Highest Good model. Right now we are hooked into a world economy that has been a blessing in terms of the opportunities it creates to share some resources and products and for some degree of ingenuity. But it is also a monster, not only for the environmental damage, but also because we have no idea, in our everyone-for-themselves economic model, of how to improve the quality of life for all people. This damage has happened even though, as we have pointed out many times, we have all the resources and manpower to have life be abundant, nurturing, and fun for *everyone.* In fact, with what is happening to the environment, a case can be made that the idea of having more or less than someone else doesn't really matter anymore. Rather, the important thing is having the absolute most available for everyone while still keeping in harmony with the planet and restoring the environment. (Of course, as we have described, living in Communities and sharing resources represents abundance rather than sacrifice.)

A USE AND ACCESS WORLD

With the Community model redefining wealth as use and access rather than as possessions and as cooperation rather than power, let's look at what would happen if we replaced the out of control, "sorcerer's apprentice" money exchange system with something that would work for the Highest Good For Everyone. First of all, with the Communities more integrated with nature and locally growing the food that is needed, we no longer have to ship food the huge distances to market (while simultaneously enjoying fresh and natural rather than processed foods). With hothouses and hydroponics, Communities could also choose to grow most foods anywhere on the planet.

While the sharing of resources locally means that we will have to produce far fewer of the products that can easily be shared, we have also, with the Highest Good model, eliminated the need for the nonsense products—since we no longer have to invent ways to individually make a living. However, we still would have many products which are necessary and helpful to people that need to be distributed across the planet. So, how could we both produce and distribute those products in a worldwide Community system? One big change would be that, in the Highest Good model, there would be the cooperative commitment to create the very best possible products that can be made. No longer bound by the profit motive, there would be no secrets, and the people with the best ideas could get together to not only produce products that would last a long time, but, with our absolute commitment to the environment and to health, would also be 100 percent safe and recyclable. Nothing but material that can easily and safely decompose need ever go into the ground—goodbye landfills.

In the U.S. the advertising expenditure per capita is about $500. Think of the resources that are tied up in that. In cooperative Communities, with the very best products being made, there would no longer be any need for the marketing industry. There would be no reason for hype or for trying to convince people that they need something, and all the information on a product would be available on computer. Then when a product is no longer necessary, the Community(ies) producing that product would simply stop making it and start doing something else to contribute to the Highest Good of the planet.

Even in our current system it would make more sense to just provide people with the best possible products as opposed to continuing our market economy. For instance, if Ontario Hydro in

Ontario, Canada gave away energy-efficient appliances to every home in the Province at a cost of $7 billion, this would save enough energy to save them from building a nuclear reactor at a cost of $17 billion. Likewise, if we produced 250 million refrigerators for prospective new buyers, and these refrigerators were seven times more energy efficient (we can already do this, even though we don't), it would save enough electricity to save building $90 billion of coal powered generating plants or $200 billion of nuclear plants. Just giving the refrigerators away costs only $6 billion. In addition, every dollar spent on building nuclear-power plants would be seven times more effective in diminishing the greenhouse effect if that dollar were invested in energy efficiency.

The same is true of both electric cars and solar energy collectors—it would be far cheaper to just provide these items than to continue our current economic approach. That doesn't even take into account the ultimate environmental costs of fossil fuel use—everyday the world's economy burns an amount of energy it took the planet 10,000 days to create. Stephen Lewis, former Canadian ambassador to the U.N., warned that we're not going to get away with anything less than "an all-out assault on the whole process of fossil-fuel combustion, everywhere, in order to save the planet." We have the technology available to stop using both nuclear and fossil-fuels for energy, but there are powerful economic forces at work that prevent this from happening. As I've said, our current system into which we've boxed ourselves seems to be really crazy.

A WORLD OPEN FOR ALL—COOPERATING FOR THE HIGHEST GOOD

In the Highest Good system, information on what is needed for people and for all life on the planet would be compiled and representatives of areas would decide which Communities would be best suited for making and providing those needs. Government in the Highest Good system is no longer a patriarchal power/money-based system, but instead would consist of rotating representatives whose job is to look for the needs of the planet and coordinate production, distribution, and assistance. In the Highest Good system, the needs of the one are the concern of everyone—where there is a need, it just gets provided. When we take out the money/power factor and its complications and replace that with unfettered cooperation, we can just do it—it really can be that simple. Remember, of course, that the people living in the Communities have also transitioned into the *consciousness* of going for the Highest Good and into seeing themselves as citizens of the world and as part of the oneness of humankind.

The "government," like the smaller Communities, would also use consensus for decision-making. There may well be a Community cluster (a global Community), which would consist of rotating representatives from all the regions of the world. Their job would be coordinating the equity distribution system and monitoring the planetary conditions. There would no longer be Third World countries (if the idea of countries still even makes sense in our new role as citizens of the world), and the quality of life would be elevated throughout the world. This would not only produce a very high quality of life anywhere on the planet but would also enable us to restore the planet's forests and ecosystems, which are currently being destroyed in good measure by the need for profit and survival in the everyone-for-themselves paradigm.

With the system of Communities, how can we transport products that may need to be shipped long distances? Well, remember that, when sharing resources and eliminating many nonsense products and products that now go to support jobs (that do not need to exist in a cooperative system), the shipping of many things will be cut down immensely or completely. However, there will still be a need to transport many items, so how can we do that if the shippers themselves are also members of Communities, yet have to travel? In the equity distribution system, there will be centralized warehouses with inventories. Then when a Community needs products, they can transport in the product(s) they produce and pick up what they need. Also, people involved in transportation in a Highest Good system can be at home anywhere by just stopping in at any Community because every Community has a certain amount of "guest" accommodations— just call ahead for space available. Airports and seaports are also still easily handled because they are the primary function and contribution of a Community or cluster of Communities. Since we are no longer in competition with others, the time factor involved with pickup and delivery is not the urgent priority necessitated by our current system. This allows us to be much more efficient in the shipping that we still have to do.

One of the things I get excited about when thinking about Communities around the globe is how much easier travel will be for all the citizens of the world. One could simply look at a computer for openings in Communities around the planet and become a part of that Community for the duration of the stay, which could be a day or a year. In fact, relocation also becomes very easy when one can come to a Community and be a full partner in that Community. Moving is no longer an ordeal as we don't have to worry about furniture and the myriad of other possessions that often create more confinement than freedom. Whatever we need is available at the next location if we so choose. If one chooses to, one could travel the world living in one area and then another and having interesting experiences with a variety of loving, supportive people.

Certain Communities will have the primary function of catering to vacationers because of their locations. Right now most of the people on the planet do not have the means to vacation at all, let alone travel far away from home, but, in the cooperative model, everyone on the planet can travel without having to worry about what it costs—because it would cost nothing. I think that most people, even in a culture such as ours, which has more access to the resources to travel, would enjoy the ability to take vacations that were heretofore unthinkable, unaffordable, and/or undoable because of the constraints of time and money. However, to people in cultures that have never been able to travel, this would create opportunities these people have never known. It's all possible when we decide to make the world work for everyone.

As the need for most traditional transportation diminishes, we can remove the vast amounts of extra concrete and asphalt and either fill up the quarry holes or we can use existing concrete-eating machines to turn most of those three million acres per year of concrete back into productive farmland. In a Community system, we can utilize group transports more because there is really no need to have a hurry-hurry, rush-rush life to be anywhere at a given time. That idea is linked to our Western world everyone-for-themselves, "If you snooze, you lose" approach to life.

But what about the jobs in today's society that you may think that no one wants to do? Two things come into play with this. The first is that the very foundation of the Highest Good system is that, not only has the form of how we live together changed but also there has been a profound change of consciousness to go for the Highest Good Of All. This change is reinforced by the tremendous change in lifestyle with increased abundance on all levels. So people who have come to embrace the Highest Good will want to make a contribution. We are now trained to work for money and conditioned to the struggle for money, and, with that struggle laid to rest, people are more motivated to do whatever it takes to be of service. However, the second factor that comes into play is that in a cooperative model and in a cooperative world we can creatively design products and systems up front to eliminate many of the jobs that are either unpopular or unnecessary. In our competitive model it's very difficult to eliminate these jobs because people cut corners to create profit, and then others must do the undesirable, make-work for them later to clean up the waste. For example, garbage disposal is one of those kinds of jobs. It's far easier for most companies and households to just throw "trash" away and have someone then haul it away. But, in the Highest Good system, there would be very little packaging and everything would be produced both to last and with recycling in mind. As opposed to how difficult it is now for those of us who recycle, the Community would be designed for ease of recycling and composting. Therefore, it becomes a very easy task for all of us to do, and we do it with the satisfaction that we are taking care of the planet.

Now, what of those jobs which require many years of education? Will anyone be ambitious enough to spend eight plus years to be a medical doctor? Actually, I think that we'd find that probably more people would pursue higher education in the Community clusters supporting universities. First of all, the financial limitation factor would be eliminated so that young doctors, for example, would not emerge a hundred thousand dollars in debt, and the high-pressure competitive system could be replaced by a more supportive system. Rather than the information stuffing torture that medical students are currently put through, the new system would focus on truly learning from a variety of disciplines and treating patients with loving and caring. Imagine being able to go to school in a nurturing, supportive setting where everyone is focused on the goal of learning in order to both expand one's inner wisdom and creativity and to serve one's fellow man. I think that a lot more people would choose to expand their inner wisdom in the Community University clusters.

Because we haven't laid out a complete, detailed, thousand-page blueprint on exactly how the worldwide system of Communities would work, people could easily say at this point that the system would break down here or there because we haven't addressed this or that. The intent of this book is to create a workable framework, not to present all the detail. Within the Highest Good framework, the evolving detail will be created in the consensus process for each Community. However, let's remember that the point is that what we are doing now is not working, and there is only a small window of time to do something drastically different about that. We cannot have the current everyone-for-themselves paradigm in place 50 years from now without also seeing the devastation of the planet's environment, the degradation of lifestyle for almost all of us, and probably more conflict and war as a result of people fighting over what little is left.

With the Highest Good approach, for any problem that we can identify, we can also *create a solution*. The reason that we can do that is that the Community/Highest Good model is a systems-approach to living on the planet and there would not be the blocks to doing what has to be done on *all* levels to resolve an issue. Thus, we can creatively change or alter whatever has to be changed in order to create balance and abundance. In our everyone-for-themselves paradigm, it is hard to affect workable solutions because there are so many factions and special interests with power/control and profit motives that we end up not being able to change what then usually creates more problems a few years or generations down the line. Looking at how we currently do things, it's easy to get stuck thinking that things can't change. But the model we are proposing makes things possible that are virtually impossible in the everyone-for-themselves system. Again, the key is the major change of consciousness to that of going for the Highest Good Of All. With that consciousness, with the systems-approach of the Community model, and with the magic of consensus and its innate creativity, then almost all things become possible—*for all people.* With the world living in cooperative Communities, not only are people enjoying their lives more, but also it works for all life as we return the world to more of its natural state by regrowing the forests and healing the land, the water, and the air.

I think that Thoreau best expressed the danger of the well-intentioned, Band-Aid approach (vs. the systems-approach) in trying to solve our problems:

"There are a thousand hacking at the branches of evil to one who is striking at the root, and it may be that he who bestows the largest amount of time and money on the needy is doing the most by his mode of life to produce that misery which he strives in vain to resolve."

—Henry David Thoreau, Walden

Chapter 14

S E E D S   O F   C H A N G E —
A D D R E S S I N G   O U R
P L A N E T ' S   N E E D S

by Jack Reed

As I wrote before in the Highest Good chapter, individuals, cities and countries alike now use the lack of money as the excuse for not getting things done. But, if the world had a format for all of us cooperating together for the Highest Good, then money would not be an issue and we would just do whatever was necessary for ourselves, for each other, and for the Earth. We have the manpower, the resources, and the technology available to do all that we have described, so what's the worldwide problem? It's just that our systems are not set up for cooperation. We're still in the age-old system where the many really serve the few. The few think that they can have much more (except, of course, in terms of the real quality of life, which transcends materialism), and the many, blinded by thousands of years of history, are still unaware that another choice is possible.

Again, in attempting to resolve the severe challenges that now face mankind and threaten our continued life on Earth, unless we address the quality of all life all over the planet, we are simply taking a Band-Aid approach that will at best just delay the inevitable by a few years. We must take care of all life in a loving and caring way. We must address both wealth (the quality of life on all levels) and sustainability simultaneously to make life work bountifully for all. To eliminate the isolation, alienation and powerlessness that is the root of many of these problems, we must reinvolve people in the decisions that affect their daily lives.

With the technology now available, we have a tremendous source of support to have life work for everyone. You probably know that we have the capability to put cameras in satellites that can literally photograph and identify us individually. We're even working on being able to view a pin on the floor from 500 miles up. We can make "smart bombs" that can be programmed with the picture of a target, for instance a particular building within a city, and we can drop these bombs and they will go and seek out that particular target, identify it, and then destroy just that target. If we have the technology to do these kinds of things, we can produce energy and other products without pollution. We can recycle all that we make. We can create a high quality of life for all. So far, however, in the everyone-for-themselves system, science is expensive and technology follows the money that is available to be spent. The pentagon pays for most of it—70 percent of all science funded in the U.S. is paid for by the military. Worldwide, the military budgets are $800 billion per year, and $80 billion goes for military research and development. We can change all that in a cooperative system and create some really positive miraculous things to improve our lifestyles while also restoring the planet.

In revisiting the problem areas identified earlier, let's look again at the challenges facing us to see what the Community approach would do to resolve some of these issues.

ECONOMICS

The idea of some people having great wealth while others live in poverty doesn't make sense anymore because of the conditions now on our planet, specifically the environmental crisis and the diminishing resources and food production problems. Yet, what has been described here in this revolutionary approach to cooperation is that we can all live very abundantly. Remember being or seeing children at play and the issue of sharing toys and then getting into "that's mine and you can't use it"—even if you weren't playing with it at that moment? Now we are adults, and the system is not set up to share our world. It was children's toys then, but now it's our adult toys like property and possessions, even if we rarely use them.

There is enough wealth in terms of resources and manpower for everyone to have a really incredible, abundant life.

Future economics must involve sustainability, otherwise the well from which we take our resources eventually runs dry. Obviously we need to not only stop destroying the environment but to begin to restore the planet. We know that consumption— largely through the consumerism of the Western societies—uses up the vast majority of the world's resources. We also know that the trickle-down effect of the present polarization of the world's wealth has resulted in poorer countries destroying their environments to service those Western societies and the tremendous financial debt owed to them. Through living cooperatively as we have described, we can eliminate unessential jobs and the resources they consume, we can eliminate nonsense products and still have more play and pleasure in our lives, and we can cut back on many essential products through sharing. We can even provide all of the people in the world with products that are beneficial, and we can eliminate all the absurd indebtedness that has enslaved people and countries to the point where the environment and the quality of people's lives have been compromised. Thus, everyone and the environment can win in a cooperative system of Communities.

We live with the unnecessary restriction of how we see society and wealth. Isn't wealth and abundance much more than money? It's what money can do that makes it valuable, and, in an individual Community and as Communities spread across the planet, you will be able to do incredibly well. As I said earlier, we need to redefine wealth as "use and access" rather than as possession. Yet, in this transition phase, perhaps until all the people realize that we can all basically have it all, we don't want to keep people away who have more, or who like having more, so we created a model (in the "How Do We Share Our Abundance" section) that would work for them, too, during this time of transition.

In the Highest Good Community system there really is no such thing as employment because there is no unemployment— everyone in a Community contributes, even those with perceived limitations. I learned through working many years with people with disabilities that we all have abilities and limitations and that everyone can make a contribution on some level no matter what those abilities or limitations are. Welfare and social security also become archaic concepts in a cooperative system, as that which is needed can just be provided. People are naturally cared for in a Community, and, if services are needed, i.e., medical care, they can be provided for in a high quality way because they are now, with the old system out of the way, made a priority. We would have the resources and the technology to do that which was impossible in the everyone-for-themselves paradigm.

Yet, with "full employment" realized in the Community system, we have also eliminated some 80 plus percent of the existing jobs, thereby giving us both the ability to have the time to restore the planet and to have more time to enjoy our lives. Entire industries—including insurance, middlemen, sales and marketing, retailing, legal, governmental bureaucracies, and everything having to do with money—will be eliminated. The whole money system will eventually be replaced in the Highest Good system by representatives, working without the excuse of "there is not enough money," to coordinate production and distribution so that *all* the world's people can prosper. Again, until we do something about the wealth and poverty gap in the world and the corresponding rip-off of the environment, the environment that is our lifeblood will continue to decline.

Skeptics may speculate, probably based on their own feelings and lack of experience with working with people for the Highest Good, that people in Communities will become lazy and not want to work in a more idyllic life setting. However, the statistics I wrote about earlier from large cooperative systems like the Mondragon cooperatives in the Basque country prove that people willing to cooperate for the Highest Good can be far more productive. In Israel, the kibbutzim, with less than 4 percent of that country's population, were producing 40 percent of Israel's agriculture and 7 percent of the industrial exports in addition to supplying their own food, housing, medical, and entertainment needs. The ones I visited were also very pretty places to live.

THE ENVIRONMENT

Many experts feel that the major problem we're dealing with is the rampant increase in the planet's population and thus the over-taxation on the planet's finite resources. But we must look at this in a holistic way and address the causal factors of population growth. It's in the poorer countries where we see the population explosion. People have felt that they needed large families in order to survive. Ironically, the Kerala State in India is the one glaring exception in the world. Although one of the world's poorest areas, they have a fertility rate lower than America's, a 100 percent literacy rate, and even a life expectancy about the same as ours.10 The reason for this startling contradiction is that the people have chosen to cooperate to a higher degree than any populous State in the world is currently doing. Overpopulation per se is not a problem, but a symptom of our lack of cooperation in the world. The most effective birth control continues to be social and economic gain resulting in a high quality of life. There is an old saying: the rich get richer, and the poor get children. As we make the world work for everyone through Communities, the need for large families dissolves into the realization that we are all family. The Communities will provide the family support that people have heretofore looked for in biological families. Then, as we realize through the worldwide Communities that we are all one family on this planet, we can choose to spread the population around in ways that make sense beyond the issues of national borders.

In a talk before the United Nations, Robert Mugabe of Zimbabwe said, "They [the Third World peoples] know that cutting down trees and the deforestation of tropical forests will lead to soil erosion and future disasters, but their problem is survival today. To ask us to plan for our survival tomorrow when our survival today is in doubt, is to ask too much of us. For it is only when we can survive today that we can talk of tomorrow." In 1987, the World Commission on Environment and Development published the results of a four-year study on environment and development. Their report, *Our Common Future*, found that "Poverty is a major cause and effect of global environmental problems. It is therefore futile to attempt to deal with environmental problems without a broader perspective that encompasses the factors underlying world poverty and interna-tional inequality." Therefore, the report concluded that improving human welfare through sustainable development is the key to protecting the environment." Ms. Brundtland, the Prime Minister of Norway, who headed the Commission, added that there was no way to improve the environment without improving people's life conditions generally, and that, "The Commission became collectively convinced that present development patterns cannot be allowed to continue. While economic and social development suffer from severe national and global imbalances, threats to the environment are becoming global in scope and devastating in scale and effect. The survival of this planet requires that we act now."

Yet, in improving people's lives in order to try to rescue the environment, we cannot emulate the Western free market economics because the Western world's impact on the environment has been a disaster. We have been operating under the myth that nature was infinite and could absorb all our waste with no— or at least limited—adverse effects. Economic development and environmental protection must proceed together, which means sustainability and restoring the Earth's resources. We think that what we've described in this book—a system based on the Highest Good For All Life— may be the only way to do it. We're going to have to make the world work for everyone or it will work for no one.

Because we have the technology to eliminate the production of just about all the pollution (if we choose to do so), the production of pollution is mostly economically driven. So, when we combine the predicament of the Third World countries and the developed countries, we see that the environmental problems are economically based. With worldwide Communities, there no longer would be people living on the edge and having to destroy their own habitats to survive, nor would countries have to sacrifice their environments to service their massive debts. There would also be Community based agriculture rather than the economically driven system of eradicating nature from vast tracks of land for large-scale agriculture. Here and in the Third World we will be putting back trees and ecosystems to replenish the topsoil and provide natural insect control so that there is no longer a need for harmful chemicals and pesticides which pollute both our planet and our bodies. Also, with education and the nutritional way our Communities will prepare our food, we'll be using less meat and dairy, which will help restore the land and improve our health.

In a Highest Good Community system, there is no reason why we cannot restore the Earth to the state of being the green planet, a virtual ecological paradise that is a pleasure to see—with clean air, water and land. There no longer have to be landfills, vehicles that pollute, or even traffic. Yet, at the same time, all people have more time and access to see more of this magnificent planet.

Remember the boiled Frog syndrome that I described earlier? How do we get the people of this planet to respond to the environmental changes before it's too late? I believe that the answer is to show the frog that there is a much better pond available. That better pond is a Highest Good For All way of living on our planet.

HEALTH

As I understand it, the key factors in health are our mental/emotional state, good water, good air, and nutritional food. According to experts in longevity, with these factors in place, we should now be able to live healthily in excess of 120 years of age or so. The Communities will enable us to greatly improve our health on all levels. Perhaps most important is the freedom from stress that we will experience as we are involved with a loving, supportive family of people, as our work actually becomes meaningful for everyone, and as our lives are greatly simplified in the Highest Good paradigm. Currently in the U.S., all seven top selling drugs are for stress-related diseases, and Zontac, the top selling drug in the world, treats ulcers. Further reducing stress and adding to our well-being on all levels, regular exercise and play in nice surroundings with nurturing people become daily Community activities rather than events to try to squeeze into our too-busy lives. Even regular massage becomes commonplace for all rather than a luxury for the few that can afford it.

Given the reallocation of manpower and resources in the Community system, there will be more resources available to all for medical treatment. Of course, with better water, air, and food and with less stress and more of a holistic approach to preventative medicine, we will also have a tremendous reduction in the medical drug industry as well as much less of an incidence of many of the preventable diseases that are caused by stress, pollutants, and improper nutrition. Still, medical services will no longer be limited by insurance or to those who can afford them. In our current system, we have made some tremendous medical advances, but, with spiraling medical costs, it has more and more become medicine for the rich. Health services are all too often determined not by need but by money. Meanwhile, a major injury or health crisis can devastate many families. We also can't afford to get regular preventative treatment, which would cost less in the long run. Worldwide, millions of people die from preventable diseases. To me, that's a tragedy that is attributable to our everyone-for-themselves system and preventable in a Highest Good system. All the planet's people deserve and can have access to needed, preventative, and vitalizing health care.

Do you know that in some countries whole villages of poor people are selling their "spare" body organs just to survive financially? The organ brokers take these organs and sell them to those who can afford this service. Excuse me, this not only gives me the creeps, but is just plain wrong. This is not "survival of the fittest," but "survival of the richest."

On a personal note, pain is one of my least favorite things. Since we can plan our planet in a way that alleviates the most possible pain on all levels, including emotionally and mentally for all people, there is no really good reason not to do it. We have just had thousands of years of everyone-for-themselves which has blinded us to the possibilities.

SOCIAL

I previously proposed that isolation and alienation are two of the key causal factors for the dysfunction in the world today. As a consequence of this, people have tried to escape their feelings of powerlessness through crime, drugs, cynicism, resignation, and lapsing into uninspiring lives. With the support, nurturing, and creativity available within the Communities and with abundance being a given in our lives, the key factors to the escapist behavior of addictions and crime are eliminated. We also can end the separation we impose on people with disabilities and people who are elderly as they become valued, integrated members of our Communities. Obviously there would also no longer be homelessness or refugees as we make the planet work for everyone.

What would you really like to do with your life if you really had the freedom to choose and the time to express that choice(s). Would it be to express yourself more creatively, perhaps even for the benefit of humanity, or would you like to have a peaceful life in beautiful surroundings that would support you to go inside and discover more of who you truly are? Whatever your dream for self-actualization, in your life as it is now you may feel that you just don't have the time to pursue your dreams. With the unessential jobs and products eliminated via a cooperative world of Communities, people not only will have more time to enjoy themselves but also more time and cooperative resources for actualization—and we're talking about *all the world's people,* including those that have heretofore been disenfranchised by their struggle to survive.

In going for what works for all of us in the Highest Good system, we find things getting simpler. There are fewer responsibilities to fill up our lives, especially in the stressful area of finances and security, and there is more natural space to facilitate our attuning within. Who knows, we may even spend a lot less time as media spectators, as we choose to participate more than watch. Given the choice through accessibility to a variety of fun pursuits and fun people to participate with, I think that most of us would rather play than to watch others play. Of course, there would still be the opportunity to enjoy the performances of others, but you no longer would have to pay big bucks to watch multi-millionaires play and perform. Instead, you would see good and talented people perform for the joy of it.

Awhile ago I talked with a person from Armenia who told me that, while poverty was rampant in her country, the people in the area she was from were much happier than the people here. When I asked her why, she said that the people would sit down and talk with their neighbors and do things together. She said they had a sense of community there and that that was the big difference. Here, a lot of the older houses have porches, but who even knows their neighbors anymore, let alone participates with them. In the abundant Highest Good Communities, the support would be phenomenal and opportunities for nurturing, play, creativity, and having needs met would be almost unlimited for all the people. Imagine living in a happy/loving world.

POLITICAL

It's interesting that I saved this area for last. In one of Buckminster Fuller's talks, he said, "I hear a lot of people say 'I don't like machinery and technology, it's making a lot of trouble, upsets all the old things.' So we're going to take all the machinery away from all the countries of the world, all the tracks and wires and the works and dump it all in the ocean. And you'll discover that within six months two billion people will die of starvation having gone through great pain. So we say, 'That's not a very good idea; let's put the machinery back the way it was.' Then we're going to take all the politicians from all the countries around the world, and we're going to send them for a trip around the sun, and you find that we keep right on eating. And, with the political barriers down … the scientists say very clearly that you could make the world work and take care of 100 percent of the humanity … but you can't do it with the barriers; … it is an organic whole." Bucky Fuller, perhaps our foremost futurist, knew that we are going to have to change business-as-usual to free up the resources for everyone. He said that "The only way we can possibly take care of everyone is through a design revolution—doing more with less." Also, he noted that "Our bedrooms are empty two-thirds of the time, our living rooms are empty seven-eights of the time, our office buildings are empty half the time, it's time we gave this some thought."

Of course, the basis of the design revolution has to be on the level of how we choose to live together, it has to be choosing to live in a way that works for everyone, and, as Fuller correctly noted, sending politicians around the sun would be helpful. The political process in our everyone-for-themselves world has virtually always broken down into power struggles between two or more groups, political parties, or power brokers positioning themselves for financial gain. The bulk of humanity has been left on the outside of this struggle—while also being at the effect of the struggle—with no one really getting their needs met in terms of the real quality of life.

The only way we can change is to show something completely different—as different as a Highest Good system is to our everyone-for-themselves institution. We must reinvolve people in the decisions that affect their daily lives and help them learn effective, harmonious communication. In Communities operating for the Highest Good Of All Concerned, the fundamental difference between the Communities' method of making decisions by consensus and other traditional forms of decision making is that we have fundamentally similar ideas rather than that we are fundamentally different. Of course, this depends on the consciousness of the people, but, in seeing that the Highest Good can benefit all and having the commitment to go for that, we can have a revolution in making the world work for all. It becomes much easier to give up something, like a holdout dissension position, when people can see that through cooperation they can have so much more in return, both in terms of the quality of their lives and actually having more say in the decisions that affect their daily lives.

As this educational process spreads across the planet through worldwide Communities, the power will go to the people, and the political process will be taken away from the power brokers and the accompanying philosophy currently committed to protecting the status quo. In a peaceful, evolutionary/revolutionary process, the power will be taken away from the few controlling the many through their philosophy of conflict and the hoarding of the resources. We will then have essentially sent the power brokers around the sun. If they still want to play, they will find an ever-shrinking audience. Besides, the quality of their lives would also improve by choosing to become part of a Community and finally experience the caring and Loving that they were trying to seek through having control over others.

There are good things about countries and certainly about cultures, and we need to move into peace and cooperation. In the Community model, we can let go of nationalism, racism, sexism, etc., where everyone has a point of view that is "right"—a position that probably can be justified on any side by hundreds or thousands of years of history. However, because of the destruction of the environment, we must now be willing to move into a greater oneness, into the brother/sisterhood of all humankind. That means that we must make life work very well for everyone everywhere to eliminate inequity, one of the key sources of againstness. We are now all interconnected because of the world's environmental problems and economics, and practicing nationalism and other "isms" has led us away from the solutions.

While we're at it, let's also discuss religious differences because they have too often been the source of conflicts between individuals and groups for thousands of years. We must move into acceptance and understanding, which are qualities beyond merely tolerance, where everyone can pursue whatever Spiritual path they choose—as long as they don't inflict on others and as long as their choice includes an absolute respect for all life. Within the Communities and their Highest Good consciousness, that will be the requirement. I think it's great to have diversity in religion as long as there is acceptance and understanding for the choices of others. We are all on our path to realizing who we truly are, and there are likely different approaches that work best for different people. Even if one disagrees with that, demonstrating a happy life, acceptance, and loving service to others without expectation is always more persuasive than any other approach.

Now is a good time to address the possibility that some people may, in seeing that the Highest Good system is not the "acceptable" capitalistic system, mistakenly put an erroneous label like socialism or communism on our model. In many cases, the people who sit on the boards of the print and broadcasting media are the same ones who sit on the boards of the multinational corporations. Through the propaganda of corporate America, free enterprise has come to be equated with freedom, which equals nationalism, which equals Christianity, which equals God. However, as we've noted, "free" enterprise has enslaved the world economically, and more and more people fall into poverty as more and more gets concentrated into the hands of fewer and fewer. Meanwhile egalitarianism has come to equal equality, which equals socialism, which equals unionism, which equals communism, which equals Satan. Remember, though, that American communities began with the Plymouth pilgrims who set up our first towns by pooling their resources. Also, the early Christians practiced communal living and held all things in common. Funny how times have changed— these early Americans and Christians would now be seen as anti-Christian and branded as evil.

With capitalism, communism, and socialism alike, the power is in the hands of the state and the ruling elite, and thus these models are basically more alike than they are different. The Highest Good For All Community model that we have described is fundamentally different from any existing models because we are a group of individuals who make decisions for ourselves at the Community level—not the State level—and everyone is involved in those decisions. There is no elite group controlling everyone else. Also, remember that what is unique here is that the Highest Good model is the marriage of the consciousness of the Highest Good to the *form* of the Highest Good. It has never worked to impose the form on everyone—the consciousness of the Highest Good has to be there. If it is not, then we are not talking about the same thing. This is, therefore, neither socialism nor communism nor a State-controlled social welfare system. Some of the social welfare countries, i.e., New Zealand and Sweden, are not doing well because they try to do it on a State level within an everyone-for-themselves paradigm, and this can never really deal with the intricacies of the problem, because it is not a systems-approach.

People need to be given opportunities, nurtured and cared for as individuals, and included as an integral part of a Community and not anonymously just given money. Using any current system, when we try at a State level to provide for people, then the economy supports a bureaucracy, middlemen, nonsense jobs, unemployment, and welfare—none of which would exist on the Community level. To me, capitalism, socialism, and communism, as they have been practiced, are also fundamentally more alike than different in that they are all patriarchal varieties of the everyone-for-themselves approach rather than a systems-approach of making life work for all of us. Still though, a systems-approach at any level won't work unless everyone is committed to the Highest Good, and that's an educational problem that people must first see demonstrated.

Interestingly, if we were to use a consensus decision-making approach to deciding how we as people would live together on this planet, we would eventually come up with a system or form of living that would work for everyone and for the planet. That form would probably look a lot like the one that we have described. It would be a decision that worked for all us on the planet: it would encompass sustainability, it would put nurturing, fun, and joy into our lives, and it would eliminate unnecessary jobs and give us more time and fun and less stress. We would also stop polluting and unnecessarily using up our planet's resources and get back in touch with nature. Politically, it's time we start choosing to make our planet work for everyone.

If we do not start making our world work for everyone, the United States Commission on National Security 21st Century has some sobering predictions. This report was put together using our best security advisors. The report forecasts: "Thanks to the continuing integration of global financial networks, economic downturns that were once normally episodic and local may become more systemic and fully global in their harmful effects. Isolated epidemics could explode into global pandemics." Also, "... disparities in income will increase and widespread poverty will persist." Because history tells us that desperate and disenfranchised people will do desperate things, the report also offers the dire prediction that "... mass-casualty terrorism directed against the U.S. homeland was of serious and growing concern." and "A direct attack against American citizens on American soil is likely over the next quarter century." Even then will we have the wisdom to start making choices that support all life on the planet or will we go down the traditional road of separation, revenge, and retaliation. In order to change course, it's going to take a new paradigm of living together and relating together for the Highest Good For All, and this must be first demonstrated on a Community level.

"The dramatic threat of ecological breakdown is teaching us the extent to which greed and selfishness—both individual and collective—are contrary to the order of creation, an order which is characterized by mutual interdependence. Modern society will find no solution to the ecological problem unless it takes a serious look at its lifestyle."

—Pope John Paul II

"To commit a crime against the natural world is a sin. We're all connected—there is no separation. Polluting the environment is blasphemous—we are ruining God's work. There's only one planet and one people."

—His Holiness Bartholomew I

A competitive system will always have people at the bottom who have little to balance those at the top who have too much.

Chapter 15

T H E   N E X T   (R) E V O L U T I O N

by Jack Reed

Just like the Sorcerer's Apprentice in Fantasia, we, as a planet, now stand on the precipice, watching the seemingly out-of-control results of what we have created threaten the very survival of the planet or, at the very least, cause a greatly diminished lifestyle for almost everyone, as the ability of the planet to support life drastically erodes over the next 50 years. It's ironic that in this post-Cold War era, it's become increasingly clear that the real threat to our survival maybe never was nuclear war because no one really wanted to do something which would have been so fast and final. Rather, the threat we face is more insidious than war because the destruction of the earth's environment has been happening so much more slowly in its inextricable marriage to our everyone-for-themselves paradigm. Having taken place over hundreds of years, so many economic forces are involved in our world economy that it's now too complicated for anyone to bring into balance. All our efforts to date have at best been Band-Aid approaches, and the destruction continues. Therefore, we now find ourselves in World War III — the War Against The Earth. This war is not only against the environment but also against the quality of life which that environment supports.

OUR PLACE IN HISTORY

With all our crises, mankind now teeters at the precipice of its out-of-control creation. Which way are we going to go? If we do not in the next few years have a major (r)evolution in the way we go about life on this planet, it is absolutely predictable how historians will write about this period of time. What will they say fifty years from now when the quality of life on this planet is greatly diminished and as our depleted planet is no longer able to provide food and other basic needs for the ever-increasing population? The historians will say that we engaged in financially-driven chemical experimentation with the various products we made, which had devastating long-term effects on the air, land, and sea. They will also write about how we basically raped the planet's resources, treating them as if they were limitless, with no concern for future generations. Although those things are sometimes reported now, the historians will be unmerciful in describing how, even at the start of the 21st century, we still allowed many known poisonous products to be widely used because of the political/economic factors. They will write about how we the people bowed to big money and power broker interests, and then they will report that it didn't even work out for those people as the planet self-destructed.

The historians will compare this time to the decadence in the fall of the Roman Empire. They will decry us for choosing temporary greed over the well-being of the planet and of our grandchildren, and they will cite numerous examples of how we attempted to justify our economic decisions at the time while ignoring the long-term results of our choices. They will point out how television and the media became the opium of the masses by fixating people on the momentary sensational stories like the allegations against Michael Jackson, the Tonya Harding Olympics story, the emasculating of John Wayne Bobbit, the Menendez brothers' murder trial, the two-year daily coverage of the O. J. Simpson story, Monicagate, and Eilian Gonzales. They will also report how increasingly bizarre talk show topics and "Survivor"-type reality shows became all the rage.

The historians will question why, with what we knew about the depletion of the planet, we stuck or heads in the sand and focused on sensational momentary issues and profit instead of our using the media 24 hours a day to report about the seriousness of the environmental issues. They will indict us for not using the media as a forum to explore possible solutions that would begin to restore our planet and keep the Earth healthy for generations to come. It's like there's a huge black cloud coming that can suffocate the world, and, although we have the evidence that it's coming, we choose instead to bicker about balancing the budget, affirmative action, taxation, crime, drugs, family values, etc. If that cloud finally settles upon us and it's too late, we'll say, "Oh, we should have been dealing with the issue that was looming over us with the capacity to destroy our way of life instead of arguing about what we now realize were, in comparison, petty differences."

The historians might say that we considered the planet's long-range problems to be too scary and too overwhelming to even think about, and thus most of us felt too impotent to really do what it would take to heal the planet. Sticking our heads in the sand, we hoped that the problems would just go away. It's sort of like what happens in a dysfunctional family. The family makes an unspoken covenant not to talk about the dysfunction because, if they did start to really talk about it, then they might have to start doing something about it. They might also have to face the reaction of the power brokers. Our planet is like that dysfunctional family. It was interesting to me to note that in President Clinton's 1995 State Of The Union Address, nothing was said about protecting and restoring the environment, even though Vice President Gore's, *Earth In The Balance*, detailed the environmental threat to the planet. Then, in his 1996 address, when the Republicans were more vulnerable on environmental issues, Clinton chose to say something.

Perhaps, though, the current alarming rate of environmental destruction and the rapid decay of social, political, and environmental systems can be seen as a good thing because they will force us to look for long-term solutions for survival. We will be forced to choose either cooperating and having more for all of us or continuing our everyone-for-themselves approach and watching our quality of life rapidly decline. So, even though it may not look that way now, our destructive changes can be seen as good. As Martin Luther King once said, "Only when it is dark enough do you see the stars." Think of the billions of people already in absolute have-not situations. Many of these people have been there for generations, even lifetimes as they daily live in abject poverty on the edge of starvation and survival. Long ago the planet stopped working for them. To restate one last time the simple truth that is the key to changing things while there is still time: if we choose to make life work for everyone, there are enough resources and manpower on the planet for all of us to live very abundantly.

THE (R)EVOLUTION

The problem has been that we're still choosing to go with the age-old, tired, and archaic everyone-for-themselves way of going about life. We've used the survival of the fittest philosophy as the justification for how the rich and powerful have continued to oppress the poor and disenfranchised. The philosophy is useful to the "haves" because, if God set the planet up as a "survival of the fittest" paradigm and that's just the way it is, then the "haves" get to exploit the people, the planet and its resources, and feel no guilt while doing it.

The solution is to change the way that we as people live together. Now, with the survival of the planet in question, it is truer than when Patrick Henry first spoke these words, "We must hang together or we will surely hang separately." We must now adopt a new "Declaration Of Independence" for the Next (r)Evolution. This must be a Declaration of Interdependence simply stated as "We choose to make life work for all of us, for The Highest Good Of All Life on the planet."

"The overall thrust of AGENDA 21 is that the global community must be set on a bold new course—a course which strives for a sustainable future for humanity—a course which fully implements an understanding of the impact of humanity on the natural world.

"The world scientific community has seen into the abyss of environmental collapse and has sounded an urgent alarm. The leadership of the world has finally grasped the consequences of the failure to heed the warning to step back from the brink. AGENDA 21 is the call for an unprecedented global partnership among all nations and all citizens to confront and overcome the problems. It is now up to individual citizens to

understand and grasp the crucial nature of the twin global problems of environmental destruction and poverty.

"The responsibility for our common future is in our own hands. The prospect of inevitable global environmental disaster or world-wide social upheaval must not be the legacy which we leave our children. Within the lifetime of a child born today, we have the opportunity to create a world in which concern for life is paramount—a world in which suffering is not taken for granted—a world in which nature is revered and not exploited—a world which is just, secure and prosperous—a world in which our children's children are assured of enjoying the bounty of nature and the splendor of life.

"This particular point in history offers a unique opportunity for humanity to make the transition to a global community which provides a sustainable living for all."

—AGENDA 21

Indeed, as AGENDA 21 points out, "The responsibility is in our hands," but we cannot depend on nations, politicians, and vested multinationals to make the changes. Instead, we must boldly show on the level of Community how we can not only save our planet's environment but also create the opportunity for all people to lead inspired and abundant (on all levels) lives.

We're not preaching sacrificing yourself to take care of others. We still want and need people to take care of themselves, but the old win/lose method is just not going to do it. Win/win is the only way to truly look out for Number One. Going for The Highest Good Of All is really the tremendous commitment to one's true self as we realize that immediate self-indulgence is the immaturity that has caused us to threaten the survival of our planet. The mature person knows that we are all interconnected and that one's own welfare is intrinsically linked to the well-being of all life on the planet.

If we can act for The Highest Good Of All and create a model to demonstrate how to do this, there will be a revolution like no other that there has ever been. This Next (r)Evolution will be how we choose to live together for The Highest Good Of All and how we came to have respect for all life on the planet. This (r)Evolution will change competition into cooperation. Technology will no longer serve greed but will be for the betterment of all. This (r)Evolution will redefine wealth and ownership and even what countries are until this truly is OUR WORLD. This (r)Evolution will change isolation and alienation into joy and loving and rediscovering play and creativity in our daily lives. This (r)Evolution will start because we choose to stop blindly going about our lives the way we have for thousands of years and start doing what will work for all of us. It will be a (r)Evolution perhaps a hundred years in the process as it spreads from the first model to all peoples throughout the planet.

People may respond to our solution by saying it's too simple to work or by saying that there would be economic chaos. It's easy to be a critic, and it's easy to be critical, but the truth is that the approach of making life work for everyone is very simple, and it's never been tried as we've described it. For thousands of years, out of the consciousness of againstness and everyone-for-themselves, we have complicated life to the point of not even considering that there could be a simple approach that would work for everyone. Remember also that the key to change is both having the model and the consciousness of The Highest Good. We will avoid chaos because the Next (r)Evolution will occur one Community and one cluster at a time at first until people really get the change of consciousness that is necessary. The key to creating a utopian society is to have fairly utopian people. Books have been written about utopian societies, but there's never been the consciousness and the tools to do it on a large scale. Now, with media coverage, technology, and our diminishing quality of life, people are seriously looking for a different approach, and that different approach is possible.

The truth is also that life as we've been doing it is no longer a viable choice for preserving life on the planet, so, despite how easy it is to be critical, we still have to do something radically different, and we have to do it while there is still time. So, as we learned from our experience with consensus decision-making, if you can see a problem with the approach we're suggesting, let's synergize creative solutions that keep us going along the path of having life work for everyone.

When I think about the Next (r)Evolution, what gives me goose bumps is the realization that this greatest of all revolutions will be different than all the others. I have a good friend who defines peace as "the cessation of againstness." We must no longer be against poverty, hunger or pollution, but rather we must be for all life.

Created without any againstness towards anyone or any country, the Next (r)Evolution will be a totally nonviolent revolution as it sweeps the planet. Unlike other revolutions, there doesn't have to be any againstness because everyone's lifestyle will be improved as people experience not only more abundance in terms of access, but also more abundance in terms of having much more fun, creativity, and Loving in their lives. The isolation and alienation that most of the people experience will be replaced with truly connecting with each other. It is only logical that the greatest (r)Evolution ever on the planet will be that we chose to make it work for everyone. All the great spiritual teachers have talked about it, now it's time to do it.

A part of The Next (r)Evolution will be that we also take back our lives. It is all too commonplace now that people spend all their time and energy in pursuit of a better life, and, in that struggle, they lose all hope of a better life. Truthfully, the quality of our lives is not the amount of money or possessions that we have but rather the amount of loving, nurturing, fun, creativity, friendship, and time spent in nature that we have access to. We can transform life into a less stressful and more enjoyable place for all.

Having brought the world to the place where it will no longer support us if we continue on our same path, we are not unlike the sorcerer's apprentice whose own creation was about to destroy himself. Can we find the Wizard within us so that we finally realize that we are all one.

From the postscript of the Community Planet description:

"We believe that the keys to world peace and prosperity are recognizing our oneness with all life, having a consciousness of sharing and cooperation, and acting in loving. If we lived in these ways, we could eliminate hunger, poverty, and the isolation and alienation of those who are perceived as being different from ourselves. The idea of Community has come forth to provide a working model for living together in greater harmony with ourselves, each other, and all life on the planet.

"It is our hope that historians will look at this time and write something like: 'The people of the early 21st century recognized that they

had to wake up and stop doing life as it had been done for thousands of years. They realized that to survive, it could no longer be 'me vs you' or 'us vs them,' but that it had to be just US. They finally realized that they had all the resources and manpower to make life work for everyone, and they just did it.'"

Let me leave you with a prayer that I wrote a few years ago:

MY PRAYER

Let us realize that we are all one.
Let us see that when there is even one amongst us
that needs assistance and loving,
that it is the concern of each one of us.
Let us know that there is enough for all of us,
that the world is for all of us to share and take care of.
Let us let go of the need to individually have more,
and move into the consciousness
that we can all have everything.
Let us look upon each one of us as sister and brother.
Let us see and experience the presence of God
within ourselves, in everyone, and in everything.

Never having written a book before, this process has been an odyessy. Please forgive any style or writing errors. I would rather have been at the beach, but this book had to be written by someone. I now issue you a challenge:

If you feel so moved, please join with us, and LET'S MAKE THE WORLD WORK FOR EVERYONE.

We Love You & God Bless,
Jack Reed, Jen Chendea, & Jim Costa
jack@communityplanet.org
www.co-opvillagefoundation.org

Appendix A

LEGAL ENTITITES

by Jim Costa

LEGAL ORGANIZATIONS

Several corporations would be required in order to always protect the land and buildings from a lawsuit and to facilitate financing and securing grants.

Legal protection is gained from using multiple corporations. In the practical world, two things must occur in order to get sued for the big payoff. First you must have a "deep pocket" (i.e. assets that can be taken), AND secondly, you must do something to harm another. Therefore to protect itself, one entity would hold all the assets but do nothing while another entity would have no assets but perform all activity. This makes attorneys very reluctant to take a case to go for the big bucks.

The suggested corporations are as follows:

Co-op Village Holding, Inc.

Type:	Non-Profit, Community Land Trust
As Defined: By:	The Community Land Trust Handbook The Institute for Community Economics ISBN: 0-87857-401-8 www.iceclt.org
Purpose:	To own all land, options to purchase adjacent lands, all buildings and infrastructure attached to the land. The land and buildings would then be leased to Leasing, Inc.

Membership: All bona fide residents of the Co-op Village.

Voting Rights: All members would agree that each member would have one vote and each member would have one additional vote for every $1,000 invested in Co-op Village Financing, Inc., as of January 1 or June 1, prior to voting, whichever is the closest in time.

Board Members: 5

Board Action: The Board would be primarily concerned with land acquisition, construction financing, mortgages, and stewardship as spelled out by the Community Land Trust Agreement. Day to day operations would be left to the Focus Groups.

Co-op Village Financing, Inc.

Type: Non-Profit

Purpose: To raise money to finance Co-op Village Holding, Inc.

Membership: All bona fide residents of the Co-op Village that invests a   minimum of $1,000 in this corporation. Voting Rights: Each member would have one vote.

Board Members: 5

Board Action: The Board would be primarily concerned with borrowing money from investors,   paying dividends, and lending mortgage money to Co-op Village Holding, Inc.

Co-op Village Leasing, Inc.

Type: Non-Profit

Purpose: To lease the property from Holding, Inc and sub-lease or give life estates to the residents.

This would shield Holding, Inc. from lawsuits making Financing, Inc. more attractive to investors.

Membership: All bona fide residents of the Co-op Village.

Voting Rights: Each member would have one vote.Board
Members: 5

Board Action: The Board would be primarily concerned
granting leases, life estates and possible managing a HUD
Section 8 Rent Assistance program.

Co-op Village Operations, Inc.

Type: For Profit, Limited Liability Corporation

Purpose: To collect revenue for all operations of the
village, excluding rent income.

Membership: All bona fide residents of the Co-op Village
who meet the membership requirements of the corporation.

Voting Rights: Each member would have one vote.

Board Members: 5

Board Action: The Board would be primarily concerned
with supporting all Focus Groups.

Co-op Village Health Benefits, Inc.

Type: For Profit, Limited Liability Corporation

Purpose: To collect revenue from General Operations,
Inc. and provide health benefits to members.

Membership: All bona fide residents of the Co-op Village
who meet the membership requirements of the corporation.

Voting Rights: Each member would have one vote.

Board Members: 5

Board Action: The Board would be primarily concerned
with budgeting and administration of the group health
program.

Co-op Village Library, Inc

Type: Non-Profit

Purpose: To provide a library for the community and receive grants for that purpose.

Membership: All persons who meet the membership requirements.

Voting Rights: Each member would have one vote.

Board Members: 5

Board Action: The Board would be primarily concerned with budgeting and administration of the library.

Printed in the United States
105062LV00004B/109-129/A